IN SEARCH OF THE ROMANS

Fresco from the house of Terentius Neo in Pompeii, often thought to represent Neo and his wife. They are both smartly dressed. He holds a papyrus, she a stylus and wax tablet, highlighting their education and intellectual aspirations.

IN SEARCH OF THE
ROMANS

JAMES RENSHAW

Bristol Classical Press

First published in 2012 by
Bristol Classical Press
an imprint of
Bloomsbury Academic
Bloomsbury Publishing Plc
50 Bedford Square
London WC1B 3DP, UK

CIP records for this book are available from the
British Library and the Library of Congress

ISBN 978-1-85399-748-8

Typeset by Ray Davies
Printed and bound in Great Britain

www.bloomsburyacademic.com

Contents

Preface

In Search of the Romans has been written as a companion volume to *In Search of the Greeks*. Together, I hope that the two books will provide a strong and broad foundation for students embarking on Classical Civilisation courses.

This book is the product of more than one mind, and I would like to acknowledge all the help and support I have had from a large number of people, including many pupils. In particular, the BCP committee have continued to offer advice and encouragement, but also shown the faith to let me get on with it. I have also been most grateful to various academic specialists for their input – Ray Laurence of the University of Kent has been ever helpful in response to my questions on Pompeii; Sarah Court of the Herculaneum Conservation Project and Christian Biggi of the Herculaneum Centre were able to enlighten me on many aspects of this fascinating site; Toph Marshall of the University of British Columbia gave me great insight into Roman drama. Moreover, James Morwood of Wadham College, Oxford has once again proved an invaluably wise mentor in the true Homeric tradition! Nonetheless, any errors which remain are of course entirely my responsibility. Finally, I should like to dedicate this book to my family.

Introduction

'All right, but apart from the sanitation, medicine, education, wine, public order, irrigation, roads, the fresh water system and public health, *what* have the Romans ever done for us?'

'Reg' in *Monty Python's Life of Brian*

No ancient civilisation has had a greater influence on the modern world than that of Rome. It flourished for hundreds of years in the lands of Europe, the Middle East and North Africa, meaning that ancient Rome is in the cultural DNA of modern countries as far apart as Iraq, Libya, Morocco, Spain, France, Germany and Scotland. Indeed, if one includes all the other countries which were established or colonised during the period of European expansion from the 15th century, then there are few places in the world that have not been influenced by the Romans.

This book concentrates on six key areas of the Roman world. The first chapter gives an overview of the many centuries of Roman history, from the traditional story of the foundation of the city in the 8th century BCE to the collapse of the Roman empire in the 5th century CE. This synopsis should give readers a framework in which to place all else that they read about Roman civilisation. The following chapter examines Roman religion, which was central to both public and private life. After this comes a chapter on Roman society, which explores how Romans lived their everyday lives. The book then moves on to focus on entertainment, and the topics such as baths and gladiators for which the Romans are perhaps best known today. The final two chapters describe Pompeii and Herculaneum respectively, two sites which give us an extraordinary picture of life in the Roman world. Each section in the book is concluded with review boxes, in which students are challenged to answer questions, read further (R), and write essays (E).

So what is the legacy of Rome? On the one hand, we can marvel at the achievements of a culture which produced great art and architecture, extraordinary technological advances, and remarkable literature. Many modern systems of law and government derive from Rome, while the Latin language has directly influenced some of the major world languages today, including English, French and Spanish. We can admire the Romans for their commitment to civic order and structure, and be impressed by their tolerance of most religions.

Introduction

On the other hand, there is no escape from the very dark side of their civilisation: their achievements were interwoven with great cruelty, be it in the crushing of opponents, the treatment of slaves or the gladiatorial shows where huge crowds celebrated the torture and murder of fellow human beings. As with every powerful empire, brilliance went hand in hand with terrifying brutality.

Ultimately, the many centuries of Roman rule have had a profound influence on our world today. By learning about the Romans, we can come to understand our own societies more deeply.

Rome – What's in a name?

It is hard to be sure where exactly the name 'Rome' came from, although there are a number of theories:

* Legend told of the city being named after its founder, Romulus.
* The name may have originated from the ancient name for the river Tiber, Rumen or Rumon, which is linked to the word *ruo* – 'to flow'.
* Another possibility is the Etruscan word *ruma*, meaning 'teat', and perhaps referring to the she-wolf which suckled Romulus and Remus.
* The Greek biographer Plutarch suggested that the city may have taken its name from the Greek word for 'strength', *rhômê*.

Ultimately, the origins of the city's name have almost certainly been lost forever. However, it is interesting to note that the theories above show the diverse cultural influences on the city – Latin, Etruscan, and Greek.

1

A History of Rome

'Rome was not built in a day.'

This saying is so well known that it is easy to forget the truth which lies behind it. Although the city of Rome grew to control one of the largest empires in the ancient world – stretching from Scotland in the north to Egypt in the south, and from Portugal in the west to Iraq in the east – it started its life in the 8th century BCE as a small pastoral settlement in central Italy, and took another 500 years to expand its power beyond central Italy. However, from the end of the 3rd century BCE the Romans conquered vast swathes of Europe, North Africa, and the Middle East, creating an empire which would last until the 5th century CE.

This chapter aims to cover briefly this vast period of history, giving an overview of how Rome developed from a small town into the capital of one of the largest empires the world has ever seen. The chapter is divided into three main eras of Roman history, each of which reflects a different period in the city's political structure; these are the **Kingdom** (753-509 BCE), the **Republic** (509-31 BCE), and the **Empire** (31 BCE-476 CE). As you read through this chapter, you will find it useful to consult the Chronology on pp. 372-3.

I. THE KINGDOM (753-509 BCE)

It is very hard for us to know with any certainty much about Rome's early centuries. The first Roman historians did not appear until after 250 BCE, while most of the city's early written records were destroyed when Rome was sacked and burnt to the ground by the Gauls in the early 4th century BCE (see p. 19).

Our main written source is the historian Livy (*c.* 64 BCE-17 CE), who set out to write a history of Rome from its foundation up until his own day; it consisted of 142 books, 35 of which still survive, including those which cover the city's earliest history. To his credit, Livy was himself sceptical about the accuracy of the traditional stories of early Rome:

'I intend neither to confirm nor deny those traditions which describe events before and leading up to the foundation of the city. Such traditions are better suited to poetic fiction than to genuine records of historic fact. But a city with a long history is entitled to blur the distinction between the human and the supernatural in order to add dignity to its past. And if any nation deserves to be allowed to claim divine ancestry, surely Rome does.'

Livy, *Preface*

As Livy recognises, by his time the history of early Rome was really a series of legends. However, that does not make the stories unimportant – for one thing, the legends people tell about themselves can be very revealing of their values and beliefs; moreover, as we shall see, the archaeological evidence suggests that there is more than a grain of truth in some of them.

1. The legends

There are two complementary legends about the foundation of Rome: one which traces Roman origins back to the heroic age of the Trojan War in Greek mythology, the other which is based in native Roman folklore.

Aeneas

The legend of the Trojan War had been a key part of Greek storytelling for hundreds of years. It recounted the abduction of Helen of Sparta by the Trojan prince Paris, which set the Greeks and Trojans at war with one another. The legend tells of many great heroes, both Greek and Trojan, including Achilles, Hector, Agamemnon and Odysseus. It was a heroic world with which the Romans were keen to associate themselves after they began to come into contact with Greek culture in the 3rd century BCE, and it is probably during this period that the Aeneas story was developed at Rome.

According to the legend, after the Greeks had sacked Troy, a Trojan prince, Aeneas (whose mother was the goddess Venus), was allowed by the gods to escape and lead any surviving Trojans to found a 'new Troy' in the west. After a long journey and many hardships, these Trojans arrived in central Italy, near the site of Rome. Aeneas made a treaty with the local people, the Latins, and married Lavinia, the daughter of their king, Latinus. Aeneas founded a new city, Lavinium, where the Trojans and the Latins lived together as one people. Aeneas' son, Ascanius (also known as Iulus), later founded another city nearby, called Alba Longa.

The greatest quality which later Romans admired in Aeneas was his *pietas*. This is not an easy word to translate, but it means something like 'sense of duty', with the duty being specifically to one's family, country and gods. Aeneas is often seen as the first and finest of this dutiful Roman; in particular, one famous moment of *pietas* in his life-story was often portrayed in paintings and statues: as Aeneas escaped from the flames of Troy, he carried his elderly father Anchises on his shoulders and led the young Ascanius by the hand; Anchises himself carried the household gods of Troy (the Penates – see p. 134), as grandfather, father

1. A History of Rome

This mosaic shows the poet Virgil writing the *Aeneid*. On either side of him are the muses Clio (History) and Melpomene (Tragedy).

Virgil's *Aeneid*

The story of Aeneas was taken up by the Roman poet Virgil (70-19 BCE), just after Augustus had become the first Roman emperor (see p. 41). Virgil set out to write an epic poem, the *Aeneid*, in the style of the great Greek poet Homer, who had composed his *Iliad* and *Odyssey* several centuries earlier about the legendary age of the Trojan War; in this way, Virgil hoped to associate the Roman people with the same heroic world. Moreover, Virgil's work also contains many references and subtle comparisons to his own time, and so it informed contemporary Romans about their heritage, culture and values.

The ancient biographer Donatus relates that when Virgil was on his deathbed in 19 BCE, the poem was not complete and so he ordered that it be burnt. Thankfully, the emperor Augustus intervened and it was preserved. Romans soon came to regard the poem as the greatest work of Latin literature, giving it the same standing as the works of Shakespeare have in the English language; fortunately, it still survives for us to read today.

A sculpture by the 17th-century artist Bernini depicting Aeneas carrying Achises from Troy, with Ascanius following behind.

and son all escaped from the city to found a new Troy. This image of familial, civic and religious duty symbolised for later Romans the *pietas* expected from each one of them.

Romulus and Remus

The second legend recounts the foundation of Rome itself. Twelve generations after Ascanius, his descendent Numitor was overthrown as king of Alba Longa by his wicked brother Amulius. Amulius wanted to eliminate any threats to his power, and so he had Numitor's sons killed and his daughter, Rhea Silvia, instituted as a Vestal Virgin (see p. 92),

This mosaic shows Romulus and Remus at the moment Faustulus and a fellow-shepherd discover the she-wolf suckling them.

meaning that she would never be able to marry or have children. However, at this stage, the god Mars intervened by making love to Rhea Silvia, so that she gave birth to twin sons, Romulus and Remus.

Upon discovering this, Amulius was furious and ordered that the twins be drowned in the river Tiber. However, by a lucky accident of fate, the boys were washed onto a dry patch of land, where they were found and suckled by a she-wolf. Soon afterwards, they were discovered by a shepherd named Faustulus who, along with his wife Acca Larentia, brought them up as his own children. When the twins reached manhood, they discovered their true identity and took revenge on Amulius, killing him and restoring Numitor to his rightful throne.

At this point, Romulus and Remus decided to found a city of their own near the point of the river Tiber where they had been exposed as infants. Livy takes up the story:

The she-wolf suckling Romulus and Remus. This bronze wolf masterpiece was probably made by an Etruscan artist in *c.* 500 BC. The figures of Romulus and Remus were added 2,000 years later during the Renaissance, but may have replaced original figures.

'Since the brothers were twins, and neither had seniority over the other, it was decided that the gods who kept watch over the site would choose by augury (*the flight of birds – see p. 90*) which brother should give the new city its name, and be its first king. So Romulus took the Palatine Hill for his observation point, and Remus chose the Aventine. Remus is said to have seen the first augury – a flight of six vultures – but as soon as he had announced it, Romulus reported seeing twice that number. Each brother was duly saluted as king by his own followers, Remus on the grounds that he had seen the first heavenly sign, Romulus because his augury had been twice as big.

Angry words followed, the two groups came to blows which led to bloodshed, and Remus was killed. But a more common version of the story is that Remus taunted Romulus by leaping over his newly-built city walls. At this Romulus, in a rage, killed his brother and added this threat: "Death to anyone who leaps over my city walls." In this way, Romulus gained sole power, and the city was founded and named after its founder.'
                                                                    Livy 1.6-7

The traditional date for the foundation of Rome was 753 BCE, although this was based on the guesswork of a much later writer, Varro (116-27 BCE), and has no basis in any archaeological evidence. Nonetheless, after Varro, Romans counted their years from this date, which was the equivalent of the year 1 in our era. Therefore, the year 653 BCE would have been for the Romans 100 AUC (*ab urbe condita* – 'from the foundation of the city').

6

The Sabine women

In a further legend, Romulus is supposed to have populated his new city by offering citizenship to men from nearby settlements – whether slave or free. The population swelled, but Rome was now very short of womenfolk. After trying unsuccessfully to make marriage alliances with people from nearby cities, the Romans came up with a different plan.

They invited people from these cities to a chariot racing festival. Among the visitors were the Sabines, a local tribe, who brought their women and children with them. During the festival, a signal was given and each Roman snatched one of the Sabine women and took her off as his wife. The Sabine men were naturally enraged by this, and a battle followed. The Sabine women, however, had come round to their new status, and famously ran in between the two battle lines and spoke to their fathers as follows:

> 'Turn your anger against us. We are the cause of this war, we the cause of husbands and fathers lying wounded and slain. Only one side can win this fight. As for us, it is better to die than to live, for we must do so either as widows or as orphans.'   Livy 1.13

Moved by these words, the two peoples came to terms with one another and formed an alliance which joined them together as one.

'The Intervention of the Sabine Women', a 1799 painting by the French painter Jacques-Louis David.

What are we to make of such a violent foundation story involving fratricide? There are two points which could be highlighted; the first is that through much of its later history Rome was dogged by civil wars, and so it was perhaps no surprise that Romans believed that their city had been founded at a moment of intra-family strife; secondly, the story is a very patriotic one, since Romulus sets the example that nothing – not even a tie of blood – is as important as defending one's city.

The Seven Kings

Romulus was the first of seven kings of Rome who, according to legend, between them ruled from 753 to 509 BCE (it is clearly very unlikely that the city had just seven kings over such a long period – perhaps these seven were those who were worthy of being remembered in legend). Romulus' six successors were Numa Pompilius, Tullus Hostilius, Ancus Marcius, Tarquinius Priscus, Servius Tullius and Tarquinius Superbus. Each king is credited with new innovations to the city. For example:

- Romulus is said to have introduced a senate (see p. 360).
- Numa Pompilius to have set up Rome's priesthoods and cults, as well as inventing a 12 month calendar (see p. 369).
- Servius Tullius is credited with reorganising both the army and the Roman constitution.

Both Tarquinius Priscus and Tarquinius Superbus were, according to tradition, not Roman but Etruscan, while Servius Tullius, although of Latin origins, had married Priscus' daughter. The Etruscans, from Etruria (a region centred on what it is today Umbria and Tuscany – see map on p. 17), had become the dominant power in central Italy, including Rome, by the middle of the 7th century. According to Livy, these Etruscan rulers became increasingly tyrannical; eventually, they were so unpopular at Rome that in about 509 BCE the Etruscan ruling class was driven out of the city by an uprising of Roman aristocrats. The catalyst for this revolution was apparently the rape of Lucretia, the wife of a Roman noble called Collatinus, by Sextus, the son of Tarquinius Superbus.

Sextus, who was killed in revenge, seems to have symbolised the arrogance and abuse of power associated with the Etruscan kings; in fact, the Latin word *superbus* actually meant 'proud' or 'arrogant'. The uprising which followed Lucretia's suicide was led by a noble Roman called Brutus, a friend of Collatinus. Yet Brutus was to suffer personal tragedy in the course of events. For when his two sons were found to be conspiring with the enemy, they were sentenced to death. Brutus was

Lucretia

In Livy's account, Sextus was on campaign with other young nobles when they fell into a debate about whose wife was the most virtuous. They decided to find out by heading home to see what their wives were up to while they were away. When they got there, all the women except Lucretia were out dining and partying; by contrast, Lucretia, by contrast, was at home spinning with her maids.

When Sextus laid eyes on Lucretia he was overwhelmed with desire. A few days later, while Collatinus was away, he came to her house and raped her. Full of shame, Lucretia summoned her father and husband, told them what had happened, and made them swear to take revenge on Sextus; both were very supportive, laying no blame on her, and immediately swore the oath. However, despite their sympathy, Lucretia next took a knife and plunged it into her heart, uttering these final words:

'I absolve myself of wrong, but not from punishment. Let no unchaste woman in the future continue to go on living because of the example of Lucretia.'   Livy 1.58

Romans saw in Lucretia the ideal of a virtuous woman, and her dignified behaviour was often held up as an example to later generations.

A severe archaic bronze traditionally believed to portray Brutus.

duty bound to support these sentences and watched in silence as they were both beheaded – another example of a man from Rome's early history putting patriotic duty ahead of ties of blood.

Although Tarquinius had been driven into exile, he wasn't beaten yet, and set out to recapture his throne. He formed an alliance with a nearby Etruscan king, Lars Porsenna of Clusium, whom he persuaded to declare war on Rome. Livy's account of this war is a masterpiece of Roman propaganda (as the historian presumably knew!). For if his version is to be believed, Porsenna was so impressed by the bravery and heroism of the Romans that he agreed to come to terms with them and leave them in peace.

Three brave Romans

In particular, Livy (2.9-13) recounts the stories of three noble Romans which highlight the heroism shown in this war:

- **Horatius Cocles**. The Etruscans marched on Rome, which was well defended apart from one weak point, a wooden bridge across the Tiber. Horatius bravely held off the enemy as they attacked the far side of the bridge, while one of his compatriots furiously worked to cut it down. Once this had been achieved, he dived into the river in full armour and swam to the other shore safely, surviving a hail of arrows.
- **Mucius Scaevola**. The Etruscans now began a siege of Rome. Gaius Mucius, a noble young man, devised a daring plan to assassinate Porsenna. He crept into the Etruscan camp but killed the wrong man; Mucius was arrested and Porsenna threatened to burn him to death, but he simply thrust his right hand into a nearby brazier to show that he did not care. Porsenna was so amazed by Mucius' courage that he released him. Upon returning to Rome, he was given the name *Scaevola*, meaning 'left-handed'.
- **Cloelia**. Porsenna now offered peace terms to the Romans, on the condition that they provide some hostages as a sign of goodwill. One of these, the noble woman Cloelia, led a group of young woman on a breakout of the Etruscan camp, after which they swam back across the Tiber to Rome. Porsenna was so impressed with her courage that he told the Romans that, if she alone was returned to him as a hostage, he would leave the Romans in peace. She returned willingly, after which Porsenna released her again, along with some other hostages of her own choice. Porsenna now withdrew from Rome and the city was finally free of its Etruscan rulers.

With the departure of the Etruscans, the Romans decided to abolish the monarchy for good. They wanted to come up with a system of govern-

Mucius Scaevola thrusts his right hand into the fire. An 18th-century sculpture by Louis-Pierre Deseine.

ment which prevented any one individual from taking – and abusing – complete power in the city. The new system they devised they called the 'Republic', and for hundreds of years afterwards the Latin word *rex* ('king') was a hateful one to Roman ears.

2. The archaeology

How much truth is there behind these legends of early Rome? Are they merely tales made up to impress and educate later Romans about the values of their city? Today, archaeology can give us evidence about the past which was not available to ancient historians, and it is in this direction that we must look for clues about the accuracy of the stories which Livy relates.

The archaeological evidence in Rome suggests that from about 1000 BCE (at the start of the Iron Age) small villages of herdsmen, living in simple huts, developed on the main hills in the area, particularly on the Palatine and the Esquiline (see Appendix 1 to read about the geography of ancient Rome). Initially, these were separate settlements of different tribes, but by the 7th century, soon after Romulus was said to have founded Rome, these villages had merged into a single, unified community.

By this stage, these early Romans were trading with other places such as Etruria and Greece, as well as producing their own pottery, figurines and weapons. However, they were primarily farmers and hunters, who grew barley and wheat, and reared animals such as goats and pigs.

An Etruscan bronze mirror and holder.

(*opposite*) A detail from an Etruscan tomb showing dancers. The tomb dates to the first half of the 5th century BCE.

1. A History of Rome

The Etruscans

The most powerful people in Italy at this time were the Etruscans, and they came to have a profound influence on the development of early Rome. Archaeology suggests that these people did have a firm presence in the city in the 7th and 6th centuries, just as Livy's account suggests. It is unclear, however, whether Rome was actually taken over and ruled by Etruscans (as the legends suggest) or whether it simply came under the political and cultural influence of these powerful neighbours.

The Etruscans themselves are a great mystery to historians, for a number of reasons:

- **Origins**. It used to be thought that they had migrated to Italy from Lydia (a region in what is now Turkey), but archaeologists now believe that they had been settled in Italy for some centuries before the rise of Rome.
- **Buildings**. Since they mainly built in wood, few of their buildings, apart from their stone tombs, have survived.
- **Language**. Although they used an alphabet based on the Greek script, no one has yet been able to decipher their language. However, it is clear that it was not connected with any other tongue spoken in Italy at that time.

On this Etruscan funerary urn, the deceased woman holds a libation saucer for pouring offerings to the gods.

The best evidence for their civilisation therefore comes from the elaborate tombs which they built for their aristocracy. These often depict people feasting, dancing and taking part in athletic contests; they are dressed elaborately, with fine jewellery, and, interestingly, women seem to have been given more status in their society than in other contemporary societies.

The Etruscan economy was based around both agriculture and trade, and their craftsmen produced a high standard of metalwork. They were a seafaring people who had much cultural and trade contact with the Greeks of southern Italy, as well as with those in the eastern Mediterranean. They also exchanged their metalwork, iron and copper, with gold, silver and tin from Carthage, and traded with many other peoples: their products have been found in France, Germany, Britain, and even as far away as Scandinavia.

The heartland of the Etruscan world was central Italy, in the modern regions of Tuscany and Umbria. It was here that their major cities developed, the twelve most important of which were joined in a loose confederation (the modern city of Perugia was one of these twelve). By the 7th century they expanded their power to the south into Latium and Campania, where they founded the city of Capua and probably influenced the early development of Pompeii (see p. 257). Other Etruscans headed north to the Po valley as far as the Alps, where they founded towns, some of which are still important today, such as Milan, Bologna and Ravenna.

Etruscan towns were carefully planned and laid out in a structured pattern, often surrounded by stone walls with a monumental gateway.

14

The civilisation produced brilliant engineers, who introduced the arch to Italy, and their cities show evidence of containing underground drains and cisterns, aqueducts, bridges, tunnels and temples.

Etruscan influence on Rome

There is no doubt that the Etruscans had a huge influence on the physical development of Rome. They probably built the first city walls, as well as the great temple of Jupiter on the Capitoline hill (see p. 71). Moreover, their engineering skills allowed them to drain the marshland between the Capitoline and Palatine hills; they did this by building a huge sewer, the *Cloaca Maxima*, which ran out into the Tiber; it was used by Romans for hundreds of years, and its outlet can still be seen today.

Engineering was not the only field in which the Etruscans made their mark. The Romans were clearly influenced by their religious practices, not least their belief in divination – being able to predict the future through signs (see p. 99). There were other influences too – gladiatorial fights and chariot racing may have come from the Etruscans, while Roman camps were always set out on the pattern which the Etruscans laid out their towns.

Archaeology suggests that Etruscan power in Italy waned at the end of the 6th century – just at the time when Tarquinius Superbus was said to have been expelled from Rome. In 474 BCE, the Etruscans in the south of Italy were severely defeated by the Greeks, while 50 years later the key town of Capua was captured by the Samnites (who are described in more detail on p. 21), and the Gauls to the north of Italy drove them out of the Po Valley. They were left to live in their heartland of Etruria, which in time the Romans would conquer, allowing little trace of Etruscan civilisation to survive.

Review 1

1. Define the following terms: *ab urbe condita, pietas.*
2. Why do you think the Romans wanted to link their history to the heroic world of the Trojan War?
3. How believable do you find Livy's stories of early Rome? Does our culture have similar stories about the distant past?
4. How important are the examples of courageous women to the stories of early Rome? What might this tell us about Roman culture?
5. Find out what you can about Etruscan civilisation.
R. Read Livy's account of the story of Romulus and Remus (1.3-6). Which elements of the story do you think might be based in truth?
R. Read Livy's account of the stories of Horatius, Scaevola and Cloelia (2.9-13). Which qualities does Livy emphasise in their characters?
E. Write an imaginary newspaper report of one of Livy's stories from early Rome, including analysis and interviews with key characters in the action.

II. THE REPUBLIC (509-31 BCE)

After the expulsion of the kings, the victorious Roman aristocrats took care to devise a new political system which aimed to prevent any one individual from taking control. Each year, a series of magistrates was elected by the people; the most important of these were the two consuls who ran the city together – no decision could be taken unless they were both in agreement. These consuls and the other magistrates were advised by an assembly of aristocratic landowners, the senate. The Romans called this system of government the 'Republic', and you can read about it in more detail in Appendix 2.

By the time that the republican system of government finally collapsed in 31 BCE, in the wake of Octavian's final victory in the civil wars, Rome was a city which controlled lands all around the Mediterranean, a vast contrast to the small town with surrounding farmland of 509 BCE. The early centuries of the republic saw Rome first consolidate its place in central Italy, and then expand its power through the entire peninsula, which it achieved by 270 BCE.

1. The Early Republic (509-264 BCE)

The young republic now had to fend for itself, and the other Latin cities (named after the surrounding region of Latium), soon felt threatened by a newly independent Rome. They formed an alliance – known as the Latin League – and in 496 the two sides fought an indecisive battle at Lake Regillus to the south of Rome. As a result, the Romans had little choice but to enter into an alliance with the League in 493; its terms bound Rome and the Latin cities to provide equal shares of a common defensive army, and to split any spoils of war.

During the 5th century, the Romans and their Latin allies were generally engaged in protecting the fertile plain of Latium from three fierce tribes from the neighbouring hills, the Aequi, Sabini and Volsci, as well as from the Etruscans. Livy tells a number of stories from this period, two of which – those of Cincinnatus and Coriolanus – are especially famous.

Cincinnatus
In 458, one of the consuls, Minucius, had allowed most of Rome's army to be trapped and encircled by a division of the Aequian army. In this emergency, the Romans decided to summon as their leader Cincinnatus, an aristocrat who had recently served as consul, but who preferred the

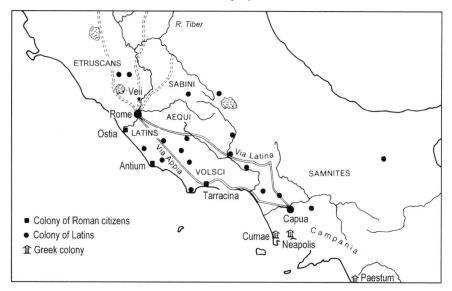

Rome and the surrounding peoples in the 5th century BCE.

simple life of working his small farm outside the city. Livy picks up the story:

> 'Cincinnatus was the people's only hope ... the messengers found him ditching, or ploughing perhaps, at any rate working on his land. After an exchange of greetings, he was asked, together with a prayer for the success of himself and the state, to put on his toga and listen to the senate's instructions. "Is everything all right?" he asked in surprise, and told his wife Racilia to run and get his toga from their cottage. Then wiping off the sweat and grime, he put the toga on. As he approached the envoys they congratulated him and summoned him to Rome, explaining the terrible plight of the army.'
>
> Livy 3.26

Cincinnatus was appointed dictator – a military leader of the state chosen only in times of emergency (see p. 358). Within 16 days he had defeated the enemy, saved the army, resigned as dictator, and returned to his farm again.

Later Romans revered Cincinnatus as an example of the sort of man who had helped mould the Roman nation: a tough farmer and soldier, who lived a simple life and had no interest in fame and power for its own sake, but simply wanted to serve his city. The Romans were not the only people to be inspired by his example – the city of Cincinnati in Ohio, USA was founded in 1788 by settlers who hoped that their own city would be built on similar virtues.

17

This statue of Cincinnatus was set up in the city of Cincinnati in 1988. In his right hand Cincinnatus hands back the *fasces*, the symbol of authority, while in his left he holds the plough, intending to resume his life as a farmer.

The *mos maiorum*

Later Romans loved the noble examples from their early legends. They looked up to Cincinnatus and others we have read about, such as Brutus, Lucretia, Horatius Cocles, Mucius Scaevola and Cloelia, believing that they represented a simple and honest period in Roman history, when people worked the land and served their city unselfishly.

The qualities which these legendary figures embodied were known collectively as the *mos maiorum* ('the custom of our ancestors'), and some of them can be seen in the Latin words which are still recognisable in English today: *gravitas, industria, simplicitas, pietas, benevolentia*, and most of all *virtus*, which literally meant 'the qualities which make a man'. Later Romans often complained that their own corrupt and self-seeking society was a far cry from these early days – although we should remember that these legends were probably told to inspire good examples in later generations, and we have no way of knowing if the Romans of the city's early history were any more virtuous than those which followed.

Coriolanus

While Livy held up men such as Cincinnatus as heroic examples of Roman *virtus*, his account of another early Roman, Gnaeus Marcius Coriolanus, warned against the dangers of treachery. Coriolanus was an aristocrat who reportedly earned his name after playing a leading role in the capture of the Volscian town of Corioli in 493. Yet he soon became unpopular by opposing the distribution of grain to the common people, and was exiled on a charge of wanting to become a tyrant.

Not to be outdone, Coriolanus defected to the Volsci and became their leader in the war against Rome; in two victorious campaigns he captured a number of Latin towns and led his forces to the gates of the city. The alarmed senate twice sent envoys to sue for peace, but both times Coriolanus sent them back empty-handed. At this point, Coriolanus' mother Veturia and his wife Volumnia, together with his two small sons, came out to meet him. Coriolanus ran to embrace his mother excitedly, but Veturia first challenged him:

> 'Before I let you kiss me, I would like to know whether I have come to an enemy or to a son, and whether I am in your camp as a prisoner or as your mother ... If I had never had a son, I would have been able to die a free woman in a free country.'   Livy 2.40

Coriolanus was shamed into retreat. As Livy put it, the women had achieved 'by tears and prayers' what their menfolk had not managed by weapons – saving their city. As for Coriolanus, Livy says that there were differing versions of his fate, but himself claims that he lived a long life pining for his home city. Another version was later recorded by Plutarch, in which the Volsci had him executed on his return from Rome.

On one level, the story of Coriolanus is a morality tale offering two lessons: that traitors do not prosper and that aristocrats should treat the common people fairly. However, it may also have been a way for the Romans to justify why they suffered so many defeats to the Volsci at that time – in their view, this could have happened only with a Roman in charge of their enemy. Whatever the truth, the story inspired Shakespeare to write his play *Coriolanus*.

The Gauls sack Rome

By the end of the 5th century, Rome had come to dominate the surrounding territory and to exert a decisive influence in the alliance with the Latin League. In 406, the Romans attacked their greatest rival, the Etruscan city of Veii, finally conquering it in 396 under the command of a brilliant general, Camillus. The Romans were brutal in victory, slaughtering the entire male population of the city and enslaving all the women and children. Rome was now master of the whole of southern Etruria.

'The Gauls in Rome', a 19th-century illustration by Alphonse de Neuville. The Gauls are depicted staring at the statue-like figure of a senator.

However, in 390 (or 387 according to some), disaster struck for the Romans. A marauding tribe of Gauls from northern Italy defeated the Roman army at the River Allia, a few miles north of Rome, and advanced on the defenceless city. They found it deserted, apart from a garrison on the Capitoline Hill, and also the senators, who had chosen to remain in their houses, dressed in togas and wearing the full insignia of their rank. As the Gauls entered these houses, they came upon these noble Romans seated in their courtyards in ceremonial chairs. Livy describes the reaction of the invaders:

> 'Awestruck, they looked at the seated figures whose robes and decorations were more impressive than those of ordinary men and whose expressions, calm and majestic, made them look like gods – they might have been statues in some holy place. Then one of them, Marcus Papirius, when a Gaul tried to stroke his beard, struck him on the head with his ivory staff. That was the beginning. The barbarian killed him in a fury, and the other senators were butchered where they sat. From then on nothing was spared. Houses were ransacked and the empty shells set on fire.' Livy 5.41

Only the garrison on the Capitoline Hill held out for any time, but after a long siege it too surrendered. Luckily for Rome, the Gauls were not interested in conquest but rather in acquiring booty, and the Romans agreed to pay them 450 kg of gold if they would leave Rome alone. In the words of Livy, 'a thousand pounds of gold was agreed on as the price of a people that was destined to rule the world'.

Rome had been humiliated and was enormously weakened. The senate even debated whether the city should be relocated to the ruined site of Veii, but Camillus persuaded them otherwise. In the years which followed, its people found the will to fight back and made a series of reforms to strengthen the state; in particular, they built a substantial set of defensive walls around the city for the first time (see p. 351), and also reorganised the army, devising more flexible fighting techniques and improving its weapons and armour. These innovations produced results: by 350, they had thoroughly defeated the Etruscans and taken full military control of the Latin League.

In 340, the discontented Latin cities demanded that the Romans restore them to an equal status. In 338, Rome won the ensuing war and dissolved the Latin League, signing separate treaties with each city – thereby isolating them from one another. This was a key moment in the process of Roman expansion. The Romans were aided in this campaign by the Samnites, a loose confederation of tough hill tribes who lived in the Apennine Mountains of central and southern Italy (see map on p. 17).

The Samnite Wars
However, Rome was to spend the next half century at war with the Samnites. In fact, the Romans had already fought a successful campaign

A bronze statuette of a Samnite warrior from the 6th century BCE. He would have originally had a crest on his helmet and carried a shield and spear.

against them between 343 and 341, when coming to the aid of the Campanian city of Capua. The victory in 341 allowed the Romans to exert their control over Campania – one of the most fertile regions of Italy – which the Samnites also had their eyes on. A series of conflicts followed: the Second Samnite War lasted from 327 until 304, and from 311, the Samnites were boosted by Etruscan support. At times it was touch and go for the Romans – most famously, in 321 the city narrowly avoided a total disaster when its army was trapped in a mountain pass known as the Caudine Forks.

The peace of 304 did not last long, and the two sides resumed hostilities again in 298. This time, the Samnites were supported by an alliance of Etruscans, Umbrians and Gauls. However, by 290 Rome had thoroughly defeated all of them. Through conquest and alliance, the city now dominated northern and central Italy. Only the Greek cities of the south stood apart, and they were next in the line of fire.

Magna Graecia

Greek settlers had started to arrive in the south of Italy and on the island of Sicily in the 8th century BCE, and within 300 years many Greek cities lay dotted around the coastlines, so much so that this region was collectively known as Magna Graecia – 'Great Greece'. The Greeks had long traded with the Romans and Etruscans, and the peoples had generally had good relations. By 282, however, Tarentum, the most powerful Greek city in the region, was growing very nervous of the encroaching power of Rome.

Seeking to boost their own military resources, the Tarentines summoned help from King Pyrrhus of Epirus in north-west Greece. He

This clay disk, dating to about the time of Pyrrhus, depicts a war-elephant carrying a battle-tower.

arrived in Italy with a force of 20,000 skilled professional infantry, 3,000 cavalry, and about 20 elephants. This was the greatest army yet faced by Rome, and Pyrrhus won the first two battles in 280 and 279.

A Pyrrhic victory

Pyrrhus is famous for giving us the phrase 'a Pyrrhic victory', describing a victory which is achieved at such a cost that it is not worth the effort.

When Pyrrhus' army defeated the Romans at Asculum in 279, the losses on his own side were extremely heavy: a majority of his soldiers lay dead, including almost all his closest confidantes and commanders. The story goes that when he was congratulated on his victory, Pyrrhus replied: 'One more victory like that over the Romans, and we'll be completely ruined!'

After this, however, Pyrrhus answered a call for help from the Sicilians, and while he was away his Greek and Italian allies changed sides. When he came back to Italy in 275 he was defeated, and decided to head home to Epirus. Tarentum surrendered to the Romans three years later, and by 270 the whole of Magna Graecia was under Roman control. Within another five years, the Romans had brought the whole Italian peninsula under their sway.

Reasons for Roman success

Rome was now a major player in the Mediterranean, and international recognition soon followed: Ptolemy II of Egypt, one of the most powerful rulers of the day, sent envoys to Rome to make a pact of friendship. How had the city achieved such success?

Clearly, military strength was a key factor, but the Romans also followed up conquests with enlightened and progressive leadership. Rather than trying to oppress conquered peoples ruthlessly, they created a political confederacy of all Italian peoples, giving to each city one of three statuses. Some peoples were given full Roman citizenship, and in turn they were expected to pay taxes; a second group enjoyed the status of 'Latin allies', involving some of the advantages of citizenship, while a third group, the 'Italian allies', retained independence on domestic issues, but had their foreign policy dictated by Rome.

In addition to this, Rome founded new settlements – called colonies – of Roman citizens at key strategic points in Italy (19 were established between 334 and 263), and these helped ensure loyalty and support in the peninsula. Crucially, all allied peoples had to provide troops for Rome, and were able to share in the profits of war. A census taken in 220 revealed that the total number of Romans and allies able to bear arms was more than 700,000 infantry and 70,000 cavalry. They were now in a position to expand beyond the seas.

23

Review 2

1. Define the following terms: *Magna Graecia, a Pyrrhic victory.*
2. Do we have anything like the *mos maiorum* in our society today? What
   words do you think best communicate the best of modern values?
3. Find out what you can about the life of the Roman general Camillus. Why
   do you think the Romans revered him so much?
4. What can you find out about the following Greek cities of *Magna Graecia*:
   Syracuse, Tarentum, Paestum (also known as *Poseidonia*)?
R. Read Livy's accounts of Cincinnatus (3.26-29) and Coriolanus (2.33-40).
   What values do you think that the historian is trying to highlight here?
R. Read Livy's account of the sack of Rome by the Gauls (5.41-48). How
   does he make this story dramatic?
R. Read Livy's account of the battle of the Caudine Forks (9.1-6). Why do
   you think that the Roman people were so traumatised by this episode?

---

2. Expansion beyond Italy (264-133 BCE)

Over the following 130 years or so, the Romans moved from controlling
Italy to being masters of most of the Mediterranean. They did this predominantly through two different sets of conflicts – one with the
Carthaginians of North Africa, and the other with the Greek kingdoms
to the east.

i. The Punic Wars

In the early 3rd century, the greatest power in the Mediterranean was
Carthage, a city in north Africa (its site lies in what is today Tunisia)
apparently founded in the 9th century by settlers from Phoenicia (modern Lebanon). The Phoenicians were notable traders and travellers, and
their Carthaginian descendants continued this tradition, taking control
of the major maritime trading routes into the western Mediterranean.
In particular they were the greatest power in the fertile island of Sicily,
which lay in a key strategic position for the shipping routes. It seems
that until 264 they had maintained reasonably good relations with the
Romans, although they must have viewed their growing power in the
Italian peninsula with some nervousness.

At this date, however, the two cities entered into the first of three
conflicts which were to be fought during the ensuing century or so.
These wars were known as the 'Punic' wars – the Romans called the
Carthaginians *Poeni*, the adjective of which was *Punicus*. The word
Poeni was itself derived from the Greek *Phoenikikos* ('Phoenician').

24

The 1st Punic War (264-241)

The first war started in Sicily in 264 when the two cities supported opposing sides in a local conflict, which soon escalated into a full scale fight for control of Sicily. The Carthaginians were a strong naval power, and the Romans had no hope unless they could fight at sea. Therefore, they built themselves a fleet for the very first time, and had some successes with their tactic of using boarding ramps to clamber onto Carthaginian ships and fight them hand to hand. Nonetheless, the Romans also suffered great disasters – effectively losing two fleets – and it was only with a rebuilt fleet that they defeated the enemy and took control of Sicily for good in 241. The island now became Rome's first overseas province.

A relief showing a Roman warship with a fully armed crew.

Regulus

One of the Roman commanders during the 1st Punic War was Marcus Atilius Regulus, about whom a famous story is told, even though there seems to be more than a hint of legend and propaganda about it.

In 255, Regulus was leading an army in north Africa when he was captured by the Carthaginians. They sent him to Rome with terms for peace but first made him swear that, if the terms were rejected, he would return to Carthage as a captive. Upon his return to Rome, Regulus apparently convinced the people not to accept the conditions. However, being a man of his word, he returned voluntarily to Carthage, where he was tortured to death.

The 2nd Punic War (218-201)

In the aftermath of their victory in 241, the Romans soon seized the islands of Sardinia and Corsica, seriously harming Carthaginian trade and prosperity. Carthage therefore looked to open up new markets and expanded its control in Spain where it founded new settlements, taking control of a large part of the peninsula. This mission was led by a Carthaginian noble called Hamilcar Barca, a veteran of the 1st Punic War who hated the Romans with a passion. Hamilcar had a young son, whom he made swear undying hatred of the Romans. That boy's name was Hannibal, and he was to become synonymous with the next, and decisive, conflict between the two peoples.

The Romans became nervous about the growing power of the Carthaginians in Spain, and a full scale war broke out in 218 after Hannibal besieged Saguntum, a Spanish town allied with the Romans. The Roman plan was to send a fleet over to Spain to fight Hannibal there. However, their opponent had other ideas, believing that attack would be the best form of defence – so he set out on an overland march to Italy with an army of about 90,000 infantry, 12,000 cavalry, and a battalion of elephants.

It was a treacherous journey, with terrible weather conditions and various conflicts with local tribes, all of which paled in comparison with the crossing of the Alps, a journey of about 15 days which resulted in enormous loss of life – the army is said to have arrived in Italy with only 26,000 men and 21 elephants. However, the following passage describes the dramatic moment when they arrived in Italy:

> 'When they set out at dawn and the column was moving sluggishly through the unending deep snow and weariness and desperation could clearly be seen on everybody's face, Hannibal went ahead of the standards and told his soldiers to halt on a ledge from which there was a vast extensive view.
>
> He showed them Italy and the plains beneath the Alps around the river Po, and said that they were now scaling the walls not only of Italy but also of the city of Rome. The journey ahead of them would be downhill and easy. And in one or at the most two battles, he said, they would have Italy's citadel and its capital in their grasp.' Livy 21.35

Initially, Hannibal's optimism was well founded, since he inflicted three early defeats on the Romans at the River Trebia, Lake Trasimene, and most spectacularly in 216 at Cannae, about 290 km (180 miles) to the south-east of Rome. The Roman army was wiped out, with at least 50,000 men being killed. The city of Rome was now at the mercy of Hannibal, but the senate held its nerve and refused to give in: they ordered that the city walls should be manned by slaves, boys and old men.

Hannibal's cavalry commander, Maharbal, begged Hannibal to send

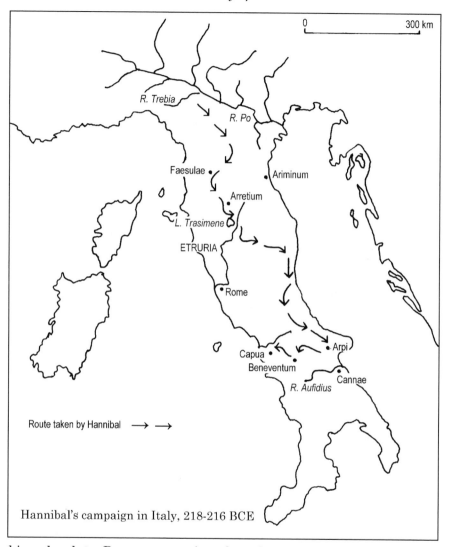

0   300 km

R. Trebia

R. Po

Faesulae •

• Ariminum

Arretium

L. Trasimene

ETRURIA

• Rome

• Arpi

Capua •

Beneventum

Cannae

R. Aufidius

Route taken by Hannibal → →

Hannibal's campaign in Italy, 218-216 BCE

him ahead to Rome, suggesting that they could be dining on the Capitoline Hill within three days. Yet Hannibal hesitated, unsure of his ability to hold the city with his shattered troops. Instead, he preferred to pursue a policy of undermining Rome's strength by attempting to win over its allies. Maharbal told his leader sadly: 'You know how to win, Hannibal, but you do not know how to use your victory.' With help from its Latin allies, Rome rebuilt its armies and Hannibal withdrew to southern Italy, where a stalemate ensued.

By 205, the Romans were strong enough to make a decisive move, sending an army into North Africa to threaten Carthage itself. Hannibal

Scipio Africanus.

was forced to return to defend his homeland, and in 202 the Romans won a great and final victory at Zama – their general, Publius Cornelius Scipio, became known ever afterwards as 'Scipio Africanus'. The Romans imposed severe peace terms on the conquered Carthaginians, cutting their navy to ten ships, stripping them of their possessions outside Africa (the Romans took control of Carthaginian territory in Spain, which they divided into two provinces in 197), forbidding them to declare war on others, and forcing them to pay 800,000 pounds of silver over a 50 year period.

The 3rd Punic War (149-146)

Despite this disastrous defeat, Carthage quickly recovered economically and started to pay off its levies. It became a small but prosperous city which posed little threat to Rome. However, there were many Romans who felt that it should have been wiped out completely after Zama; most notable among them was the senator Cato the Elder, an arch-conservative who always ended any speech, no matter its topic, with the words *delenda est Carthago* ('Carthage must be destroyed').

These hawks were given their opportunity in 150 when Carthaginians attacked a neighbouring city, thereby breaking the terms of their surrender after Zama. The Romans sent a force led by Scipio Aemilianus (the adopted grandson of Scipio Africanus). The city was burnt to the ground and its inhabitants sold into slavery. The surrounding area was annexed and turned into the province of Africa; by 146, Rome had six provinces, five of which had been gained through the wars with Carthage.

Hannibal's legacy

Hannibal himself was spared after the battle of Zama and remained in Carthage to help the city recover. However, the Romans soon grew afraid of his continued presence, and he was forced to flee to the east, where he fought for various kingdoms in their wars against the Romans. Eventually, Rome demanded that he be surrendered; rather than let this happen, Hannibal committed suicide some time after 183.

The memory of Hannibal cast a dark shadow over the Roman psyche. It was said that he had taught the Roman people the meaning of fear – Roman parents apparently told their children brutal stories about him if they misbehaved. In one sense, then, Hannibal came to be seen as Rome's ultimate bogeyman; on the other hand, many writers also displayed a grudging admiration for such a brilliant and brave opponent, and statues of him were even put up in Rome to show how worthy an enemy the city had managed to defeat.

This bust is believed to depict Hannibal. If it is indeed Hannibal, this is the only surviving likeness of one of Rome's greatest enemies.

ii. Rome and the East

To the east of Italy, the predominant culture in the Mediterranean world was Greek, and had been since the 320s, when the Macedonian king Alexander the Great had conquered vast swathes of land all the way to northern India. After his death, his vast empire had been split into various kingdoms; the three largest were those of Macedonia (covering most of central and northern Greece, as well as the lands to the north of the Aegean Sea), the Seleucid kingdom (covering modern Turkey, Syria and the middle east), and Egypt. In Greece itself, there were other smaller states – we have already read of the kingdom of Epirus in the northwest; many of the southern cities remained independent, but formed alliances in one of two political Leagues – the Aetolian League and the Achaean League.

During the 2nd Punic War, the Macedonian king Philip V made an alliance with the Carthaginians, hoping to benefit if they defeated the Romans. Rome did not have the manpower to launch a full-scale attack in the east, but instead formed an alliance with the Aetolian League, which was itself an enemy of the Macedonians. The half-hearted conflict lasted between 214 and 205, and was known as the 1st Macedonian War. Having conquered Hannibal in 202, however, the Romans had more time to concentrate on the east.

In 200, the League asked Rome for help in the continuing conflict with Macedonia. A 2nd Macedonian War ensued, in which the Romans

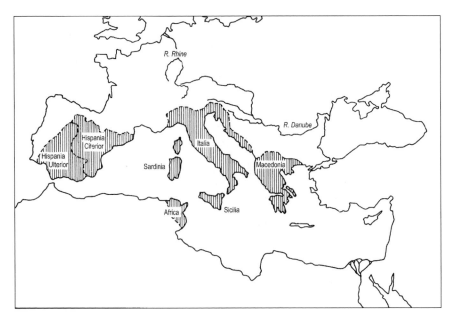

Territories under Roman control in 146 BCE.

portrayed themselves as 'liberators' of the Greeks from the Macedonian king Philip V. The Roman commander Flamininus even 'announced' their liberation – to reportedly rapturous enthusiasm – at the Isthmian Games at Corinth in 196. Over following decades, the Romans continued to be involved in Greek affairs, most notably during a 3rd Macedonian War between 171 and 167, by the end of which they had destroyed the kingdom of Macedonia. However, throughout this period, Roman policy remained one of alliance with supportive Greek peoples rather than of conquest.

This changed in 149, by which time the Romans had grown tired of the infighting amongst the Greeks, and their policy turned to one of conquest. The following year, Macedonia was annexed as a Roman province; in 146 (the same year as the destruction of Carthage), the Achaean League was defeated too and the city of Corinth was razed to the ground – all the men were killed and the women and children were sold into slavery. Within the space of a few short months, Rome had all but obliterated two of the great cities of the Mediterranean world.

Hellenisation

By the 2nd century, the Greek world had a rich cultural and artistic heritage, which had developed over many centuries. As the Romans came into contact more with the east, Greek art (especially sculpture), architecture, philosophy, drama and literature had a profound effect on Roman culture, in a process known as Hellenisation (from 'Hellas' – the ancient name for Greece). As the poet Horace later put it: *Graecia capta ferum victorem cepit* ('captured Greece captured her savage conqueror').

There were mixed Roman responses to this eastern influence, with some taking to it whole-heartedly, and others disapproving. Scipio Africanus, while staying at the Greek city of Syracuse, was accused by his critics of becoming a 'soft' Greek, with a dress and demeanour 'which were un-Roman, and not even soldierly; he strolled about the gymnasium in a Greek cloak and sandals, and wasted his time over books and physical exercise' (Livy 29.19). One of the greatest critics of Hellenisation was the conservative senator Cato the Elder, who wrote as follows to his son:

> 'I shall show you the results of my own experience at Athens: that it is a good idea to dip into their literature, but not to learn it thoroughly. I shall convince you that they are the most wicked and obstinate people, and you may take my word as the word of a prophet: if that people ever bestow its literature upon us, it will corrupt everything.'
> quoted in Pliny's *Natural History* 29.13

Yet Cato failed to halt the spread of things Greek: over the following centuries, Greek literature came to influence greatly Roman writers of many genres, including epic and lyric poetry, drama (both tragedy and comedy), the novel, philosophy, and history.

Review 3

1. Explain the following terms: *delenda est Carthago, Poeni, Punicus.*
2. Read pp. 139-47 and 223-41 and summarise the influence that Greek civilisation had on Roman education and Roman drama.
E. Research the life of Hannibal and write an obituary for him.
E. Read Livy's account of Hannibal's journey over the Alps. Imagine that you are a soldier in his army and write an account of your experiences.

---

3. The Fall of the Republic (133-31 BCE)

Over the following century, Rome extended her dominion much further still (see map on p. 39). In the east, king Attalus of Pergamum (a region which is now part of northern Turkey) bequeathed his kingdom to Rome, and this became the province of Asia in 133. Roman legions also subdued the inland regions of Spain, as well as territory north and south of the Alps: Transalpine Gaul ('Gaul the other side of the Alps') became a province in 120, while Cisalpine Gaul ('Gaul this side of the Alps') followed in 81. Back in the east, Bithynia et Pontus, Syria, Cyrene and Crete all became provinces after Rome's campaigns of 75-64, joining Cilicia (a region in what is now southern Turkey) which had already been annexed in 102. During the 50s, Julius Caesar, in a series of campaigns of astonishing violence, added the rest of Gaul – an area roughly covering today's France, Belgium and Holland (in 55 and 54, he also made two forays into Britain, but left the island unconquered).

Nonetheless, these conquests could not mask growing troubles at home. The fact that Rome had acquired an empire very quickly brought with it a mountain of social problems, key amongst them were:

- **Governance**. By 133, Rome had seven provinces, but still the political structure appropriate merely for a city-state. Many provincial governors were corrupt, so alienating local peoples.
- **Social inequality**. Vast riches poured into Rome from its new territories; however, almost all of this wealth went to the aristocrats, so widening the gap between rich and poor.
- **Land inequality**. With huge numbers of slaves now being brought to Italy, wealthy landowners developed large farming estates (known as *latifundia*) to be worked by these captives. These landowners often took land which had been set aside for public smallholdings (*ager publicus*), in the process pushing labourers and small farmers off their land and leaving them with little choice but to start a new life in the city.
- **Vested interests**. The senate, the most important ruling body (see p. 360), was dominated by a small number of about 20 noble

families. They showed no interest in facing up to these new problems, and simply looked to further their own interests. As a result, their authority came to be challenged and thus led to the collapse of the republic.

Farmland was one of the key issues in this crisis. Alongside the growth of the *latifundia*, Rome also started to import grain cheaply from abroad and this contributed to putting many small farmers out of business. Moreover, it was law that all serving soldiers in the army had to own a certain amount of land, and so the city lost some of its military manpower; this meant that there was now a large number of unemployed, poor and angry citizens. Rome was a social and political tinderbox.

The Gracchi
The situation came to a head in 133, when the tribune of the people (see p. 360) Tiberius Sempronius Gracchus attempted radical social reform: he introduced a law limiting the amount of land which any one individual could own; the resulting land surplus was to be redistributed to the poor, thereby allowing them to serve in the army once again. Unsurprisingly, this reform met with furious opposition from the senators, many of whose farms were threatened; when Tiberius stood for re-election the following year, several senators marched to the forum and clubbed him to death, together with some 300 of his supporters. However, the push for reform could not be halted.

In 123, Tiberius' younger brother Gaius was himself elected tribune, a post which he held for two years. He too fought for social justice, bringing in a more wide-ranging set of reforms than his brother had done. He aimed to see that all Roman citizens, not just the ruling class, benefited from the spoils of empire, while he tried to make those who governed the empire more accountable for their actions. His new laws included reforms of provincial administration and taxation, guaranteeing a subsidised grain supply to poorer citizens (the *annona* – see p. 151), as well as judicial reform, and supporting his brother's land reform.

Once again, the senate vigorously opposed these measures; the final straw came in 122 when Gaius proposed extending Roman citizenship to the Italian allies. In 121 he too was murdered at the instigation of the senate and, by the end of that year, most of his new laws had been repealed. Nonetheless, the Gracchi brothers had shown the Roman people that it was possible to stand up to the ruling class.

Marius and Sulla
The crisis at Rome did not go away. In the following generation, the city faced military threats in every part of its empire; these included a war in Africa against the Numidians, ably led by their King Jugurtha, a slave revolt in Sicily and an invasion of northern Italy by two German

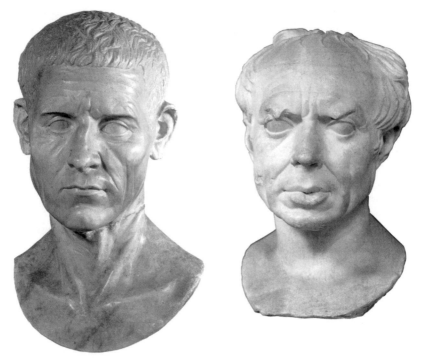

Sulla.   Marius.

tribes, the Cimbri and the Teutones. The senate handled these crises badly, and was only rescued from disaster by the genius of an ambitious general called Gaius Marius. When Marius was elected consul in 107, he was a *novus homo* ('new man'), a term which described someone who was the first in his family to be elected consul or serve in the senate. He went on to hold the consulship an unprecedented seven times in all.

Although Marius solved the military crisis, he also introduced a reform in 107 which in time would lead directly to the break-up of the republic: this was to allow any citizen to serve in the army, regardless of whether or not he owned land. The landless poor now came to rely on the generals to recruit them and give them work; moreover, they also hoped that, if they served well, then their general would reward them with a small-holding when they had reached the end of their service. The balance of power in the state had shifted decisively – it was now the generals who could control and manipulate the masses, and the ensuing decades were fundamentally a story of these generals fighting like warlords for power and diminishing the status of the senate.

In 91, the tribune Marcus Livius Drusus was assassinated after proposing, as Gaius Gracchus had, that Rome's Italian allies should be given citizenship. Many of the allies, who provided so much manpower for Rome's armies, now despaired of ever winning equal rights and revolted. This **Social War** (from the Latin *socius*, meaning 'ally') lasted until 89, when the Romans managed to overcome the allies; however, the senate sensibly recognised that it was in Rome's long term interest to extend citizenship rights, and all free inhabitants of Italy were given Roman citizenship soon afterwards.

In the same year, a war broke out in the east. Mithridates, king of Pontus, a region bordering Roman territory in Asia Minor, was provoked into invading after a border dispute; he was welcomed as a liberator by many provincials. In 88, the senate sent one of the consuls at the head of an army to confront the foe. The consul was Lucius Cornelius Sulla, who had once served in Marius' army but was now on bad terms with his former general. Marius, who wanted the command for himself, arranged for one of the tribunes to persuade the plebeian assembly (see p. 362) to overturn Sulla's appointment and appoint himself instead.

Chaos ensued. Sulla marched on Rome at the head of an army, driving out Marius and heading off to the east with his troops. Marius himself then marched on the city in 87, massacring his opponents and seizing power. Although he died the following year, his cause was taken up by his ally Cinna, and when Sulla returned to Rome in 83 the stage was set for a full-scale civil war. After a series of bloody battles, Sulla emerged victorious in 81 and had himself appointed dictator. He posed as the conservative leader of the aristocracy, launching a brutal reign of terror against his opponents, and reforming the constitution by strengthening the senate and removing most of the tribunes' powers. He then served as consul for a two further years, after which he retired from public life in 79, dying just months later. One key aspect of his legacy was clear – political domination could be secured at Rome by the use of force.

Optimates and populares

As the tension between the conservative senate and the common people grew during the final century of the republic, ambitious politicians broadly sought to make a career by identifying with either one or the other. Although it is a simplification, a helpful rule of thumb is that those who sided with the people, such as the Gracchi and Marius, were known as *populares* ('those favouring the people'), while others, such as Sulla, who sided with the senate were known as *optimates* ('the best men').

Caesar and Pompey

Sulla's reforms were quickly undermined by other generals, notably Gnaeus Pompey and Marcus Licinius Crassus, the one a brilliant young military leader, the other the richest man at Rome. They were elected joint consuls in 70 and undid many of Sulla's reforms, in particular

Pompey.

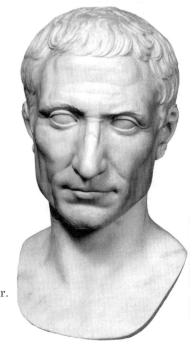

Julius Caesar.

returning full powers to the tribunes. The senate's last chance to dominate the state had disappeared.

The following years were troubled ones at Rome as the struggle continued between the senate and the generals. Mob violence was common
in the city and, in 63, a young noble called Catiline was caught plotting
to overthrow the state; the consul Cicero (see box on p. 40) swiftly had
many of his supporters executed (Catiline himself was killed in battle
soon afterwards). A decisive moment came in 60 when Pompey and
Crassus chose to join forces with another rising military star, Gaius
Julius Caesar, to form a 'Triumvirate' – a ruling board of three men,
which had the support of the army and people (it subsequently became
known as the 'First Triumvirate'); the senate was left powerless.

Caesar was consul in 59 and enacted all the measures his partners
wanted. However, the Triumvirate was always an alliance of conven-
ience and often showed signs of strain. When Crassus died in 53, Caesar
had been away for five years on his extraordinary conquest of Gaul and
the tension grew between the two surviving triumvirs. Pompey felt
threatened by Caesar's military power and success, and so he became
more and more closely aligned with the senate. On January 1st 49, the
senate voted that Caesar, who was still in Gaul, should lay down his
command. Caesar had to choose between humiliation and a return to
Italy to fight a civil war.

> **Crossing the Rubicon**
>
> The river Rubicon in northern Italy was the boundary between the province of Cisalpine Gaul and Italy itself. No general was allowed to lead his army into Italy – to do so was considered an act of treason. Therefore, when Caesar arrived at this river, he hesitated – knowing that once he had crossed, there could be no going back on fighting a civil war. Today, the phrase 'to cross the Rubicon' therefore means 'to go beyond the point of no return'. Apparently, when Caesar did finally decide to cross the river he uttered another famous phrase: *alea iacta est* – 'the die is cast'.
>
> In fact, Caesar was rather good at coming up with catchy phrases. In 47, he fought a victorious campaign at lightning speed in Pontus, about which he famously said: *veni, vidi, vici* ('I came, I saw, I conquered').

Against all the odds, Caesar won. By brilliant generalship he defeated his opponents in Spain (49), Greece (48 – after which Pompey fled to Egypt and was murdered), the Middle East (47), Africa (46), and Spain again in 45. He returned triumphantly to Rome in that year, and in 44 had himself appointed 'dictator for life'; he now embarked on a series of important reforms to relieve hardship, improve administration of the empire, and reform the Roman calendar (see p. 369). However, many at Rome were alarmed at his power, thinking that he was trying to become the first monarch for 500 years. Led by Brutus, one of Caesar's closest friends, a group of assassins stabbed him to death on the Ides of March in 44.

This coin depicts Brutus, a leading conspirator on the Ides of March (left). The reverse of the same coin (right) shows the Cap of Liberty between two daggers.

Yet the conspirators' victory was short-lived. Two of Caesar's lieutenants, Mark Antony and Marcus Aemilius Lepidus, joined forces with his adopted heir, Octavian, to lead a campaign against them. In 43, they formed the 'Second Triumvirate'; unlike the First Triumvirate, this second version was an official, legally established institution. As a result, it managed to sideline the role of the senate, so signalling the end of the republic.

Shakespeare and Roman history

William Shakespeare was one of many who have been fascinated by this bloody period in Roman history, to the extent that he wrote two history plays set during these times, *Julius Caesar* and *Antony and Cleopatra*. It is in the first of these that Caesar utters the famous words at the moment of his death: '*et tu, Brute?*' ('You too, Brutus?'), which have become synonymous with any act of betrayal by a close friend. However, according to our main source, Caesar's final words were actually in Greek: the historian Plutarch records him as exclaiming: '*kai su, teknon?*', which means something more like 'You too, my child?'.

In 42, Antony and Octavian scored an overwhelming victory over the conspirators' army at Philippi in Macedonia. The triumvirs now divided the empire between them, with Octavian ruling in the west, Antony in the east, and Lepidus in Spain and Africa. However, Octavian and Antony were both ambitious men, and they too soon fell out. For a while, Lepidus managed to distance himself from their frequent quarrels; yet in 36 he made a fatal political move in trying to take control of a number of Octavian's legions. This allowed Octavian to accuse him of attempting rebellion; Lepidus was stripped of nearly all his titles and removed from the political scene.

Mark Antony (left); Cleopatra (right).

The Roman world was now run by two men who held a deep mutual loathing. Antony was based in Alexandria, living openly with Queen Cleopatra of Egypt, who bore him three children (despite his still being married to Octavian's sister!). Back in Rome, Octavian managed to stir up the people against Antony, and further conflict followed. The last great battle of the civil wars came at sea in 31 at Actium, off the southwest coast of Greece. Octavian won and pursued Antony and Cleopatra back to Egypt where, the following year, they both committed suicide. Octavian was now the single most powerful man in the Roman world, and the republic was well and truly dead.

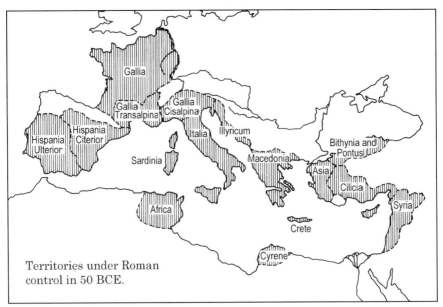

Territories under Roman
control in 50 BCE.

Cicero.

39

Cicero

A key figure in the final decades of the republic was Marcus Tullius Cicero (106-43 BCE). Cicero came from a wealthy family of Arpinum, a hill town about 100 km (60 miles) from Rome; however, his family had never played a serious role in Roman politics and so Cicero, who became quaestor in 76 and consul in 63, was a *novus homo*. The young Cicero made his name as a barrister, brilliantly prosecuting Verres, the governor of Sicily, for corruption in 70.

Throughout his political life, Cicero fought for the preservation of the republic, vainly hoping that the senators and the merchant class, the equites (see p. 361), could learn to work together in harmony. Although he took no part in the assassination of Caesar, he clearly approved of it: in February 43 he wrote a letter (*Ad Fam. 10.28*) to Trebonius, one of the conspirators, which began: 'How I wish that you had invited me to that most glorious banquet on the Ides of March!' Cicero was executed later that same year on the orders of Mark Antony, against whom he had delivered a series of savagely critical speeches, known as the *Philippics*.

Yet Cicero's legacy is far more than political. He is acknowledged as the greatest prose writer in the Latin language, and a vast body of his works has survived, including speeches for the law courts, philosophical treatises and poems. He was also a great letter writer, and 35 books of letters remain – 16 to his family and friends, 16 to his closest friend Atticus, and 3 to his brother Quintus; these throw a very detailed light on the Rome of his day. Cicero's legacy is therefore enormous, and today the Latin studied in schools and universities worldwide is centred on what is known as 'Ciceronian Latin'.

Review 4

1. Explain the origin and meaning of the following words and phrases: *alea iacta est; optimates, populares, to cross the Rubicon; veni, vidi, vici.*
2. Find out what you can about the lives of the following: the Gracchi brothers, Marius, Sulla, Pompey, Crassus, Cicero, Julius Caesar, Cleopatra.
3. Why do you think that the Gracchi have sometimes been thought of as among the earliest 'socialists' in recorded history?
4. Find out about the conspiracy of Catiline. Do you think that Cicero took the right course of action?
5. Research the story of Antony and Cleopatra. Why do you think this has captured the imagination of so many people down the ages?
E. Choose one of the personalities mentioned in Question 2 and write an obituary for them.

III. THE EMPIRE (31 BCE-476 CE)

1. The Rule of Augustus (31 BCE-14 CE)

In essence, Rome was once again back to one-man rule. Although Octavian was careful to appear to restore power to the magistrates, assemblies, and senate, in reality he kept hold of the reins himself by two very simple measures: he ensured that he was always elected a tribune of the people, while he also held supreme power over the provinces and the legions which policed them (you can read more about the constitution of the empire on p. 364). Octavian assumed the name Augustus

This statue portrays Augustus as a Roman general. The cupid at his leg is a reference to his supposed descent from the goddess Venus.

('revered'), and was often referred to as *princeps*, or 'the first citizen'. He was Rome's first 'emperor' – this English word is derived from the Latin *imperator*, meaning 'commander' or 'general'. The following passage from the Roman historian Tacitus, who wrote disapprovingly of Augustus about a century later, gives an insight into how he achieved his status:

'He won over the soldiers with gifts of money, and civilians with cheap food: both alike were beguiled by the delights of peace. His powers grew step by step as he took over the functions of the senate, the public offi-cials and even the laws. No one stood in his way, as his boldest oppo-nents had been wiped out by war or execution. As for the other aristocrats, the more slavish their obedience, the greater the riches and rewards bestowed upon them. The revolution had brought them pros-perity, so they preferred the safety of the new government to the dangers of the old one.'   Tacitus, *Annals* 1.2

For the next five centuries, Rome would be ruled by emperors, and so this period of its history is referred to as the 'empire'. While the Roman people lost their democratic rights and, under some emperors, much of their freedom of speech, Augustus had given them a system of govern-ment which brought lasting stability to the Roman world.

Caesar
Augustus also took on the name 'Caesar' after his adoptive father. From then on, Caesar came to be one of the titles of the Roman emperor. The word has also survived in many modern languages to mean 'ruler' – the Russian 'Tsar' and the German 'Kaiser' are two famous examples.

Augustus faced a mammoth task to get the empire back on its feet after the devastating years of civil war. Yet he was so successful that by the time of his death in 14 CE, he had brought peace and prosperity to the Roman world – so much so that he was able to revive the ancient tradi-tion of closing the gates to the temple of Janus (see p. 78) to indicate that the whole empire was at peace. This had happened only twice before in the long centuries of Roman history, but it occurred three times during Augustus' reign. His success was based on placing Rome's 28 legions at strategic points around the empire, and on developing an efficient sys-tem of civil service and management in the provinces.

Back in Rome, Augustus was keen to beautify the city, making it wor-thy as the capital of such a vast empire. A large number of new build-ings were commissioned and, according to the biographer Suetonius, Augustus boasted that he found Rome a city of brick and left it a city of marble (see p. 351). He also tried by various means to make the city safer for its inhabitants, introducing a rule limiting blocks of flats to a height of 18 metres (see p. 126), while he also tried to fight the fires which were a perennial problem:

> 'As far as human agency could, he made the city safe for the future ... He instituted nightly guards and regular watches against fires, and to check floods he widened and cleared the channel of the Tiber, which had been blocked with debris and building projects.'   Suetonius, *Augustus* 30

The new fire brigade consisted of 7,000 men known as *vigiles*. They were permanently on patrol in the city, although at times they could not prevent disasters from happening, as in 64 CE (see p. 212).

Another aspect of Augustus' rule was his encouraging of Romans to return to (what he thought was) traditional morality and religion – many of the new and restored buildings were temples – thereby connecting them with their past and improving standards of behaviour. Not everyone was so keen to follow him in this, however: in 8 CE he decided to banish the poet Ovid to the Black Sea after he had published a racy love poem, *Ars Amatoria*, which advised men how to chase women successfully for love affairs (including adulterous ones); worse still for Augustus was the fact that his daughter Julia was said to have had numerous affairs – she was even exiled for five years to a tiny island, where no men were allowed to be in her presence and she was banned from drinking wine!

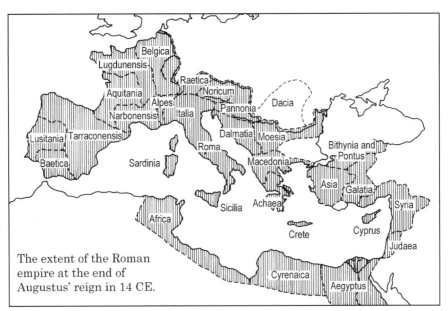

The extent of the Roman empire at the end of Augustus' reign in 14 CE.

A golden age of Latin literature

During the final decades of the republic lived some of Rome's greatest writers, perhaps because Latin literature was now so heavily influenced by Greek models through Hellenisation. In particular, prose writers such as Cicero and poets such as Catullus took the Latin language to new heights.

Augustus was keen to make use of this literary revolution as he sought to bring peace and prosperity to the empire. He was fortunate in having as a key friend Maecenas, a notable patron of the arts, who supported and encouraged great writers such as Virgil, Horace and Livy, all of whom were writing during Augustus' reign. The expectation was that, in return for the emperor's support, they would write in a style supportive of the new regime. However, even those writers who were close to Maecenas managed to retain some independence – and to produce literature which has had a profound effect on European and western literature ever since.

---

2. The 1st century CE

The immediate successors of Augustus came from his own family, and are known as the Julio-Claudian emperors. The first was his step-son **Tiberius**, who immediately deprived the Roman people of their right to vote in elections – in future, all the magistracies would be chosen by a vote of the senate. Two army rebellions were quickly suppressed, and Tiberius was able to get away with this move because he was a good administrator of the provinces and kept the peace, as the writer Strabo commented:

> 'Never have the Romans and their allies enjoyed such peace and prosperity as was given to them by Augustus from the moment he assumed absolute power, and is now being provided for them by his son and successor Tiberius, who is basing his own administration and laws on those of Augustus.'   Strabo, 4.4.2

Yet Tiberius did not have the self-confidence of Augustus and became paranoid that people were conspiring against him. He withdrew to the island of Capri for the last 11 years of his reign (where, according to Suetonius, he led a life of disgusting immorality), leaving Sejanus, the prefect of the Praetorian Guard (the garrison of soldiers which protected the city of Rome – see box below), to preside with cruelty over affairs at Rome; ironically, Sejanus was himself caught conspiring against his master and put to death.

When Tiberius died in 37, the Roman people breathed a collective sigh of relief, and welcomed his great-nephew and heir **Gaius** with open arms (he was more commonly known as '**Caligula**', meaning 'Little Boots', since at a very young age he would accompany his father, the

44

general Germanicus, in a miniature soldier's uniform). Yet he too soon became drunk on power and ruled with great cruelty, so that he was assassinated after four years in power.

The Praetorian Guard

Upon becoming *princeps*, Augustus realised that as sole ruler of the Roman world, he would need strong military protection in Rome itself. He therefore established the 'Praetorian Guard', consisting of nine cohorts with 1,000 soldiers each. In 21 CE, under the orders of Tiberius, a large barracks was built for the guardsmen just outside Rome. The guardsmen's role was to patrol the city, with one cohort always on duty at the imperial palace.

The Praetorian Guard soon gained huge political power in Rome, as it was hard for an emperor or the political class to go against the wishes of such a large number of soldiers. They were often easily bribed and, for the right amount of money, could turn against emperors or even the people of Rome. As a result, the commander of the Praetorian Guard, known as its 'prefect', could be a key figure in Roman politics, as can be seen from the careers of both Sejanus under Tiberius and Burrus under Nero.

Caligula died without naming a successor and so the senate began discussing a return to the republican system, but the Praetorian Guard had other ideas. When they found Gaius' 50 year old uncle, Claudius, hiding behind a curtain in the imperial palace, they immediately proclaimed him emperor (his promise of 15,000 sesterces for each guardsman may have helped!). **Claudius** was a most unlikely emperor – crippled by polio as a boy, he spoke with a stammer and was seen as a quiet intellectual lacking the confidence to rule. However, he added new provinces to the existing frontiers, including Mauretania (in Africa) and Thrace (to the north of Greece) while, in 43, he successfully launched a full-scale invasion of the island of Britain. He also reorganised the civil service, and promoted large numbers of freedmen to positions of power. Yet Claudius was a victim of his own dysfunctional family. His fourth wife, Agrippina the Younger (who was also his niece), persuaded him to adopt her son **Nero**, in preference to his own son Britannicus. No sooner had he done this than Agrippina had Claudius poisoned, and Nero came to the throne in 54. He too was initially popular with the masses and seems to have ruled well in his early years, being guided by his tutor, the philosopher Seneca the Younger, and Burrus, the prefect of the Praetorian Guard. Things changed in 59, however, and within six appalling years he had discarded all his advisers and arranged the murders of Britannicus, his mother Agrippina and his wife Octavia, while Seneca was forced into suicide.

Nero was obsessed with the arts, and often competed in theatrical contests and chariot races, a fact which appalled the aristocratic elite

Nero.

but delighted the masses. Yet his popularity with them was soon severely strained too by the events surrounding the great fire of Rome in 64; after the poorest area of the city had been devastated, Nero claimed the land for himself rather than help re-house his people. He put the blame on the Christians (see p. 118), having hundreds executed in horrific ways. Eventually, the armies in Gaul and Spain could take no more and marched on Rome in 68. Nero fled in fear and committed suicide. This was a key moment in the history of the empire, as Tacitus observes:

> 'Nero's death caused an initial outburst of joy and relief; at the same time it evoked a variety of emotions, not only in Rome, among the senators, people and city garrisons, but also in all the legions and their generals – for one secret of imperial politics had been revealed – an emperor could be created elsewhere than in Rome.'
>
> Tacitus, *Histories* 1.4

Tacitus' words here also underline another key fact – that an emperor could not hope to stay in power unless he had the support of the army. Nero was the last of the 'Julio-Claudian' emperors who had started with Augustus.

In the aftermath of Nero's death, a power struggle ensued, during which Rome had four emperors in the year 69 – Galba, Otho, Vitellius and Vespasian – all of them powerful army commanders. After months of civil wars, **Vespasian**, the commander of the forces in the east, was proclaimed emperor. He left his son Titus to finish the process of crushing the Jewish Revolt (see p. 117) and returned to Rome, where he ruled

46

Vespasian.

successfully for the next ten years. From the outset he sought to work with the senate, governing with wisdom and fairness. One of the key achievements of his rule was the construction of the Colosseum (see p. 212).

He was succeeded in 79 by **Titus**, who had won much acclaim for his victories against the Jews. He proved a popular and effective ruler, not least when trying to arrange support for those affected by the eruption of Mt Vesuvius (see p. 263). However, just two years later he was dead, to be replaced by his younger brother **Domitian**, a ruthlessly efficient administrator but also extremely arrogant – he even ordered that he should be addressed as 'Lord and God'! He disregarded the opinions of the senate and rarely consulted it, so that conspiracies arose against him. In response, Domitian began a 'reign of terror', culling all those who he felt were against him. In one example, some books were published in praise of two philosophers critical of the regime: the authors were executed and the books publicly burnt in the forum by the emperor's agents, as Tacitus relates:

47

The Arch of Titus was set up in the Roman forum in 81 CE by Titus' brother and successor Domitian. It celebrates the triumph awarded to Titus after his capture of Jerusalem in 70 CE.

'They believed that this fire was exterminating the voice of the people, the liberty of the senate, and the conscience of mankind. Teachers of philosophy were banished, together with every honourable study in case anything decent might offend the emperor's eyes. And we senators gave a remarkable example of subservience. Our ancestors saw the heights of liberty, we the depths of slavery: the fear of spies made us deaf and dumb, and we would have lost our memories if it had been as easy to forget as to keep silent.'   Tacitus, *Agricola* 2

When Domitian was assassinated in 96 without leaving a named successor, it fell to the senate to determine the future for the first time in more than a century. They chose not to revive the republic, but instead elected another emperor, presumably believing that the vast complexity of the empire needed the certainty of one ruler, rather than the deliberation of committees.

The senate's decision worked well, as the empire now entered into a period of greater peace and prosperity, under the rule of the 'five good emperors' who ruled from 96-180. Edward Gibbon, the 18th-century historian of the Roman empire, wrote about these years, surely rather too idealistically, as follows:

> 'If a man were called to fix the period in the history of the world, during which the condition of the human race was most happy and prosperous, he would, without hesitation, name that which elapsed from the death of Domitian to the accession of Commodus (in 180).'
>
> *The History of the Decline and Fall of the Roman Empire* 1.78

The first of these five emperors, **Nerva** (96-98), was a respectable elderly lawyer who, in his brief reign, made some sensible changes, and in particular went back to consulting the senate regularly and submitting legislation to it for approval.

Philanthropy

Nerva set up a remarkable philanthropic practice which lasted for over 200 years. Large sums of state money were set aside to provide loans for farmers at a low rate of interest, meaning that farmers were guaranteed their livelihood. More importantly, the interest on these loans was used to support and educate orphans and the children of the poor.

---

3. The 2nd century CE

Nerva named as his successor **Trajan** (98-117), who was born and raised in Spain and so was the first non-Italian emperor. This reflected the increasingly cosmopolitan nature of the empire, and by now more and more senators were drawn from all parts of the Roman world; especially important were those from Asia Minor and the other eastern provinces, where the Greek-speaking population was becoming increasingly involved in imperial administration. During Trajan's reign, the empire reached its greatest extent (see map on p. 50). His campaigns along the Danube to incorporate the province of Dacia (a region which is today the country of Romania) are recorded in a series of sculptured reliefs spiralling up the massive pillar known as Trajan's Column, which can still be seen in Rome today.

Following Trajan came **Hadrian** (117-138), who came from the same town in Spain. He was keen to make the empire's borders more secure, believing rightly that the Romans had overstretched themselves under Trajan. He withdrew from the territory Trajan had conquered in the Parthian empire (modern Iran), fortified the frontier in Germany, and in Britain built the wall for which he remains famous. This was one of

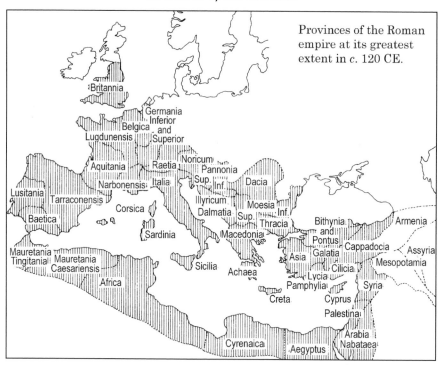

Provinces of the Roman
empire at its greatest
extent in *c.* 120 CE.

Trajan's Column.

Hadrian.

many great architectural wonders completed in the reign of the art-loving Hadrian. Others which can still be seen today include the Pantheon in Rome (see p. 87), the temple of Olympian Zeus in Athens, as well as his extensive villa complex near the hills of Tivoli outside Rome.

The rule of Hadrian's successor, **Antoninus Pius** (138-161), was recognised even then as a golden age. Antoninus was a moderate and fair emperor, who placed a maximum cost on gladiatorial games to save money, which helped him to pay for new buildings and repair old ones. He was devoted to his wife Faustina and set up a charity for homeless girls called the *Faustinianiae* in honour of her. Moreover, he was reluctant to go to war, claiming that he would 'rather save a single citizen than a thousand enemies'.

After Antoninus came **Marcus Aurelius** (161-180), who is today best known for his book of *Meditations*, which set out his ideas on stoic philosophy (see p. 103). However, although Marcus was an intellectual at heart, he was forced to spend most of his reign in frontier campaigns, as barbarians on the far banks of the Rhine, Danube and Euphrates rivers tried to migrate into the empire. He had to raise taxes and conscript thousands of men into the legions; vast sums of money were required to sustain the empire. Moreover, plague spread from the east throughout the empire, causing grievous loss of life. By the time he died, dark clouds seemed to be looming over the Roman world.

As Gibbon suggests, the reign of Marcus was later seen to be the end

Marcus Aurelius.

of a high point which Rome never regained. The contemporary historian Cassius Dio wrote that 'our history now descends from a kingdom of gold to one of iron and rust'. The first problem was Marcus' heir; all the emperors since Nerva had nominated successors from outside their own families, but Marcus returned to the practice of the early emperors by choosing his son, **Commodus** (180-192). Commodus was little interested in fighting barbarians and soon made terms with them, giving away much of the progress made by his father. He headed back to Rome,

Commodus is here shown dressed as Hercules, suggesting the emperor's high opinion of himself.

where he lived a life of luxury and sadistic pleasure, just as some of the early emperors had. Cassius Dio wrote of him that he was 'a greater curse to the Romans than any plague or crime'.

The end of Commodus

Eventually a plot to assassinate Commodus was hatched by the prefect of the Praetorian Guard and various other of his allies. The final straw for them had been learning of the emperor's plan to kill the consuls and appoint gladiators in their place (Commodus was a great lover of gladiatorial combat – see p. 216). His mistress Marcia was one of the conspirators and fed him poison, but he was so drunk that he vomited it up! However, they finished the job by having him strangled by an athlete.

After Commodus' demise, there followed a period of unrest and infighting until in 193 **Septimius Severus**, the commander of the army in Pannonia, claimed the prize.

4. The 3rd century CE

Severus, who came from a wealthy north African family, ruled until 211. These years were marked by warfare with tribes on the borders of the empire, particularly with the Parthians, after which campaign he erected an arch in the Roman forum which can still be seen today. His relationship with the senate was always poor, and he had many senators killed for conspiring against him; they were replaced with his own favourites, and the principate was once again turned into a ruthless mil-

Septimius Severus.

itary dictatorship. Yet he was popular with the people since he stamped out the corruption of Commodus' era. In particular, Septimius had the support of the army, not least because he raised the annual salary of a soldier from 300 to 500 denarii! According to Cassius Dio, his dying words to his sons (and co-heirs) were:

> 'Stick together, spend your money on the troops, and let everyone else go hang!'   Cassius Dio, 76.15

Yet from the outset Severus' elder son **Caracalla** ignored the first part of this advice – within a few months he had his brother and co-emperor Geta murdered (along with various other members of his family), ruling on his own until 217. Like his father, Caracalla indulged the army, raising their pay by 50%. To fund this, he gave citizenship to every free-born inhabitant in the empire – thereby hugely increasing the number of people eligible to pay tax. Today, Caracalla is perhaps best known for the magnificent set of baths he had constructed in Rome (see p. 243).

When Caracalla was murdered in 217, a power struggle followed after which Rome was ruled first by the praetorian prefect **Macrinus** (the first non-senator to become emperor); after he was assassinated, a 15-year-old religious fanatic called **Elagabalus** replaced him, supported by his grandmother Julia Maesa. Yet he too was murdered, and replaced by his 13-year-old cousin **Alexander**. He reigned from 222 to 235, but the real power behind the throne lay with his mother Julia Mamaea, who was the virtual empress of Rome. In fact, these years were ones of peace and stability for the empire, as the rulers avoided frontier conflicts.

Progressive policies

Alexander and Julia also put forward many progressive initiatives to benefit citizens of the empire: teachers and scholars were subsidised; landlords who improved their property were excused taxes; everybody engaged in a trade or industry that benefited the city of Rome was enrolled in a specific guild and carefully supervised.

Yet the progress of Alexander's reign did not last. When the German tribes threatened the Rhine frontier, the legions mutinied and the emperor was killed in a riot.

The empire now entered an era of great instability. Between 235 and 284, more than 50 emperors or heirs were named by different armies. Two parts of the empire broke away: for 15 years there was a separate 'empire of the Gauls', which included Spain and Britain, while in the east Queen Zenobia of Palymra (in modern Syria) for a few years set up an empire which stretched from Asia Minor to Egypt. Within the borders of the Roman empire, a series of disasters struck: barbarians seeking a better life invaded, plague and famine devastated many provinces, while heavy taxation ruined people all over the Roman world. As a result, many ran off and joined groups of outlaws and army deserters, who ransacked and burnt vast areas of the provinces. The population dropped heavily, so barbarian mercenaries had to be employed to defend the borders.

These civil wars slowly came to an end, and political order was restored by **Diocletian**, who reigned from 284 to 305. Diocletian concentrated on strengthening the army, and soldiers became the privileged class in place of the landed aristocracy. Retired centurions were given huge grants and promoted to the equestrian order; equites, rather than senators, were now appointed as provincial governors and legionary commanders. In fact, the senate lost almost all its power – after 280, it never issued another decree and simply acted as Rome's city council.

Splitting the empire

Diocletian made huge changes to the administrative structure of the empire. Most significantly, he felt that the empire was too large to be ruled by one man alone, and so he divided it into two halves, east and west. Each half was to be ruled by an emperor, known as 'Augustus', and each emperor was given a successor and deputy, known as a 'Caesar'. In practice, each Caesar was given a large province to govern, so that the empire was really split into four parts, a structure now known as the 'Tetrarchy'. Diocletian became the Augustus in the east, while a fellow soldier, Maximian, was the Augustus of the west.

This statuette of the Tetrarchs dates from the 4th century CE and portrays the four rulers embracing in a sign of harmony.

5. The 4th century CE

Diocletian resigned in 305 and persuaded his fellow Augustus to do the same, intending that the two Caesars would take over. However, within months the new system broke down, as four army commanders once again vied for power. One of them was **Constantine**, who fled to Britain, where his troops declared him emperor in 306. Constantine believed that the division of the empire into four parts had been a mistake, and for years a series of civil wars ensued. By 323, however, he had defeated all his rivals and become sole emperor.

After Augustus, Constantine was perhaps the most influential emperor in all Roman history. His reign, which lasted until 337, was significant for two enormous changes:

- **Constantinople**: he decided to relocate the empire's capital to the east; by this time, the eastern half of the empire was far more prosperous and needed more defending from barbarians. Constantine lavishly rebuilt the Greek city of Byzantium on the Bosphorus, renaming it Constantinople ('the city of Constantine'), and making it the imperial capital.
- **Christianity**: the other key change was the acceptance of Christianity as an official religion of the empire. This change is explained in more detail on pp. 116-23.

Constantine.

56

The conversion of Constantine eventually led to the union of church and state. Imperial taxes went into the coffers of the church, bishops became civil servants, and the titles, rules and regulations of the empire pervaded the Church. Moreover, Constantine supported the building of a huge number of Christian basilicas, including the Church of the Holy Sepulchre in Jerusalem, and the original Basilica of St Peter in Rome.

Constantine was succeeded by his son **Constantius II**, who reigned from 337 to 361. He continued his father's policy of Christianizing the empire, but was hampered by continuing civil wars during his reign, particularly in opposition to his rival Magnentius, who at one stage managed to develop a break-away empire in Spain, Gaul, Britain and Africa. He was eventually defeated in 353, but at great cost to Constantius' troop numbers. According to the contemporary historian Ammianus Marcellinus, Constantius was as ruthless in suppressing treachery as any ruler in Rome's history.

After Constantius' death, the military commander Julian took power. He was a fierce opponent of Christianity, and so became known as **Julian the Apostate** (an 'apostate' being someone who rejects a religion). Julian wished to return Rome to its pagan gods, which he felt gave people a more pragmatic and traditional focus for their beliefs. He was undoubtedly turned off Christianity by the numerous splits and rifts which took place within the church, while he was also unimpressed by seeing Christian friends and relatives commit all sorts of appalling crimes, for which they felt that they only had to express repentance to their God to be forgiven.

Yet Julian ruled just two years, and had little success in his efforts to turn back the clock. Christianity continued as the dominant religion, and was soon recognised as the only official religion of the empire under **Theodosius I** (379-395). He outlawed sacrifice and haruspicy (see pp. 95 and 99), had the eternal flame in the temple of Vesta extinguished and the Vestal Virgins (see p. 92) disbanded, ended the Olympic Games in Greece which had been held in honour of the god Zeus since 776 BCE, and closed down pagan religious sanctuaries such as Delphi; many hallowed pagan buildings were destroyed. The empire was now fully Christian, although the new religion could not save it from the invading peoples who were about to overrun it.

6. The Fall of the Roman Empire

The empire in the west was no longer strong or wealthy enough to defend itself against peoples outside who wanted to share the spoils and wealth of the Roman world. In 367, many armies were overrun and three Germanic tribes – the Goths, Suebi and Vandals – set up their own

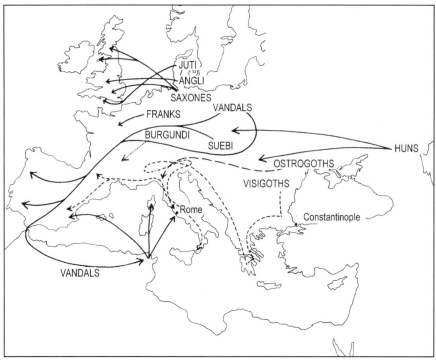

The barbarian invaders of the Roman empire.

kingdoms within the boundaries of the empire. Theodosius managed to reverse this, but in 408 Alaric the Goth (who was himself a Christian) entered Italy and famously sacked Rome two years later. Before long, the Goths and Vandals had occupied Spain, while eastern Gaul was held by the Burgundi, and northern Gaul by the Franks (from whom France takes its name).

The final collapse of the empire in the west was slow and painful. In 429, the Vandals occupied north Africa, while in the 440s Italy faced invasion from Attila, the savage king of the Huns, a tribe originating from lands in what is today southern Russia. Although he eventually withdrew, Rome was soon afterwards sacked by Vandal pirates so thoroughly that half of the city was left derelict, while the population dropped to a meagre 20,000. In 476, the last emperor of the west (who was, ironically enough, called Romulus Augustulus) was defeated by a group of mercenaries led by the German Odoacer. The empire in the west was finished for good.

In the east, however, the empire still remained, centred on its capital Constantinople. In fact, it continued on until 1453, when the city was sacked by the Turks. Today, it is known as the Byzantine empire, taken from the city's original name of Byzantium. However, historians conventionally place this in another era of history. The fall of Rome and the western empire is traditionally seen as the end of the ancient world and of more than a millennium of Roman history.

Review 5

1. Define the following terms: *Augustus, Caesar, imperator, princeps, tetrarchy.*
2. Find out about the lives and works of the historians Suetonius and Tacitus. How do their styles and approaches to writing history differ?
3. Research and write an account of the lives and works of some or all of the following Roman writers: Virgil, Horace, Ovid, Livy, Martial, Juvenal.
4. Compare the reigns of Augustus and Constantine. Why do you think that they are considered two of the most important Roman emperors?
5. Find out about the building of the city of Constantinople. How was it made a fitting capital of the empire?
E. Research the lives of two emperors of your choice, and write your own obituary notice for each of them.

2

Roman Religion

Religion has been a bedrock of every human society until very recently, and this was just as true in the Roman world as it has been elsewhere. Roman society was dominated by its religion, which was closely linked to the state and to the rituals of everyday life, and the main part of this chapter examines key aspects of this traditional religion. The chapter then moves on to look at the alternatives which developed alongside or in place of it – philosophy, mystery religions, and then Christianity, which ultimately became the empire's official religion.

I. ROMAN STATE RELIGION

1. The character of Roman religion

The English word 'religion' comes from the Latin *religio*, which meant something like 'that which binds together'. Roman religion certainly bound together all areas of Roman life in a manner which has all but disappeared from modern western society. However, in many parts of the world today, religion remains central to people's everyday life and understanding of the world, just as it has done throughout history for most human civilisations.

i. Ancient and modern

Where Roman religion was most similar to modern religions was in giving structure to the daily lives of its followers. This is evident in a number of ways, such as:

- **Family life**. Religion was particularly prominent in the day to day life of the family, and this is examined in detail on pp. 133-6 of the Roman Society chapter.
- **Rites of passage**. As today, religion was central to rites of passage such as birth, coming of age, marriage, and death; all of these are also described in the Roman Society chapter.
- **Festivals**. Festivals gave a structure to the cycle of the Roman year, just as modern religions base their year around festivals such as Diwali, Eid, or Christmas.

However, Roman religion lacked some of the key characteristics of a religion today, and it is important to be aware of these differences from the outset; there are three areas in particular: the lack of a scripture and a moral code, the lack of optimism about the afterlife, and the lack of desire to convert people from other religious traditions.

Scripture and morality

Roman religion had no formal scripture to speak of (although the Sibylline books did offer some advice in specific areas – see p. 67). This meant that there was no set of beliefs to which everyone had to subscribe. In fact, for the Romans, religion was about 'doing the right thing' (in terms of sacrificing and honouring the gods properly) rather than 'believing the right thing'.

Perhaps because of this, Roman religion contained no moral code equivalent, for example, to the Ten Commandments in Judaism and (later) Christianity. The Romans did not look to their religion to tell them how to behave towards one another; they were only concerned about treating the gods in the right way, so hoping that they would win their favour. Romans instead looked to law codes such as the Twelve Tables (see p. 360) to guide them on ethics; more educated Romans might also follow ethical beliefs put forward by philosophies such as those of the Stoics and Epicureans.

The afterlife

At the heart of most religions today is an optimism about an afterlife and, alongside this, a belief that moral behaviour in this life will be rewarded in the next (or, conversely, that immoral behaviour will be punished). For example, both Christianity and Islam promise paradise in reward for a faithful life; alternatively, Hindus and Buddhists believe in a cycle of reincarnation, whose ultimate goal is release into nirvana.

None of this was the case in Roman religion, which inherited the gloomy view about death held by the Greeks, whereby the souls of the dead went down to the Underworld to join the 'shades below', ruled over by the god Pluto. In Graeco-Roman myth, those who had lived very wicked lives (such as Sisyphus and Tantalus) live in endless torment, while the heroic live in the Elysian Fields, a kind of paradise; however, the vast majority of souls reside in a place of gloomy shade, pale shadows of their former selves.

The point about this view was that it was the present life which mattered. Those who wanted a more hopeful view of death looked elsewhere – to the mystery cults or to Christianity, which are examined later in this chapter. Roman religion, however, aimed to help people live this life as effectively as possible.

Dead sinners being punished in the Underworld: Sisyphus forced to roll a stone forever, Ixion used as a revolving wheel, and Tantalus unable to eat or drink.

Conversion

The Romans had no concept of converting others to their religion, and generally held a tolerant attitude towards the religions of other peoples, in many cases believing that they worshipped the same gods by different names. In this respect, Romans probably looked at other religions in the same way as we look at foreign languages today – the language you speak depends on the culture or country you are born in, but ultimately it fulfils the same purpose as any other. For example, each language might have a different word for 'mountain', but they are all describing the same thing.

The Romans were therefore usually accepting of other gods (although not always), and many foreign gods and cults were introduced into the Roman world over the centuries, especially if it was felt that they could help the Roman people. Moreover, the Romans often merged their own gods with those of other cultures; an excellent example of this is the building of a shrine in Aquae Sulis (modern Bath) to Sulis Minerva – a merging of the British and Roman goddesses of healing. One consequence of this attitude was that there was far less violence and warfare stirred by religion in the Roman world than there is in our world today.

The only religions which the Romans found it hard to accept were those, such as Judaism and Christianity, which insisted on exclusivity – claiming that their one god was the only acceptable one. Romans expected all the inhabitants of their empire to worship their gods as well as any others, fearing the anger of their gods if they were not worshipped properly.

ii. Origins and development

Our knowledge of the early development of Roman religion is very limited, and based upon Roman writers who lived many centuries later. However, as Rome started out as a small farming community looking to defend itself, it is fair to imagine that its earliest gods were those associated with farming and warfare.

Farming as an act of worship

The close relationship between farming and religion in early Roman times can be seen in the double meaning of the Latin verb *colo*, some forms of which have the stem *cult-*, and which can mean either 'I till the land' or 'I worship', This suggests that for the Romans farming was in itself an act of worship and a prayer for blessings. Interestingly, the double meaning has survived into English: we still talk of 'agriculture' and 'viticulture' to describe types of farming; in addition, the word 'cult' is used to describe a closed-off group of religious believers.

Another word which has come into English via a similar path is 'pagan', since ancient religions are often called 'pagan' religions. The Latin word *paganus* meant something like 'villager' or 'countryman', suggesting that pagan religion had its origins in the worship of country folk.

One feature of the religion was that it was **polytheistic** (from the Greek, *poly:* many, *theos:* god), in other words it had many gods – in fact, a vast number, each one responsible for a specific area of life. St Augustine, a Christian writer of the late Roman empire who aimed to discredit the traditional religion, mocks this feature in the following passage:

> 'How could I possibly record ... all the names of the gods and goddesses? (The Romans) were not willing to entrust care of all their land to just one deity, but instead assigned their fields to the goddess Rusina, mountain ridges to the god Jugatinus, hills to the goddess Collatina, and valleys to Vallonia.'

This illustrates how the Romans saw their gods in every part of nature, with gods and goddesses inhabiting woods, groves, springs and rivers. However, as St Augustine goes on to explain mockingly, it was not just in the countryside that the gods were to be found:

A statue personifying the Tiber as a river god.

> 'The early Romans assigned three gods to the task (of guarding the door): Forculus for the doors, Cardea for the hinges, and Limentius for the threshold. Thus, Forculus was not capable of guarding both the hinge and the threshold as well as the door.' Augustine, *City of God* 4.8

A Roman might have countered Augustine's mockery by arguing that polytheism had clear advantages. In particular, since each god had certain spheres of responsibility, a person knew exactly who to worship in each and every situation. For example, he or she might pray to Ceres for a good harvest, Jupiter for rain, Mars for help in war, Neptune for a safe sea voyage and Apollo for success in a musical contest. Moreover, he or she might feel a close personal link to a god who played an important role in his life (for example, a sailor might feel an affinity with Neptune).

Another feature of Roman religion was that the gods were **anthropomorphic**. In other words, they were represented in human form (in Greek, *anthrôpos:* human being, *morphê:* shape). There were countless statues of the gods, all of them portrayed with human bodies. In fact, the gods were 'human' in more than their appearance. Roman gods had the faults and imperfections of human beings, a far remove from the modern idea of a God who is wholly good and perfect. Roman gods could be cruel or kind, helpful or vindictive, and all had their human favourites.

Etruscan and Greek influence

It is hard for us to disentangle early Roman religion from the religion of the Etruscans, who were so influential over the developing Roman society in the 6th century BCE (see p. 13). It is clear that Etruscan religion had a major influence on the Romans, who adopted some of its gods and

A reconstruction of an Etruscan temple. The principal deity worshipped here was Menvra, whom the Romans later adopted as Minerva. The temple shows the wide eaves, which were designed to protect the mud-brick walls from the weather. One key feature of Etruscan temples was their high podiums, an element which the Romans adopted.

The Temple of Poseidon at Paestum in southern Italy. Paestum, originally founded as Poseidonia by Greek colonists in the 7th century BCE, was one of the many Greek cities of Magna Graecia.

practices. Some important gods, such as Jupiter, Mars and Minerva, clearly had their origins in Etruscan culture. Moreover, it wasn't just gods who were borrowed: the first Roman temples were built in the style of Etruscan temples, while the Romans also took beliefs about divination – predicting the future – from the Etruscans; in particular, haruspicy (see p. 99) was an Etruscan skill.

The second influence on Roman religion was even greater: the religion of the Greeks. The Romans (and indeed the Etruscans) had much contact with Greeks from early times, and especially with those who lived in the many Greek communities of Magna Graecia in southern Italy and Sicily. As the Romans became more influenced by their neighbours, they started adopting Greek gods as their own or, more often, merging their own gods with their Greek equivalents. Therefore, for

The Sibylline Books

One very important Greek influence on early Roman religion were the Sibylline Books. In Greek religion, a 'Sibyl' was a woman with special powers of prophecy, and in southern Italy there was a Sibyl at Cumae, a Greek settlement just north of the Bay of Naples (see map on p. 256). According to legend, the Sibyl of Cumae came to the Roman king Tarquinius Superbus the Proud (see p. 8), and offered him nine prophetic books which would help the Romans in times of trouble. The king, however, scoffed at her asking price, and so she threw three into the fire and then asked the same price for the remaining six; the king laughed at her again, so she burnt another three books; at this stage, Tarquinius grew worried that he had made a mistake and agreed to pay for the three remaining books at the original asking price. He placed them in a vault beneath the temple of Jupiter on the Capitoline Hill.

There was a special group of priests responsible for interpreting the books (see p. 91), and they were aided by two Greek translators, since they were written in Greek hexameter verse. The books were not strictly prophecies of the future (as, for example, some people claim that those of the 16th-century seer Nostradamus are), but offered, in times of crisis, guidance about the religious actions needed to divert or overcome a disaster. Dionysius of Halicarnassus (4.62.6) says that the senate was the only body that could order the consultation of the books, and that this happened 'when civil disorder grips the city, or some great disaster has befallen the Romans in war, or some great prodigies or apparitions, which are difficult to understand, have been seen by them'.

The books frequently recommended the introduction of a Greek deity or cult to the Roman world. One of the earliest examples is the building of a temple to Demeter, the Greek goddess of the harvest (who was later merged with the Roman Ceres), on the Aventine Hill in 496 BCE after a devastating famine. The books were consulted throughout Roman history, as we know of consultations in the 4th century CE. There is little doubt that they played a key role in the growth of Greek religion at Rome.

example, the great Roman sky god Jupiter was matched up with Zeus, the king of the Greek gods, while the war god Mars was likened to his Greek equivalent Ares and the agricultural goddess Ceres was compared to the Greek Demeter.

This process gathered pace during the 3rd century BCE, when Greek literature and culture were having a profound impact on the Roman world. In the middle of this century, a writer called Livius Andronicus (see p. 224) produced the first ever translation of Homer's *Odyssey* in Latin, so that Romans learnt more about Greek mythology. In early Roman religion, there were few such stories about the gods (except those relating to the foundation and well-being of the city), since gods were seen merely in terms of their functions. Greek mythology captivated the Romans, and they soon adopted its stories for their own gods. By the time that the poet Ovid (43 BCE – *c.* 18 CE) came to write his famous poem on mythology, *Metamorphoses*, Roman and Greek mythology were almost one and the same.

iii. The relationship between gods and men

The Romans were not expected to 'love' their gods, as followers of some modern religions would be, but to 'honour' them. Most Romans believed that the world was run by beings far more powerful than them, and that they needed to be treated with reverence and respect. In return, they hoped that their gods would help them in every aspect of their lives, be it health, marriage, work, or warfare.

The key way to ensure the support of the gods was to offer them gifts; these could come in many forms (discussed on pp. 95-102), but the most important was blood sacrifice – the sacrifice of an animal, which was a common feature of all ancient religions. In offering this gift, a person or group of people hoped that they would secure a god's favour. This has sometimes been seen as a rather cynical arrangement of 'you scratch my back, I'll scratch yours' (or in Latin: *do ut des* – 'I give that you may give'), but this view does not do justice to the respect and awe in which the gods were held by the many Romans who genuinely believed that these powerful beings deserved their gifts.

A key feature of Roman religion was its role at the centre of the life of the Roman state. Politicians and generals would never take a major decision without consulting the gods, while there was even a set of priests appointed to ensure that when the Romans went to war, they did so with the gods' support. At all times, the Romans were careful to ensure the *pax deorum* ('the peace of the gods'), and to avoid at all costs the *ira deorum* ('the anger of the gods'). Foreigners were often very impressed by the piety – or devotion to the gods – of the Romans, and some even believed that this lay behind their success in winning such a great empire. The Greek historian Dionysius of Halicarnassus, writing in the 1st century BCE, comments on their earlier conquests thus:

> 'For those who do not know the piety which the Romans practised in those times it may now seem surprising that all their wars ended so well. For you will see that they conducted the beginnings and basics of all of them with immense piety and for this reason in particular had the gods on their side in times of danger.'
>
> Dionysius of Halicarnassus, *Roman Antiquities* 2.72.3

Review 1

1. How would you define the word 'religion'?
2. Draw up a table listing the similarities and differences between Roman religion and a modern religion of your choice.
3. How does the relationship between the Roman gods and humans compare with that of a modern religious believer?
4. How central to modern religions with which you are familiar are the following: (i) a moral code; (ii) the afterlife; (iii) scripture; (iv) conversion?
5. Do politicians use religion to justify their behaviour today? Do you think that they ought to?
6. How different do you think it would be to live in a society where everyone followed the same religion?
R. Read Book 6 of Virgil's *Aeneid*. What can we learn of the traditional Roman view of the Underworld here?
E. What do you find to admire and what do you find to criticize in the character of Roman religion?

---

2. The Roman gods

From the time when the Romans merged their native gods with those of the Greeks, the most important gods were the twelve Olympians – but it should not be forgotten that there were hundreds of others besides, some particular to just one village or region.

i. The Olympian family

The Olympians took their name from the fact that they were believed to live on Mt Olympus in the north of Greece. However, Olympus was also perceived to be a fictional place in the sky, much in the way that some people today talk about heaven.

Like the Greeks, the Romans believed that their gods were both immortal and ageless, meaning that, after their childhoods, each of them was always imagined to be frozen at the same age; Jupiter was always a fatherly figure in healthy middle-age, while Apollo was ever in youthful manhood. There were twelve Olympians, six gods and six goddesses, all of whom belonged to one family. There is much inter-marriage within the family (for example, Jupiter is married to his sister Juno), a common feature of all polytheistic systems.

The many faces of the gods

Each god was actually responsible for many different areas of life and was given an adjective (known as an epithet) to describe them accordingly. For example, a farmer might have prayed to Jupiter Pluvius (the rain-giver) for rain, politicians might worship Jupiter Optimus Maximus (the Best and Greatest – a god of sovereign power), while a variety of people might have appealed to Jupiter Lapis (the god of oaths). Meanwhile Juno could be invoked as Regina (the queen of the gods), Lucina (goddess of childbirth), Moneta (protector of the Roman mint) and Pronuba (the patron of marriage). Temples were often dedicated to one specific version of the god. For example, Jupiter and Juno were both worshipped in the temple on the Capitoline Hill as rulers, and therefore in their guises of Optimus Maximus and Regina.

In the short descriptions which follow, the natures and roles of each god and goddess are briefly outlined.

The six gods

Jupiter: Known to the poets as 'the father of the gods and king of men', Jupiter was the patriarchal head of the Olympian family. His name is a merging of *Iov pater* ('father Iov' – with Iov being the Etruscans' name

The head of a statue of Jupiter, found in the Temple of Jupiter in Pompeii (see p. 290).

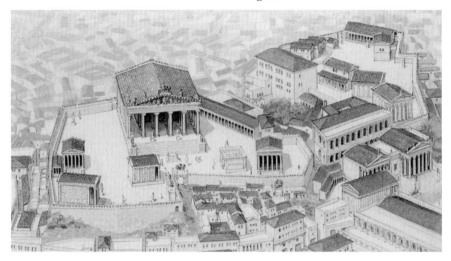

A reconstruction of the Temple of Jupiter Optimus Maximus on the Capitoline Hill.

for their great sky god), and he is also commonly referred to as Jove. Since he was originally a sky and weather god, he is often portrayed holding a thunderbolt; he is also often seen holding a sceptre, the symbol of political power. Jupiter was the Roman version of the Greek god Zeus and took on most of the related myths. Many of these refer to his numerous amorous conquests, which caused the jealousy of his wife Juno.

In Rome, the Temple of Jupiter Optimus Maximus on the Capitoline Hill was the largest and most important in the city; it was closely associated with the Roman state: at the start of every year, the new consuls went there to perform a sacrifice, while the senate always held the first meeting of the year there.

The Capitoline Triad

The Temple of Jupiter on the Capitoline Hill was actually home to what is known as the Capitoline Triad, a group of three vital deities – Jupiter, Juno and Minerva. Such 'triads' are a common feature of Indo-European religions, as can still be seen today in Hinduism, in which the three most important gods are the triad of Brahma, Vishnu and Shiva. The Capitoline Triad developed from Etruscan religion; inside the temple on the Capitoline, each deity had their own sacred room. As Roman power expanded to encompass new lands, the central temple of many Roman cities – in Italy and further afield – was often dedicated to this Capitoline Triad (including Pompeii's main temple – see p. 290).

The Capitoline Triad: in the centre is Jupiter, to his left his wife Juno with her peacock; to his right Minerva with her owl, a symbol of wisdom.

Neptune (who emerged from the Etruscan sea-god Nethuns) came to be associated with the Greek Poseidon. He was the brother of Jupiter and, as the god of the sea, was particularly important to sailors and fishermen. He was also believed to be the god of earthquakes and was often depicted with a trident, which he used to shake the earth. With the growth of the Roman empire, controlling and travelling the Mediterranean was vital for Roman power, and so Neptune was an essential figure. He was also closely associated with horses and so was the focus of prayers and offerings by those going to the races (see p. 194).

Vulcan was linked with the Greek Hephaestus; both were gods of fire and metal-working, who could turn rock into bronze weapons or fine jewellery. Since the Romans relied so heavily on the production of iron, Vulcan was very important to them. He was believed to live under Mt Etna in Sicily; in the Olympian family he was married to Venus, who in turn preferred the affections of Mars. According to legend, whenever Venus was unfaithful to him, he would grow angry and beat the red-hot metal so hard that it would cause a volcanic eruption. The god's festival, the *Vulcanalia*, was held on 23 August each year, at a time when crops and granaries were especially at risk of catching fire during the intense heat of summer.

As he was the father of their founder Romulus (see p. 4), Romans liked to believe that they were all descended from **Mars**. Moreover, war was central to the development and security of the Roman world, and so

2. Roman Religion

God	Responsibilities	Symbols
Jupiter (Zeus)	king of the gods; sky & weather, travellers	throne and sceptre; thunderbolt
Neptune (Poseidon)	the sea, earthquakes, horses & bulls	trident and dolphin; horses
Mars (Ares)	war; agriculture	armour
Apollo	education, music & the arts, archery, the sun, prophecy	lyre and bow
Vulcan (Hephaestus)	fire, metal-working, artisans	anvil and hammer
Mercury (Hermes)	messenger of the gods; travel and trade	winged sandals
Bacchus (Dionysus)	drama, wine and revelry	thyrsus, vines, ivy, animal skins

Mars dressed
in his armour.

he was often regarded as second only in importance to Jupiter. Yet, in early times, Mars was also a god of agriculture associated with the Etruscan farming god Maris. Even as late as the 2nd century BCE, Cato the Elder gives the following advice to farmers:

'For your cattle, for them to be healthy, make this sacrifice to Mars Silvanus (*Mars of the woods*); you must make this sacrifice each year.'

Cato the Elder, *On Agriculture* 83

As part of this agricultural role, Mars was responsible for the defence and protection of cattle, fields and farmers. In this role he therefore came to be identified with warfare and Ares, the Greek god of war, and it was in this context that he was most important to the Romans – the large exercise ground in Rome where soldiers trained was known as the *Campus Martius* ('Field of Mars' – see map on p. 352).

Apollo had no obvious equivalent in early Roman religion; the Romans simply borrowed him from the Greek pantheon. He was one of the most important gods in the Graeco-Roman world, with a wide range of responsibilities: as god of music, the arts, education, health and disease, prophecy, archery and the sun he was often portrayed as a beautiful young man with short, curly hair, who carried a lyre or a quiver full of arrows. His relationship to the sun is reflected in his common epithet *Phoebus*, which meant 'shining'.

According to the historian Livy (1.56), the Romans worshiped Apollo from early times, since he records that during the reign of Tarquinius, the king sent two of his sons to Apollo's oracle at Delphi in Greece to interpret a worrying omen. Every year in the middle of July, the *ludi Apollinares* (games of Apollo) were held in Rome for eight or nine days.

Mercury had the same attributes as Hermes, the messenger of the Greek gods; like Hermes, he is usually portrayed wearing winged sandals and a winged helmet, while carrying the *caduceus*, a herald's staff entwined with two snakes. In addition to being a god of travellers, Mercury was also the god of traders and commercial profit; in fact, his name is linked to the Latin word *merx* – 'merchandise' (cf. other English words such as 'merchant' and 'commerce'). The Romans also believed that it was Mercury who escorted the souls of the dead down to the Underworld.

The six goddesses

As queen of the gods, **Juno** was particularly important to women and oversaw both marriage and childbirth (see pp. 160 and 166). It is therefore ironic that her own marriage was unhappy; she suffered the philandering of her husband Jupiter and frequently sought vengeance on his

Mercury flies holding his
caduceus.

Juno was generally portrayed as a regal
example of a virtuous Roman mother.

lovers. On 1 March every year, Roman women held a festival in honour of Juno called the *Matronalia*, a celebration of motherhood and of women in general. However, Juno had other roles, most notably as *Juno Moneta* ('Juno the adviser'), goddess of the Roman Mint, whose duty it was to protect the finances of the Roman empire.

As the goddess of the crops and harvest, **Ceres** (whose name is linked to words such as 'cereal', 'create', and 'increase') was a vital goddess for the Romans. As we have seen, she became prominent in Rome after 496 BCE, when the Sibylline Books ordered that the Romans adopt her Greek equivalent Demeter to drive away a terrible famine which was afflicting them. At this point, her temple on the Aventine Hill in Rome was established, her most important temple in the Roman world. The *Cerealia*, a festival in her honour, was held every year between 12 and 19 April and the worship of Ceres became particularly associated with the plebeian classes, who dominated the grain trade.

The most famous myth about Ceres concerns the abduction of her daughter **Proserpina** (*Persephone* in Greek), who was picking flowers in a field one day when Pluto, the god of the dead, on a visit to the earth from the Underworld, fell in love with her and carried her off down to his kingdom below. The distraught Ceres searched all over the earth for her lost daughter and fasted in grief. As a result the crops of the earth stopped growing and there was a famine until Jupiter intervened and persuaded Pluto to return Proserpina. However, as she had eaten food in the Underworld – some seeds of a pomegranate fruit – she was forced to spend some months of the year with Pluto. Ceres fasted during these months and the crops stopped growing; thus people came to call this season 'winter'.

Goddess	Responsibilities	Symbols
Juno (Hera)	queen of the gods; women & marriage	peacock
Ceres (Demeter)	agriculture & the harvest	flowers, fruit and grain
Vesta (Hestia)	the hearth	fire
Diana (Artemis)	hunting, the moon, childbirth	moon, bow & arrows
Minerva (Athena)	wisdom, weaving & crafts, war	owl, an aegis
Venus (Aphrodite)	love & beauty	sea shell

Venus was an early Roman spirit of fertility and procreation, and so it was natural for the Romans to associate her with the Greek goddess of love, Aphrodite. Venus was particularly important to the Romans as the mother of their Trojan ancestor Aeneas (see p. 2), and she figures prominently in Virgil's *Aeneid*. She is often depicted with Cupid, her son by Mars, who can inflame human hearts with passionate desire by piercing them with his arrows.

Minerva's name is derived from the Etruscan goddess Menrva, who is believed to have been a goddess of wisdom, war, art, schools and commerce, so that she was naturally linked to the Greek Athena. In Etruscan, Greek and Roman myth, Minerva was believed to have been born from the head of her father, Jupiter. As goddess of wisdom,

Diana as a huntress in a mosaic from North Africa.

Minerva's sacred bird was the owl; she was also worshipped as a goddess of war, and one of her military symbols was the *aegis*, a goat-skin shield imprinted with the image of a gorgon's head. As goddess of weaving and handicrafts, she was important for artisans and women working in the household, while she was also the goddess of school children.

Diana, originally an early Roman goddess of hunting, became linked with the Greek goddess Artemis and her twin brother Apollo; she therefore also took on the role of goddess of the moon, in which guise she commonly known as *Phoebe* (the feminine form of *Phoebus*). However, she is most often depicted in hunting dress, accompanied by animals such as a deer and with a quiver of arrows. Diana was particularly worshipped by the poor and slaves, and the latter could receive sanctuary in her temples.

As the goddess of the hearth, **Vesta** was of vital importance to every Roman family, since the hearth was a home's source of light, heat and cooking. In addition, Vesta also had a huge role to play in Roman public life as a protector of the state, as is described on pp. 92-4. The *Vestalia*, a festival in the goddess's honour, was held at Rome between 7 and 15 June. There were few myths about Vesta; she was originally one of the Twelve Olympians, but she later gave up her place for Bacchus in order to tend to the sacred fire on Mt Olympus.

The two-headed god Janus was unusual in being a completely Roman deity. His worship was very popular among the Romans.

ii. Other important gods

The Romans also adopted Dionysus, the Greek god of wine and theatre, usually calling him by his other name of **Bacchus**, and associating him with Liber, an early Roman god of fertility, wine and growth. The rites of Bacchus, or 'Bacchanalia', formed one of the most popular and controversial mystery cults of the Roman world (see p. 106); these rites are famously, but mysteriously, depicted on the walls of a triclinium in the Villa of the Mysteries in Pompeii (see p. 319).

A specifically Roman god was **Janus**, the god of gates and doorways. While this might not seem a particularly important role, Janus came to be seen as the protector of a house, as well as a god of beginnings and endings. This is evident in his physical appearance, since he has two heads which look in opposite directions (i.e. either into or out of a house, or back to the past and forward to the future). It is therefore no surprise that the first month of the year is named after him, since January is a time when people reflect on the past twelve months and look ahead to the year to come (see Appendix 5 to read about the Roman calendar).

Pluto was the ruler of the Underworld and the god of the dead. His name is probably derived from the Greek word *ploutos*, meaning 'wealth'; in Pluto's case, his wealth was measured in the vast number of

Pluto. The god's frowning and gloomy face is fitting for the god of the dead.

The Gates of Peace

Janus was worshipped in Rome at the temple of Ianus Geminus in the Forum. According to Roman tradition, the temple's gates were only closed during times of total peace; when Augustus closed them in 29 BCE after his final victory against his rivals, it was for only the third time in Roman history.

---

souls he ruled over in the Underworld. He was sometimes also referred to as **Dis Pater** ('wealthy father'), the name of an early Roman god of the Underworld. There are few myths about Pluto as he rarely emerged from his kingdom below but, as we have seen, on one of the rare occasions when he did he abducted Proserpina and took her down below to be his wife. He is rarely pictured in art, but his symbol was often the pomegranate, the fruit which she ate in the Underworld.

iii. The cult of the emperor

With the advent of Octavian (Augustus) as the first Roman emperor after 31 BCE (see p. 41), a new cult of emperor worship began to emerge. This had precedents elsewhere in the Mediterranean world, since the Pharaohs of Egypt were worshipped as gods, as were the rulers of the

Hellenistic World such as Alexander the Great. It was clearly an effective way for rulers to make their subjects believe in the divine nature of their power, so guaranteeing their loyalty. Cassius Dio, a historian of the 2nd century CE, emphasises that the imperial cult had the benefit of unifying the Roman world in loyalty to the emperor. However, he is very clear about the limits of imperial divinity:

> 'For in the capital itself and in Italy generally, no emperor, however worthy of renown he has been, has dared to do this (i.e. have cults to himself as a living god); still, there are various divine honours bestowed after their death upon such emperors as have ruled uprightly, and in fact shrines are built to them.'   Cassius Dio, LI.20.8

The rules were quite clear: even though in many parts of the eastern empire it came naturally to worship the emperor as a god (and many did so), in Rome and Italy the practice was strictly frowned upon, and an emperor could only be deified after his death. However, his *genius* (meaning something like 'guardian spirit' – see p. 135) could be worshipped while he was living. When an emperor had died, it was up to his successor to choose whether to deify him or not; therefore, emperors who had died in disfavour with the people or after a coup (such as Tiberius, Caligula and Nero) were denied this by their successors. On the other hand, successful emperors such as Augustus, Vespasian and Trajan were deified by their successors.

Am I a god?

Ancient writers record differing attitudes to the imperial cult by 1st century emperors. Some were respectful and refrained from casting themselves as gods while still alive. However, Caligula seems to have got it into his head that he really was a god, and once apparently berated a Jewish delegation for sacrificing *for* him and not *to* him. Unfortunately for him, he was so unpopular that he wasn't even deified after death. Other emperors took the whole issue rather less seriously: Vespasian, lying on his deathbed, is said to have joked '*vae, puto deus fieri*' – 'Oh dear, I think I'm becoming a god'!

The first 'emperor' to be deified was Julius Caesar who, in 42 BCE (two years after his death), was named a god (*divus Iulius* – 'the divine Julius') by Octavian 'with the full consent of the senate and people of Rome'. Soon after his final victory over Antony at Actium, Octavian dedicated a temple to *divus Iulius* at the spot in the Forum where Julius Caesar had been cremated. Octavian was therefore able to style himself 'son of a god', so adding to his own mystique; his change of name to 'Augustus' reflects this, since the name really meant 'venerable' in a religious sense.

The cult of the emperor was served by a college of priests known as the *Augustales*; the college was instituted by Tiberius and named after his adopted father Augustus. The *Augustales* were normally drawn from the ranks of freedmen: this allowed them to play a role in public life, since they were barred from holding any other political or religious posts (see p. 182). The imperial cult therefore allowed them the chance to contribute to the society that had freed them, advance themselves and show their loyalty to the emperor. There were 21 Augustales in the city of Rome, while provincial cities seem typically to have had just 6.

Review 2

1. Explain the meaning and usage of the following words: *aegis, caduceus, Olympian, phoebos, ploutos*.
2. Design a web profile for each god and goddess. How would they describe themselves? What other information would they put on their webpage?
3. Examine the two following paintings: (i) Titian's *Bacchus and Ariadne*; (ii) Botticelli's *The Birth of Venus (Aphrodite)*. What characteristics of each deity can be observed in these renaissance works of art?
4. Find out about how the planets of the solar system came to be given the names of Roman gods.
5. Which planets feature in the composer Gustav Holst's *Planets Suite*? How does he characterise each god through his music?
6. Are there examples in the world today where political leaders (past or present) are worshipped as gods?
E. Which gods and goddesses would you have felt the most affinity with, and why?

---

3. Festivals

The Romans did not have a seven-day week with two days of rest as we do today (see Appendix 5). Instead, their calendar was organised in cycles of eight days, labelled A to H; day A was always a market day and therefore a day of rest. Confusingly, this market day was known as the *nundinae* ('ninth day'), as it was the ninth day since the last market day counting inclusively. Yet the Romans did not just have one day off in every eight; rather, their year was punctuated with many religious festivals, as well as games (which you can read about in Chapter 4) for the relaxation and enjoyment of the people. By the time of the emperor Claudius, there were 159 days in the year which were marked as holidays for one reason or another.

About 40 of these days were given over to religious festivals, many of which dated back to the earliest Roman times. Therefore, they tended to reflect the cycle of the seasons which were important both to the farmer and to the soldier, who fought only during the 'campaigning season' of March to September (the winter months being too harsh to keep an army away from home). For example, a festival to Mars was held on 1 March, when soldiers were preparing to campaign again. Then, in mid-April, when the warm weather was beginning to reappear, there was a week-long festival to Ceres, the goddess of the crops. Later in the year, when a farmer had completed all his sowing for the following year, a festival was held to Saturn, the god of sowing.

There are too many festivals to examine in detail in here (a number of them have already been mentioned above), but there follow descriptions of two of the most popular – the Lupercalia and the Saturnalia; moreover, other festivals are described elsewhere: the festival of the *Bona Dea* is described on p. 94, and you can also read about the *Parentalia* and the *Lemuria* (pp. 190-1).

The Lupercalia

The Lupercalia was one of Rome's best loved festivals. It took place on 15 February and, as spring approached, was intended to purify the city and promote fertility. Its origins were lost in the mists of time, and even Romans were unsure exactly where its rituals came from. However, it was believed to honour Lupercus, a god of shepherds; his name has clear links with the Latin *lupus*, meaning wolf, and the festival was also associated with the story of Romulus and Remus, who were suckled by a she-wolf (see p. 4).

The action of the day centred around a group of noble young men, who were selected as Luperci – priests specifically appointed for the Lupercalia. The Luperci were divided into two teams, each led by a captain, or *magister*. The day's events started in a cave on the west side of the Palatine Hill known as the Lupercal; according to legend, it was here that Romulus and Remus had been suckled by the she-wolf. In the cave they sacrificed goats and a dog; these were unusual animals for a Roman sacrifice, but they were believed to be very fertile and so were appropriate offerings at a fertility festival. The faces of the two captains were then smeared with the animals' blood, which was washed off with wool dripped in milk; at this point, the two young men had to laugh loudly. A feast was next then held, which involved the Luperci drinking lots of wine.

Now it was time for the public element of the festival. The two teams of Luperci, dressed only in loin-cloths, ran a race around the foot of the Palatine Hill. As they ran, they carried strips of skins from the sacrificed goats, with which they whipped anything in their way – trees, ground, buildings, and especially people. This was seen as a way to drive out evil and promote fertility. As one ancient writer points out, some women were actually keen to be on the receiving end:

'They (the Luperci) cut the hides of goats into strips and run through the
city, naked except for a loin covering, lashing anyone in their way
with the strips of the goat hide. However, women of child-bearing
age do not avoid the lashings, since they think that they aid in fertility, pregnancy, and childbirth.' Plutarch, *Romulus* 21.3-5

Unfortunately, there is no evidence to tell us whether being whipped by
a goat-strip at the Lupercalia really did make women more successful in
pregnancy and childbirth!

Ancient and modern

The word for the strips of goat hide used by the Luperci was *februa*, from the
Latin verb *februare*, meaning 'to purify', and this is the origin of the name of
our month February, when the Lupercalia took place.

A second suggested link to the modern world is more unlikely. It has often
been believed that Valentine's Day (14 February) is directly derived from the
Lupercalia. However, the notion of Valentine's Day being associated with
romantic love only started in the time of Chaucer, who lived in the 14th
century. The Lupercalia festival was abolished by the church in the late 5th
century and replaced with a festival to the Virgin Mary.

The Saturnalia
This festival was held around the time of the winter solstice, which has
long held importance for cultures worldwide, since the sun is believed to
be 'reborn'. The Saturnalia was originally celebrated on 17 December,
but later extended over several days. The festival honoured Saturn, who
was originally a Roman god of agriculture and sowing, but came to be
associated with the Greek god Cronos, who was the father of Zeus and
ruled over mankind during its mythological 'Golden Age', when all people were equal and lived together in peace and harmony.

As a result, the celebrations of the Saturnalia were associated with
various concepts: the rebirth of the sun after the winter solstice, the
completion of sowing the following year's crops, and the hope that one
day people would again live in peace with one another in a second gold-
en age. In this sense, it was a feast of 'peace and goodwill', just as
Christmas is for Christians today. The holiday began with a great sacrifice at the temple of Saturn in the forum (see p. 354), which was followed by a free public banquet. Daily life came to a halt during the
festival: shops were shut, schools were closed, law-courts were deserted
and there was a break from politics. The streets were full of strolling
crowds, who greeted one another with *Io Saturnalia* ('Happy
Saturnalia'); unlike the rest of the year, people were allowed to gamble
in public.

However, the most remarkable aspect of this festival was what happened at home. For it was a tradition of the Saturnalia that masters treated their slaves as equals (at least for one day), and even waited on them at table – all in the spirit of the golden age, when all people had been equal. People discarded the formal toga, instead wearing party clothes and the soft cap (*pileus*) normally worn by freedmen, which symbolised freedom. The whole atmosphere was one of feasting and celebration, and this is captured by the following lines from the poet Statius (*c.* 45-96 CE), in which he asks the patron deities of learning – Phoebus, Pallas, and the Muses – to leave him alone during December, when he doesn't want to work on his poems:

> 'Father Phoebus and stern Pallas, go away! You, too, Muses, take a vacation and go far away! I shall call you back on New Year's Day. But you, Saturn, cast off your chains and come near. You, too, December, tipsy from so much wine, and laughing Good Cheer and playful Joviality, come and be present!'
> Statius, *Silvae* 1.6.1-7

In this passage we see 'Good Cheer' and 'Joviality' personified as characters – and even as minor gods. Personifications such as these were a common feature of Roman religion.

The Saturnalia and Christmas

It is not hard to see similarities between the festivities of the Saturnalia and those of Christmas, and this is unlikely to be coincidence. When 25 December was set as the date for Christmas by the church in the 4th century, it probably looked to incorporate various elements of the pre-existing midwinter festival, including the giving of gifts and the idea of peace and goodwill. Moreover, the more recent British tradition of Boxing Day, which originated in the reign of Queen Victoria, when the wealthy would leave gifts in boxes for their servants and the poor, can clearly be compared to the Saturnalian idea of slaves being waited on by their masters for a day.

Gift-giving was also a central feature of the Saturnalia. Common gifts included wax candles and doll-like clay figures, a particular favourite of children. The poet Martial based a whole book of poems (*Epigrams 14*) on gifts given at the Saturnalia. Some were expensive, others small and humble; they included items such as dice, combs, moneyboxes, toothpicks, balls, perfumes, a parrot, tables, cups, spoons, books, and pets. The following two lines accompanying gifts suggest the flavour of the tradition:

> 'This pig will make your Saturnalia merry. He was fed acorns and pastured with the foaming boars.'
> Martial, *Epigrams* 14.70

> 'On wintry cold days of Saturnalia, Umber used to give me, when he was poor, a cape as a gift. Now he gives me a drink, because he has become rich.'
> Martial, *Epigrams* 12.81

Review 3

1. Draw up a list of similarities between the Saturnalia and Christmas.
2. How do public festivals in the Roman world compare with those in our society today?
3. What elements of the Lupercalia suggest that it went back to earliest Roman times?
4. Find out about two other Roman festivals and make a presentation to the rest of your class explaining what took place.
E. Imagine you are a Roman who takes part in either the Lupercalia or the Saturnalia. Describe the whole experience.

4. Temples and priests

i. Temples

The Latin word *templum* originally described a patch of land which had been set aside and made holy for the gods. As time went by, the word came more to describe the building situated on this holy ground, but the temple building was usually only part of a larger sanctuary; sometimes these sanctuaries were walled round and the temple building surrounded by a colonnade – the Temple of Apollo in Pompeii (see p. 291) is a good example of this.

Reconstruction of the Temple of Fortuna near the Capitoline Hill in Rome.

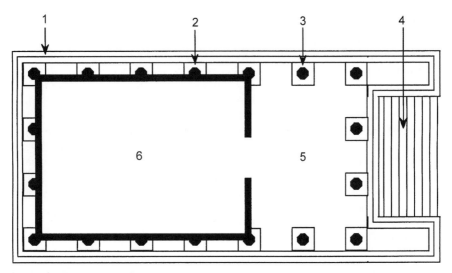

Plan of a Roman temple.

The design of Roman temple buildings was influenced first by the Etruscans and then by the Greeks. It was rectangular in shape and built on a high podium (1), with steps (4) leading up to the building (perhaps this was done to give an impression of the temple being higher and closer to the gods). In front of the building was a porch area (5), which led into the main room, the **cella** (6); the temple was surrounded by the columns of a colonnade; some of these were free-standing (3), while others were merged with the outside wall of the cella (2).

Inside the *cella* would be the statue of the god to whom the temple was dedicated; this might be decorated with gifts from worshippers, such as flowers, jewels, or other precious ornaments. Incense might be burned around the statue. Apart from this, there would be were no seats or other furniture, while the room would also be darkened by the lack of windows. The only light would come in through the front door, and the sun might perhaps cause any gold or silver on the statue to glint during the daytime. Most temples would also have a store of treasure dedicated to the god, and some temples had an underground chamber or an extra room behind the *cella* to hold this.

A Roman temple building played a different role from modern equivalents such as churches, mosques, or synagogues. The temple was believed to be the home of the god, whose presence was represented by the cult statue. No worship took place inside the temple, and the only reason a worshipper might enter the *cella* would be to look at the cult statue and perhaps to leave a gift or burn incense. The key act of worship for a Roman was a sacrifice; this took place at an altar in the open air outside the front of the temple.

The Pantheon

Not all Roman temples needed to conform to this standard form. One of Rome's most famous, the Pantheon, can still be visited today. It is believed to have been dedicated to all the gods (*pantheon* meant 'all gods' in Greek), and was first commissioned in the time of Augustus, although its present form dates to *c.* 126 CE, during the reign of the emperor Hadrian.

The inside of the temple is one grand circular space, with a spectacular curved and vaulted ceiling, in the centre of which is a central opening to the sky. Engineers still marvel today at how the Romans managed to construct such an extraordinary ceiling, which allowed worshippers to look straight up into the heavens and feel closer to their gods.

The inside of the Pantheon today.

ii. Priests

A Roman priest played a very different role from a modern equivalent. Today, we expect imams, priests or rabbis to play a pastoral role for their congregation, helping them through difficult personal times and encouraging them in their faith. Yet a Roman priesthood was a purely ceremonial and functional role. Priests were not normally attached to particular temples, but merely ensured that various religious rituals were performed correctly. In Rome, priesthoods were closely tied up with politics, and tended to go to the influential elite, since this would be a way for them to increase their power.

There were various different committees (known as 'colleges') of priests in Rome, each of which had different functions in the religious life of the state. Many of these colleges were believed to have been intro-duced by the early king Numa Pompilius (see p. 8); the most important of them were as follows:

a. The pontifices

The 'college of *pontifices'* was the most important group of Roman priests, led by the chief priest, the *Pontifex Maximus* ('Greatest Pontiff').

The emperor Augustus dressed in his role as Pontifex Maximus.

2. Roman Religion

The word *pontifex* (pl. *pontifices*) originally meant 'bridge-builder' – it is a mystery how it came to be associated with a priesthood. The *pontifices* seem to have emerged during the kingdom as the king's main religious advisers. For most of Roman history, a new *pontifex* was elected by a vote among the current *pontifices*. The number of *pontifices* in the college varied over the years, but the most common number seems to have been 15. The *pontifices* had a variety of duties, which included:

- the protection of all temples.
- the regulation of the laws regarding burials and cemeteries.
- the supervision of the religious calendar.
- the overseeing of laws regarding wills and inheritance.

Moreover, they were often consulted on points of religious law, and had to keep records in special 'pontifical books' of all the religious prodigies which occurred each year (such as, for example, thunder from a clear sky, or statues sweating blood).

The Pontifex Maximus

In republican times, the Pontifex Maximus effectively became the high priest of Roman religion, who was responsible for overseeing the college of pontifices. He had an official residence in the forum, the Domus Publica, which stood between the House of the Vestal Virgins and the Via Sacra (see map on p. 355), and he carried out his religious duties from the nearby Regia, or 'House of the King'. The office of Pontifex Maximus was a very prestigious one and therefore coveted by leading Romans; it was also only a part-time role, and so ambitious men could combine it with pursuing a political or military career – Julius Caesar was elected in 63 BCE. After the advent of empire, the emperor was automatically the Pontifex Maximus.

When Christianity became the religion of the Roman empire in the 4th century CE, the title of Pontifex Maximus was transferred over to the Pope, who is still referred to as the 'Pontiff' in English today.

The college of *pontifices* also consisted of other priests with separate responsibilities, including the 15 *flamines* (sg: *flamen*), priesthoods attached to one particular god so that, for example, there was a *Flamen Dialis* (of Jupiter) who, of course, oversaw the worship of Jupiter. However, these positions seem to have come from the earliest Roman times – many of the *flamines* were attached to gods about whom little is known, such as Falacer and Furrina. After the deification of Julius Caesar in 44 BCE, his former lieutenant Mark Antony was appointed to be *flamen* to *divus Iulius*, the first new *flamen* to be created in hundreds of years.

An augur holding his *lituus*. At his feet is a sacred chicken.

b. The augurs

The 'college of augurs' was the second most important college of priests. Their role was to interpret the will of the gods by looking for signs and omens; the best known and earliest way in which they did this was by interpreting the flight of birds, but they also used other techniques, such as observing thunder and lightning, or watching the behaviour of animals. The process of augury was known as 'taking the auspices', and was central to many public and private rituals in Roman life, such as war, business and marriage.

The historian Livy, writing in the 20s BCE, gives an account of the confirmation of Numa Pompilius as king according to the auspices. The passage highlights the use of the augur's rod, the *lituus*, which he used to define the region of land or sky from where he would read omens.

'The augur veiled his head and sat on Numa's left, holding in his right hand a bent staff with no knots in it, which they called a *lituus*. Then, looking towards the City and its land, he prayed to the gods and defined the regions from east to west: he stated that the right-hand area was to the south and the left to the north. Opposite, he mentally defined a feature at the furthest point his eyes could reach. Then, transferring his *lituus* to his left hand and placing his right hand on Numa's head, he prayed thus: "Father Jupiter, if it is right for this Numa Pompilius whose head I hold to be King at Rome, then may you give sure signs to us within those limits which I have made." Then he specifically stated the auspices which he wished to be sent and when they were sent Numa was declared king.'   Livy 1.18.7-10

Although we are not told what auspices were sent in this passage, it is likely to have been certain types of birds flying in specific directions.

The sacred chickens

Romans often took 'sacred chickens' with them on military campaigns for the purpose of augury. They would never start a battle without taking the auspices, but waiting for the flight of birds in the sky could waste valuable time if a quick attack was needed. In this situation, the sacred chickens would be released from their cages and pieces of cake dropped in front of them. If they didn't come out to eat, or flew away, or flapped their wings and cackled, it was taken as a bad sign. However, if they tried to gobble up the cake and bits fell from their beak, it was considered a favourable omen.

Some Romans clearly believed in this process more than others. Before a sea-battle during the first Punic War in 249 BCE, the Roman general Publius Claudius Pulcher was so incensed when the chickens refused to eat that he had them thrown into the sea and exclaimed: 'Since they don't want to eat, let them drink!'. When the Romans subsequently went on to lose the battle, the general was tried for impiety and fined.

---

c. Other priesthoods

The two other main colleges apart from the Pontifices and the Augurs were the *Quindecimviri Sacris Faciundis* ('the fifteen men in charge of conducting the rites') and the *Septemviri Epulones* ('the seven men in charge of feasts'). The former were the guardians of the Sibylline Books, and so were responsible for managing the introduction of Greek rites into Roman religion based on the Books' recommendation; the duties of the latter involved helping the pontifices oversee arrangements for public sacrifices and the feasts which followed them, particularly at the games. This college of priests was only introduced in 196 BCE, at which time many new public rites had been introduced to Roman religion.

In addition, we have already read about the *Augustales* on p. 81. Another important college in earlier Roman times was that of the *Fetiales*, who were responsible for the rituals involving going to war.

Such rituals had to be performed correctly to ensure that the war was supported by the gods and therefore a 'just war'. We also hear of associations of men formed for specific festivals, such as the *Luperci* for the *Lupercalia*.

d. The Vestal Virgins
The 'college of Vestal Virgins' consisted of the only major female priests at Rome. The Vestal Virgins were among the most important people in

A statue of a Vestal Virgin.

A reconstruction of the temple of Vesta.

the entire Roman state, and consisted of six priestesses of the goddess Vesta who tended the fire in her temple in the Roman forum (see map on p. 355). As well as being worshipped in the home, Vesta was also vital to the Roman state, since the fire in her temple represented the symbolic 'hearth of the state', and therefore its security; Romans believed that it would be a terrible omen for the city if this fire ever went out.

The temple of Vesta was one of the most important in Rome. It had an unconventional design, being round and smaller than most temples, while inside there was no cult statue but rather the sacred fire (with a hole in the roof for smoke to disappear through); according to Roman legend, the flame had been brought by from the ashes of Troy by Aeneas and his followers (see p. 2). There was also a store-house in the temple, which contained the *palladium*, a statue of the goddess Athena also said to have been brought from Troy, and the *fascinum*, an erect phallus which was believed to symbolise fertility.

Selection and duties

It was considered a huge honour to be selected as a Vestal Virgin, not just for the girl concerned, but also for her whole family (therefore, the Vestals were normally chosen from senatorial families). When a post became available, the Pontifex Maximus was responsible for selecting a new candidate. She had to be a girl between the ages of six and ten, who was free of physical and mental defects and had two living parents. When a girl was selected, it reflected very well on her family, and so aristocratic fathers were keen to put their daughters forward.

Once selected, the girl would be removed from the power of her family and had to take a vow of chastity. She would be expected to serve for 30 years: for the first ten years she was a novice who learnt her trade, for the next ten years she would be performing most of the Vestals' duties, while for the final ten years she would spend more time teaching novices. The Vestals had certain key duties:

- To guard the **sacred flame** and ensure that it never went out.
- To bake the sacred flour, **mola salsa**, used at state sacrifices.
- To attend certain important **state sacrifices**.
- To act as guardians of **important documents**, such as wills and state treaties (e.g. Julius Caesar and Mark Antony both left their wills in the temple of Vesta for safe-keeping).

Privileges and punishments

The Vestals, who were revered in ancient Rome, were given a number of privileges:

- An escort of a *lictor* (see p. 359) to guard them when they went out in public.

- Seats of honour at the games in Rome.
- Freedom to own property, make wills, and vote.
- A palatial residence in the forum next to the temple of Vesta. Three storeys high, it was built around an elegant open-air court-yard with a pool in its centre.

However, should things go wrong, the Vestals could suffer harsh penalties. If they let the sacred flame go out, they were whipped. If a Vestal Virgin was found to have broken her vow of chastity, then she was executed by being buried alive (while her lover was publicly whipped to death). Although it was rare for this punishment to be enacted, Pliny th Younger recounts in a letter (4.11) how the emperor Domitian had a Vestal killed in this way in the 80s CE; in Pliny's view, she was innocent.

Good and bad examples

Livy relates two legends from early Rome which offer very different examples of Vestal Virgins. On the plus side is Rhea Silvia, the mother of Romulus and Remus, who was believed to have been impregnated by the god Mars. She was therefore seen as a mother to the Roman people.

On the other hand, there is the story of a Vestal called Tarpeia, which was told as a warning to the Roman people. During the wars with the Sabines in the time of Romulus (see p. 7), Tarpeia, daughter of a Roman commander, approached the Sabine camp and offered to let them into the city in exchange for 'what they bore on their left arms', hoping for the golden bracelets which they were wearing. However, the Sabines crushed her to death with their shields which they carried on the left arm. The Romans then hurled her dead body from a sheer cliff on the Capitoline Hill, which they subsequently called the Tarpeian Rock – and which became the place of execution for Rome's most notorious traitors throughout its history.

Festivals

The Vestal Virgins were particularly prominent at festivals which promoted fertility and the health of the city. One example was the festival to Vesta herself, the *Vestalia*; another was the women-only festival of the *Bona Dea*, held on 4 December. Little is known about the *Bona Dea* ('Good Goddess'), but she seems to have been associated with fertility, healing, and women. At her annual festival, her secret rites were conducted in Rome by the wife of a senior magistrate, who was assisted by the Vestal Virgins. These rites took place in the senior magistrate's house, but on no condition were men allowed to be present. Although little is known of what took place, it is believed that the sacrifice of a pig was a central event.

A transvestite gatecrasher

In 62 BCE, the secret rites of the Bona Dea were hosted in the house of Julius Caesar (who was Pontifex Maximus) by his wife Pompeia. A young aristocrat called Publius Clodius dressed himself up as a woman and tried to attend, but he was detected and thrown out; since the rites had been tainted, they had to be held again on another day. Afterwards, Clodius was mercilessly mocked by Cicero and a bitter feud broke out between the two of them. In revenge, Clodius engineered Cicero's exile in 58 BCE.

This wasn't the only fall-out from the incident, for there had been rumours that Pompeia was having an affair with Clodius. Caesar therefore divorced Pompeia, not because the rumours were necessarily true, but because, in his words, 'my wife should be above suspicion'. The phrase 'Caesar's wife should be above suspicion' has survived to this day as a proverb, meaning that people should not only do the right thing, but should also be seen to do the right thing.

Review 4

1. Define the following words: *augur, cella, flamen, lituus, palladium, pontifex*.
2. What similarities and differences can you find between a Roman temple and a modern place of worship?
3. To what extent are women given prominent positions in modern religions, as the Vestal Virgins were in Rome?
4. How do the roles of an ancient priest compare to those of a modern religious leader?
5. Are there any modern equivalents of an augur today? To what extent do you think people still rely on interpreting omens to predict the future?
6. Research the dimensions and structure of either the Temple of Jupiter Optimus Maximus or the Pantheon. How do they compare to major religious buildings today?
E. Imagine you are either a pontifex, an augur or a Vestal Virgin. Describe a typical week in your life.

5. Sacrifice

Sacrifice was fundamental to Roman religion, and always accompanied public and private events such as festivals and rites of passage. The principle behind a sacrifice was that a person honoured the gods by giving up something valuable for them; a sacrifice might be offered to was to ask a god for help (e.g. for an upcoming journey), to thank a god for a benefit received (e.g. a good harvest), or simply to celebrate and honour a god (e.g. at the god's festival).

The most common type of sacrifice was a blood sacrifice – the killing of an animal as a gift to a god or gods. Although this is very uncommon in the modern world, the principle of giving up something valuable still remains. For example, Jews and Muslims fast on Yom Kippur and during Ramadan respectively, while there is a Christian tradition of forgoing something pleasurable during Lent.

In addition to blood sacrifice, there were various other ways in which Romans might leave gifts for their gods:

- **Food offerings** such as grain, cheese, fruits and cakes were often left on altars or by cult statues, particularly during harvest time when people were giving thanks for their crops.
- **Drink offerings** (known as libations) such as wine, milk and honey were often poured to the gods.
- **Votive offerings** were left in temples. For example, men retiring from their trade might leave the tools that they had worked with – a soldier might dedicate his arms, a fisherman his net, the shepherd his flute, the poet his lyre, etc., as a way of thanking the gods for their support during their working lives.

People believed that by these offerings they bound themselves closer to the gods. However, the most important sacrifice of all was the sacrifice of an animal.

Blood sacrifice

A Roman preparing to make a sacrifice would first go to the temple and arrange a date with the temple officials; he would also need to book the relevant officials such as the *popa* and *cultrarius* (see below). On or just before the appointed day, he would go to the market to buy an animal, which would have to be free of any blemishes. The type of animal to be sacrificed (which was always domestic) depended partly on the god involved and partly on the reasons for the sacrifice. According to Cicero, the rules were laid down in manuals held by the pontifices, and each temple had a list of which sacrifices its deity would accept.

Some of these rules were straightforward: male animals were always sacrificed to gods, and females to goddesses; white animals to Jupiter and Juno, but black animals to gods or souls of the Underworld (for example in Virgil's *Aeneid* 5.97, Aeneas sacrifices 'two black-backed oxen' on the anniversary of the death of his father Anchises). After that, rules became more specific to events: as we have seen, goats and a dog were required for the Lupercalia, while, for example, at the festival of the October Horse in honour of Mars, chariot races were held and the outside horse of the winning team was later sacrificed.

On the day itself, ribbons would be tied to the animal's tail, as well as to its horns (if it had them); a wealthy man might also be able to

The sacrifice of a bull, sheep and pig. The priest (right) prepares the altar while one of his attendants stands ready with a cup of wine to pour. This type of sacrifice was a ritual of purification known as the Suovetaurilia. In the republic this ceremony – denoting a new beginning – concluded the taking of the census of Roman citizens and marked the arrival of a new army commander.

Human sacrifice

Human sacrifice was rare in the Roman world, although it was probably a feature of the religious rituals of the earliest Romans. Moreover, it is likely that gladiatorial combats had their origins in slaves fighting to the death at the funerals of their masters (see p. 205).

During historical times, Romans generally saw human sacrifice as barbaric, something which only foreigners would do – the Druids of Gaul were held in contempt by the Romans for just this practice. However, this is not to say that it never happened at Rome in any form; in one famous example in 216 BCE, when the Roman army had suffered a terrible defeat to Hannibal's Carthaginians at Cannae, the Sibylline Books were consulted and, as a result, two Gauls and two Greeks were buried alive in the forum to appease the gods.

---

afford to gild these. There would then be a procession in which the animal would be led to the altar outside the temple – it was a good omen if the animal went willingly; on the other hand, if it struggled or tried to get away, this was taken as a very bad sign and the process would have to be started all over again with another animal!

Once safely at the temple, the ceremony was overseen by a presiding figure; in state sacrifices and at other important moments, this role was taken by one of the pontifices. However, in a sacrifice by a private citizen, he would most likely preside himself. There were rules about who else could be present: friends might be invited, but women were forbidden to attend sacrifices to Hercules or Mars, while slaves and foreigners

The relief carving on the altar of the temple of Vespasian in Pompeii (see p. 291). A popa leads a bull to sacrifice, while a priest waits and a man plays the pipes in the background. Behind the priest, another man seems to be holding a basket of mola salsa.

were banned from all but a few blood offerings. All participants made sure they were clean and wearing their best togas; they would also have to wash their hands in holy water before the ceremony began.

The sacrifice itself began with a call for silence; the only noise would be the sound of a flute, whose tune was to drown out any unwanted noises (since they were seen to be bad omens). The priest or president would cover his head with the folds of his toga, pour wine on the victim's head, sprinkle *mola salsa* on its back, and finally pass the sacrificial knife over its spine. At was at this point that a prayer was uttered, transferring the animal from human to divine ownership. A man with a club, the *popa*, then stunned the victim with a blow to the back of the head; as the animal fell to the ground, a knife-man, the *cultrarius*, cut its throat.

The animal was then dismembered and its entrails examined by the haruspex (see below). If the omens were acceptable, the ceremony continued with the cooking of the entrails, which were offered to the deity by being burnt in a fire on the altar. The rest of the animal was also cooked, but then shared out amongst the participants for the sacrificial banquet; at large state sacrifices, when a number of animals were slaughtered, the meat was shared out among the people. The Roman diet was not based around meat, and so this was probably one of the few times when they actually ate it.

The haruspex

The haruspex was a specific type of priest who examined the entrails (and in particular the liver) of sacrificial animals: he looked for any blemish (in colour, shape or size) which could be interpreted as an ill

A haruspex examines the entrails of a bull.

This model liver was found at Piacenza in northern Italy. The different areas labelled gave guidance to the haruspex as to how to interpret the omens.

omen. The image above is a bronze replica of a sheep's liver discovered in northern Italy; it is believed that this was the sort of tool used by the haruspex to 'read' the liver of a sacrificial victim. Haruspicy was an art developed by the Etruscans, and the most respected haruspices still came from the region of Etruria well into the time of empire. Although their knowledge was usually taken very seriously, the haruspices were not an official priesthood at Rome, and they never had official power as the pontifices and augurs did.

It seems that some educated Romans did become concerned about the possibility of charlatans using haruspicy for their own profit. Writing in the 1st century BCE, Cicero (*On Divination* 1.92) is concerned that the aristocratic families of Etruria, who had traditionally provided the best

---

Beware the Ides of March!

The famous phrase 'Beware the Ides of March!' comes from Shakespeare's *Julius Caesar*, but is based upon the records of Roman writers. For according to both Suetonius and Plutarch, Julius Caesar's death was foretold to him by a haruspex. Suetonius says that when Caesar offered a sacrifice a few days before his assassination, the haruspex Spurinna told him to beware of danger, which 'would not come later than the Ides (15th) of March'. Plutarch takes up the story by saying that on the day itself, Caesar was on his way to the senate-house when he greeted the haruspex cheerfully as follows: 'Well, the Ides of March have come', to which Spurinna replied softly: 'Yes, they have come, but they have not gone.' Caesar was killed just a few minutes later as he arrived at the senate-house.

---

haruspices, were neglecting the art and argues that they should be encouraged to study it again 'in case such a great art should through the weakness of men lose its true religious authority and be subordinated to trade and profit'. Elsewhere, he reports that Cato the Elder wondered how two haruspices could look at each other without laughing knowingly!

Instauratio

The Romans were very superstitious, and if any part of the ceremony went wrong, then the whole thing would have to be repeated, together with an additional offering to apologise for the mistake. This process was known as *instauratio* ('repetition'). There were numerous ways in which a ceremony could go wrong, some of which have already been mentioned – such as the animal refusing to go willingly, or its entrails giving bad omens. Other problems might have been caused by an unwanted noise such as a sneeze, or a small accident – Livy (5.21.16) tells of how the general Camillus slipped while turning to offer a prayer during a sacrifice. There were also occasions when the animal was not killed cleanly, and managed to run off after its throat was cut.

Prayer

At the moment of offering a prayer, the priest or president would turn towards the cult statue in the temple. Prayers were often very legalistic in nature, something which can be seen in advice given by Cato the Elder in his work *On Agriculture*. Cato discusses how a farmer, who needs to thin a grove of trees, should appease whichever god lives in the grove. His suggested prayer begins as follows:

'Whether you are a god or a goddess to whom this grove is sacred, as it is proper to sacrifice to you a pig as a propitiatory offering for the disturbance of this sacred place ...'

The Romans did not know the gender or identity of every single deity, and so prayers were often addressed to a 'god or goddess, whoever you may be'. This covered all bases, for they believed that a goddess could ignore a prayer addressed only to a god. The prayer then goes on to name the proper offering required in such circumstances – a pig – showing that the farmer is following religious rules carefully. This offering is described as 'propitiatory', which means 'appeasing', since the farmer is damaging the grove. He knows that he needs to make things right with the deity.

The prayer continues as follows:

'... and therefore for these reasons whether I or someone I have appointed performs the sacrifice, provided that it be performed correctly, for this reason, in sacrificing this pig, I pray in good faith that you will be benevolent and well disposed to me, my home, my family and my children. For these reasons, therefore, be honoured by the sacrifice of this pig as a propitiatory offering.' Cato the Elder, *On Agriculture* 139-40

Again, we can see a very legalistic formula at work here. Normally, it would be the landowner who would be expected to make the sacrifice, but many wealthy Romans lived in the city and appointed a farm manager to supervise their land – the prayer makes allowances for this.

Finally, the prayer asks for the favour in return – kindness and support from the deity. When the prayer mentions 'family', this means not just his relatives, but the whole of the landowner's household, including his slaves.

Vegetarianism

For the overwhelming majority of people in the Roman world, animal sacrifice was a normal part of life, and only a few small groups (who were typically thought of as weird or dangerous) refused to practise it. Among these groups were the Pythagoreans, followers of the Greek holy man (and mathematician) Pythagoras who had lived in southern Italy in the late 6th century BCE. They believed in reincarnation, and so were worried that by killing an animal, they could in fact be killing a dead relative in his or her next existence. The Pythagoreans were seen as outlandish in the Roman world, but in his *Metamorphoses*, Ovid puts into the mouth of Pythagoras himself their arguments against sacrifice:

'O my fellow-men, do not defile your bodies with sinful foods. We have corn, we have apples, bending down the branches with their weight, and grapes swelling on the vines. There are sweet-flavoured herbs, and vegetables which can be cooked and softened over the fire, nor are we denied milk, or thyme-scented honey. The earth affords a lavish supply of riches, of innocent foods, and offers you banquets that involve no bloodshed and slaughter.

Only beasts satisfy their hunger with flesh, and not even all of those, for horses, cattle and sheep live on grass. But creatures whose nature is wild and fierce – Armenian tigers and raging lions, bears and wolves – delight in butchered food. Alas, what wickedness to swallow flesh into our own flesh, to fatten our greedy bodies by cramming in other bodies, to have one living creature fed by the death of another! In the midst of such wealth as earth, the best of mothers, provides, nothing satisfies you, except to behave like the Cyclops, inflicting sorry wounds with cruel teeth!' Ovid, *Metamorphoses* 15.75-93

The mention of the Cyclops recalls Homer's *Odyssey*, in which the monstrous one-eyed giant ate six of Odysseus' men who were trapped in the cave with him. Therefore, in the view of Pythagoras here, eating meat is just as bad as cannibalism.

Review 5

1. Define the following words: *cultrarius, instauratio, popa.*
2. Draw up a table listing the events which took place at each stage of an animal sacrifice.
3. Do any modern religions have equivalents to libations or votive offerings?
4. How does the prayer of Cato quoted above compare to typical prayers of religions with which you are familiar?
5. Do you think that the way of sacrificing an animal in ancient Rome was more or less humane than the methods used to kill animals for food today?
R. Read the whole passage quoted above from Ovid (*Metamorphoses* 15.60-175). Do you agree with the Pythagorean views about eating meat? Give your reasons.
E. 'A blood sacrifice was much more than the mere killing of an animal.' Do you agree? Explain your answer.

II. ALTERNATIVE BELIEFS

In time, two developments served to weaken the religious influence of state religion. One was the influx of foreign cults, known as mystery religions, which offered a more spiritual and hopeful religious outlook. The other was a growing scepticism about the gods among more educated people; for them, Greek philosophy had a growing appeal.

1. Philosophy

From the 2nd century BCE, some educated Romans were increasingly attracted by Greek philosophy, which attempted to examine some of life's deepest questions (e.g. What is the meaning of life? How should a person live a good life?). Traditionally, the Romans, a very practical people, had disapproved of philosophy, and even as late as 161 BCE the senate ordered the expulsion of philosophers from Rome, arguing that people should use their time in more practical ways. Yet, by the end of the same century, two philosophical schools had won a limited but committed following among the educated upper class. These were Stoicism and Epicureanism, both of which promised followers a life free of anxiety and inner turmoil; however, the paths by which this was to be achieved were very different.

Stoicism was a system devised by Zeno of Citium, who taught in Athens until his death in 263 BCE (he used to teach at a large 'stoa', or colonnade, in the city centre, and his followers were therefore called stoics). Seneca the Younger, himself a stoic, is our best source of information about Roman stoicism. It held that there was a guiding spirit in the universe, sometimes called Reason (but also variously Nature, Fate, God, Destiny, or Providence). Reason had a plan for the universe, and a person could only be happy if he followed this plan, so bringing him into harmony with the cosmos. This was achieved by living an ethical life, and here the emphasis was on duty, discipline, and the suppression of the emotions. Another key element was to accept whatever fate threw at you with a calm mind, as Seneca explains:

> 'Learn this: nothing that is truly evil can happen to a good man ... He remains firm, and, whatever happens, he adapts it to his own advantage, for he is more powerful than all external events. I am not saying that he is insensible to these events, but he prevails over them and remains serene and unruffled as he rises up to meet every assault. He regards every misfortune as a training exercise.'   Seneca, *On Providence* 2.1-4

Stoicism taught that a person was made up of both body and soul; at death, the soul left the body and remained in the atmosphere for some time, before dissolving back into the great spirit of the universe.

Common humanity

One of the most remarkable aspects of stoic philosophy was that it taught that all people – Roman or foreigner, slave or free – were equally citizens of the universe and should be treated as such. For this reason, Seneca wrote a famous letter encouraging a friend to behave humanely towards his slaves (see p. 179). However, the stoics never campaigned for the abolition of slavery, which they accepted as a natural condition of the world, just that people should be treated well whatever their position in life. This philosophy probably had some impact on improving the lives of slaves from the 1st century CE onwards.

Epicureanism takes its name from Epicurus, a Greek who taught in Athens until his death in 270 BCE (he was therefore a direct contemporary of Zeno). Little of his own work has remained, and we know about his philosophy mostly from the Roman poet Lucretius (*c.* 99-55 BCE), who wrote a poem, *De Rerum Natura* ('On the Nature of Things'), which was a sort of philosophical textbook putting forward the epicurean world view.

The basic epicurean position was that the greatest good in life is pleasure. However, 'pleasure' in this context did not mean sensual enjoyment, so much as peace of mind and freedom from anxiety; to achieve this, life should be lived in moderation. For example, a person who enjoyed drinking a lot of wine at a dinner party would pay for it the next day with a hangover, a distinctly unpleasurable experience! The wise epicurean, by contrast, would drink enough wine to allow him both to

Epicurus.

enjoy the dinner and to feel well the next morning. Lucretius explains his world view as follows:

> 'How pleasant it is, when the sea is lashed and churned by gales, to watch from the shore while someone at sea struggles to keep afloat. This is not because I derive any pleasure from someone else's sufferings, but because it is delightful to realise that I have no similar problems.'
>
> Lucretius, *De Rerum Natura* 2.1ff.

How did epicureans believe that they could avoid life's troubles? As well as living moderately, they taught that people should avoid politics and public life, dedicating themselves instead to a reflective life of studying philosophy.

Another key tenet of epicureanism was to banish any fear of death. It held that the soul dies along with the body, and so Lucretius and other epicureans denounced religion, believing that it made people fearful of the gods and of what might happen in an afterlife. In order to achieve peace of mind, a man had to free himself from such concerns:

> 'If men could see that there is a definite termination point for their troubles (*i.e. death*), they would in some way have the strength to withstand

105

religious superstitions and the threats of prophets. But as it is now, they have no plan or power of resistance, because they fear eternal punishment after death.'   Lucretius, *De Rerum Natura* 1.107ff.

In other famous words (1.101), *tantum religio potuit suadere malorum* ('religion was able to stir up such evil deeds'), Lucretius is one of the first writers in history to warn about religion's capacity to do great harm. However, it would not be true to say that epicureans didn't believe in the gods – they simply didn't believe that they influenced human life in any way.

2. Mystery cults

As the Greek world came into Roman consciousness, a distinct feature of Greek religion became popular in Italy: the mystery cults. The word 'mystery' is derived from a Greek word meaning 'initiation', and a central element of a mystery cult was that its followers were initiated into its secrets, which were supposed to reveal to them the mysteries of the world. These cults often had a central myth with the theme of death and resurrection; such myths thus gave hope to initiates that they too would live again after death in a blissful afterlife. Other attractions were typically as follows:

- A code of morality and emphasis on ethical behaviour.
- A close personal relationship with the deity.
- Pastoral guidance from priests.
- Greater equality for marginalised groups, such as women and slaves.
- Lively and emotional worship, in contrast to state religion.

However, it should be emphasised that such cults were not an alternative to state religion; the former was public, while the latter were private, and an initiate would want to worship all the state gods just as piously as he or she always had done.

Since they were by nature secretive, it is hard for us to know many details of the beliefs and worship of these cults. However, there follow brief descriptions of some of those which were most influential.

i. Cybele and Bacchus

Two significant mystery cults came to Rome around the turn of the 2nd century BCE. The first was that of **Cybele**. In 205, when the Romans were unable to defeat the Carthaginians, they consulted the Sibylline Books, which told them to introduce the cult of the *Magna Mater* to Rome. *Magna Mater* ('Great Mother') was another name for Cybele, a 'mother earth' goddess from Asia Minor who was believed to be the mother of all living things.

A sculpture of the Magna Mater being led in a chariot drawn by lions.

However, Rome's rulers were soon shocked when they learnt about the new cult. Its central myth concerned Cybele's mortal consort Attis, who had been promised in marriage to a king's daughter; Cybele appeared at the wedding, whereupon Attis, in a maddened frenzy, castrated himself and died; yet Cybele protected his body and resurrected him. To commemorate this, the priests of Cybele's cult, the *Galli*, were eunuchs who had castrated themselves upon entering her service. Moreover, her initiates seemed to the Romans to act in a state of emotional frenzy, revelling in shrill and raucous music, a great contrast to the calm and orderly nature of state religion. As a result, the Roman authorities immediately put tight restrictions on the cult, including banning citizens from becoming priests.

During the same period, the cult of **Bacchus** emerged. This cult, in contrast, was not formally introduced to Rome, and it is unclear exactly how it arrived – perhaps it came with natives of the east emigrating to the city, or else with slaves from the Greek cities of southern Italy. Initiates believed that Bacchus was a saviour god who was associated with death and rebirth – most notably in his ability to bring the vine back to life again in the spring, thereby providing wine, which offered its drinkers an ecstatic release from life's cares. Drinking wine was clearly a central element of the Bacchic cult.

The festivals of Bacchus, or **Bacchanalia**, soon developed a reputation for wild behaviour and drunken orgies, with vicious rumours of corruption and immorality. It is hard to know how much truth was

A Bacchic procession. The god is at the back, holding his thyrsus (staff) and accompanied by a panther. In front of him are two followers, one playing the cymbals and the other the pipes.

contained in these rumours (similar slanders were made against the early Christians); what is certain, however, is that the Roman upper classes were deeply alarmed by the new cult, which tended to appeal to the lower classes. Believing that it posed a threat to public order, in 186 BCE the senate introduced severe restrictions: meetings were banned throughout Italy, while sanctuaries were destroyed. However, the private worship of Bacchus was still allowed, and the religion remained popular in Italy for centuries, as can be seen from the wall paintings in the Villa of the Mysteries in Pompeii (see p. 319).

ii. The cult of Isis

Egypt held a deep fascination for Greeks and Romans, many of whom believed that its ancient civilisation possessed special sacred insights; consequently, the Egyptian gods were a source of great interest. This was particularly true of Isis, a central goddess in Egyptian mythology. A loving and compassionate deity, it was said that each summer, when she saw the lands dry and the river Nile short of water, she would weep for her people and thereby cause the river to flood, so watering the fields and allowing the crops to grow once more.

Another important myth about Isis concerned her brother Osiris (who was often also known as Serapis in the Greek and Roman world), to whom she was married. According to the myth, Osiris had taught the

Egyptian people law, agriculture and religion, after discovering them submerged in cruelty; but he was then murdered by his evil brother Set, the god of chaos, who tore the body to pieces and scattered the remains over the lands of the earth. Isis collected the remains and brought Osiris back to life; after this, he became a merciful judge of the dead. Isis and the resurrected Osiris then conceived a son, Horus, god of the living.

These two myths illustrate why Isis was such a popular goddess: she was seen as a mother-figure, who cared about her people, and provided fertility and the rebirth of the crops. Moreover, the story of her revival of Osiris suggested that she also had the power to bring human beings back to life after death; from this, her followers believed that Isis would give them a happy afterlife.

The image of Isis

Isis is often portrayed in statues as a mother-figure holding the baby Horus. Such images are often strikingly similar to those of the Virgin Mary holding the baby Jesus, and some have suggested that there was a direct influence from one to the other.

On other occasions, Isis is depicted holding two important items: a jug of Nile water, which was sacred to her cult, and a *sistrum*, a type of rattle which was played as part of the loud and lively musical celebrations at her cult ceremonies.

A statue of Isis holding
a *sistrum* and a jug of
water from the Nile.

109

This fresco from Herculaneum shows priests of Isis leading
worship, while the congregation seems to be participating in
singing. Two symbols associated with Egypt are visible: the
sphinxes beside the temple, and the ibises in front of the brazier.

Worship
The cult seems to have come to Rome in the early 1st century BCE; at
times it was oppressed by the state, particularly by Octavian in the 30s
BCE since it was the religion of his rival, Cleopatra, queen of Egypt.
However, some decades later the ban was lifted by the emperor Caligula,
and by the beginning of the 2nd century it was so integrated into Roman
life that a huge sanctuary to Isis and Serapis was built in the Campus
Martius area of Rome.

A procession in honour of Isis led by a priestess who has a cobra – another link to Egypt – wrapped around her arm. Behind her follow a holy scribe with the sacred book, a prophet carrying a jug of Nile water, and an attendant shaking a sistrum.

The best written account of the cult comes in a fantasy novel, *The Golden Ass* by Apuleius, an author of the 2nd century CE from North Africa. It is narrated by its main character, Lucius, who is turned into an ass during the novel. Later, he is changed back into human form in Corinth, after he goes to a procession of the cult of Isis, prays to the goddess, and she pities him. Lucius' description of the procession gives some flavour of the cult's loud and colourful worship:

'And now the procession of the divine Saviour moved forward. The women were a splendid sight, in their white garments, accented by various kinds of finery. On their heads they wore garlands of spring flowers and, from bouquets in their arms, they scattered flowers on the pavement of the streets where the sacred procession was passing ... then came a large contingent of both men and women with lamps, torches, candles, and other kinds of light in honour of the goddess ... next, flutes and pipes and piccolos sounded a very soothing harmony. An attractive choir of carefully chosen boys, radiant in their white garments, followed singing a hymn ...'

Lucius next goes on to describe the ordinary worshippers of the cult as they pass by:

'Then there appeared streaming crowds of people who had been initiated into the divine mysteries, both men and women, of every social class and of all ages, dazzling in their linen garments of pure white.'
Apuleius, *The Golden Ass* 11.9-11

111

It is very rare to find such a description of a religious ceremony in the Roman world where participants are drawn from all walks of life – and treated as equals. Lucius goes on to relate how he himself becomes an initiate of Isis' cult at Corinth: a priest gives him instructions from the holy books and he has to go through a stage of purification and fasting for ten days, during which he performs daily service in her temple. After this, the day of initiation comes; Lucius is careful not to reveal the secrets of the mysteries, but he does claim that he experiences going down to the Underworld and then being brought back to life again.

The Temple of Isis at Pompeii

In 1765, excavators in Pompeii discovered a remarkably well-preserved temple and sanctuary, which they quickly identified as dedicated to Isis. It is likely that it had been rebuilt in the years before the eruption of 79 CE, possibly after the earthquake of 63 CE (see p. 261); the rebuilding was funded by a freedman called Numerius Ampliatus in the name of his six-year old son Numerius Popidius Celsinus, who was nominated to the town council as a reward!

The sanctuary was protected from the outside by a high wall all around (presumably to prevent non-initiates from observing events). Inside was a colonnaded courtyard, at the centre of which was the temple. In addition, there were various other key buildings:

The remains of the temple of Isis in Pompeii.

112

- A small, square building, commonly called the *purgatorium*, which contained a well of Nile water.
- An assembly-hall (the *ekklesiasterion*), for initiates to meet in.
- A living and domestic area for people including a kitchen, dining room, and a place to sleep.

Some have thought that the worship of Isis became more popular in Pompeii after the devastating earthquake. Although it is hard to know if this was really the case, images and statuettes of the goddess have been found in more than 20 Pompeian houses. Isis was clearly a goddess who appealed to many at the height of the Roman empire.

iii. The cult of Mithras

The cult of Mithras – or Mithraism – was quite different from that of Isis. For one thing, it is generally believed that women could not take part (although there is some evidence for female involvement in certain cases); secondly, the rites and worship of Mithraism were private and lacked the public celebrations practised by the followers of Isis.

Origins

Mithras was originally a Persian god but, curiously, he had little impact in the eastern Mediterranean where many mystery cults took hold. Rather, his cult seems to have predominantly developed in Italy, where the god assumed a significantly different character from the one recognisable in 5th-century Persian religion. In fact, it is probably fair to say that the cult of Mithras was a Roman interpretation of a much older god from a foreign culture.

The myth of Mithras told by the Romans is about the eternal struggle between good and evil, and the hero is often linked to the Sun-god, a symbol of good in many cultures. According to the myth, Mithras' early life was one of hardship and painful triumph. Finally, he captured the primeval bull and, after dragging it back to his cave, killed the animal in order to release its life force for the benefit of humanity: from the bull's body grew useful plants and herbs, from its blood came the vine, and from its semen all useful animals. Therefore, from the killing of the sacred bull comes life and the victory of good over evil.

Mithraea

Very little written evidence has survived of the cult, but we can learn from the temples the initiates used. A temple, known as a *Mithraeum*, was designed to replicate the cave in which Mithras had slain the bull; therefore temples tended to be found underground, in places like caves or crypts; they were dark and windowless, with a main aisle lined by raised benches and a sanctuary at the far end, often in a recess, where

The remains of this Mithraeum are today located under the church of San Clemente in Rome.

Mithras slaying the sacred bull.

the altar stood. The most important icon in the *Mithraeum* was the *tauroctony* ('bull-slaying'), a stone carving depicting Mithras killing the bull, typically accompanied by a dog, a scorpion and a snake. It is thought that these animals represented signs of the zodiac, and astrology seems to have been important to the cult – often astrological signs and stars were drawn onto the roofs of *Mithraea*.

Initiates

Mithraism seems to have appealed to traders and soldiers, who were perhaps particularly attracted by its emphasis on truth, honour and courage. Soldiers seem to have spread it around the empire and it is very visible on the frontiers of the Roman empire – including in Roman Britain. Initiates seem to have belonged to one particular *Mithraeum*; records suggest that the number of members would be between 10 and 36; a ritual meal seems to have been a key element of services. There doesn't seem to have been any religious organisation or hierarchy beyond these individual *Mithraea*.

The goal for initiates was to work up through the seven stages of initiation, each of which had a name: 1. the raven; 2. the male bride; 3. the soldier; 4. the lion; 5. the Persian; 6. the sun-runner; 7. the father. Progressing through these seven grades was seen to be symbolic of the progression of the soul, leading to immortality. Initiations may well have been painful and frightening, if these words of a hostile Christian critic are to be believed:

> 'Further, what about that ludicrous performance they undergo blindfold in the Cave? They are blindfolded in case their eyes shudder at being disgustingly degraded! Some, like a bird, flap their wings, imitating the cry of a raven. Some roar like lions. Some have their hands tied with chicken-gut and are cast over pits full of water, whilst someone comes up with a sword and breaks this gut, who calls himself the liberator.'
>
> Pseudo-Augustine, *Questions on the Old and New Testaments* 114

Some of the different grades are clearly referred to here; it seems that in the first grade, the raven, initiates merely watched (i.e. like ravens); the most common grade seems to have been the lion, since we hear most about them; men who progressed higher than this could go on to have an influential and priestly role in their *Mithraeum*.

Eclipse

Mithraism suffered from the emergence of Christianity as the state religion during the 4th century CE. Both literature and archaeology indicate that *Mithraea* were vandalised as the Christians fought for religious exclusivity. As a result, Mithraism seems to have died with the Roman empire itself in the 5th century; however, its place in the history of religion in the Roman world is an important one, as the modern scholar Ken Dowden puts it:

> 'In their exotic and slightly masochistic way, (Mithraists) assigned their members a place in the universe: they felt part of creation and its riches, they had a sense that efforts were needed for the soul to rise from its present condition ... to an ultimate association with a power which they ... saw in, or compared to, the Sun.'
>
> *Religion and the Romans*, p. 79

As with the initiates of Isis, the followers of Mithras were given a spiritual path on which to base their lives, in contrast to state religion and this was surely the heart of its appeal.

Review 6

1. What do the words 'stoic' and 'epicurean' mean in English today? How have their meanings changed since Roman times?
2. What elements of stoicism and epicureanism do you find attractive or unattractive? Explain your answer.
3. Why do you think that the Roman state felt threatened by some of the mystery cults?
4. Are there any religious organisations today which have similarities to the mystery cults? Explain your answer.
R. Read Lucretius' account of a procession in honour of Cybele (*De Rerum Natura* 2.594-632). What can we learn about the cult from these lines?
R. Read the whole of Apuleius' passage describing the cult of Isis (*The Golden Ass* 11.7-24). What else can we learn about the cult here?
E. Imagine you are an initiate of either the cult of Isis or the cult of Mithras. Describe what you think might happen when the cult meets, and why you might enjoy taking part.

---

3. Christianity

By the end of the Roman empire, a new religion had emerged which was to define European civilisation for centuries to come. The story of how a minor cult from a distant corner of the empire grew into its official religion is remarkable.

Judaism

Christianity emerged out of Judaism. In fact, until early in the 2nd century CE, many considered it to be simply a new sect of Judaism – which already had various different factions. From the 2nd century BCE, Rome had been involved in Jewish affairs, and by the 1st century CE the region was divided into provinces, and client kingdoms. The Jewish

This triumphal procession on the Arch of Titus in Rome shows the sack of Jerusalem. The seven-branched candelabrum, the menorah, was used in the temple and remains an ancient symbol of Judaism.

world was very divided within itself as to how to react to this, with some urging rebellion, while others, such as the Herods, worked with their Roman masters. A key moment in the history of the Jewish people came with the Jewish revolt against Roman rule between 66 and 70 CE. This culminated in the destruction of the temple in Jerusalem, the holiest site in Judaism. After this, many Jews were captured and deported to Rome as slaves, while others decided to leave their homeland and settle elsewhere in the empire.

Although the Romans found the Jewish concept of monotheism very strange, they generally allowed Jews freedom of worship because they were prepared to pray for the safety of the emperor, even if they did not believe in the state religion. In addition, Judaism was not a converting religion, and so there was little danger of it spreading beyond its ethnic group (although we do hear of some converts at times). However, as with Christianity, Judaism suffered periods of terrible Roman persecution, somewhat depending on the emperor of the time.

A new religion

According to the gospels, Jesus was a Jewish rabbi from the town of Nazareth who was put to death by the Romans (at the instigation of the Jewish religious authorities) for stirring up religious and civil mutiny. Jesus' death ought to have dealt a fatal blow to his mission, but his followers, convinced of his resurrection, were determined to share his message with others. The most effective of these followers in spreading the new religious teachings was Paul of Tarsus, commonly known as Saint

Paul. He held Roman citizenship and is famed for his missionary journeys which took him from Judaea to different parts of the empire (e.g. Syria, Turkey, Greece and Italy) to spread his new religion to the non-Jews.

The first non-biblical reference to Jesus of Nazareth came in 64 CE, in the aftermath of the terrible fire at Rome (see p. 212). According to the historian Tacitus, rumours started to circulate in Rome that the emperor Nero had had the fire started himself; he was quick to look for a scapegoat, and the Christians were an easy target:

> 'To put an end to the rumour that he had started the fire, Nero invent-ed charges of guilt and inflicted the most exquisite tortures on a group of people whom the Roman mob called "Christians" and hated because of their shameless activities. During the reign of Tiberius, Christus, who gave his name to this group, had suffered crucifixion under the procura-tor Pontius Pilatus; and a dangerous cult, which had been kept in check for the moment, burst forth again, not only throughout Judaea, the ori-gin of the evil, but even in Rome ... Therefore, first of all, people who admitted their belief were arrested ... (and) mockery was heaped upon them as they were killed: wrapped in the skins of wild animals, they were torn apart by dogs, or nailed to crosses, or set on fire and burned alive to provide light at night ...'   Tacitus, *Annals* 15.44

The mention here of 'shameless activities' touches on slanders against the Christians which were to re-emerge for centuries; for the most part, it seems that they were based on fear and misunderstanding. The refu-tations of 3rd-century Christian writers give us a flavour of these slan-derous rumours: Christians were suspected of sacrificing babies, whose flesh and blood they ate instead of bread and wine; Christian ritual meals, known as 'love feasts', were associated with all sorts of sexual promiscuity, while believers were also accused of incest, since they called each other 'brother' and 'sister', even if married to one another.

In this context, it is not hard to see why Romans would have seen the new religion as subversive and 'evil'. Moreover, there were other social and political factors which caused suspicion:

- The Christian refusal to worship the traditional gods would have made many believe that their gods would be angered, so threaten-ing the *pax deorum*.
- Christians also refused to eat meat from traditional sacrifices (for example, St Paul claims at 1 Corinthians 10 that 'the sacrifices of pagans are offered to demons, not to God'), so isolating them from banquets and social occasions.
- Christianity talked about the coming of a 'new Kingdom'; while this was meant in a spiritual sense, it was open to being inter-preted as a plot against the emperor, particularly since Christians refused to worship at his cult.

- Christians also tended to meet in private places, so raising further suspicions that they might be plotting against the authorities. In contrast, Roman religion tended to be practised in public – particularly at sacrifices, in which Christians refused to take part.

However, despite the threat of persecution, Christianity clearly had a powerful appeal, particularly for those in marginalised groups such as the poor, women and slaves. As with the mystery religions, the sense of community and equality must have been a strong pull for many. Moreover, Christianity was clear in promising a blissful afterlife in paradise to its followers; this meant that many went willingly to their deaths, believing that any suffering would simply be the prelude to eternal happiness.

Secrecy

In response to persecution, Christians also became more secretive about their religion. This can be seen in the secret signs which they developed. One was a cross, symbolising the crucifixion, another was a fish: the Greek word for a fish, *ichthus*, contained the initial letters of the Greek words for 'Jesus Christ, Son of God, Saviour'. Another Greek sign was the combining of the Greek letters alpha and omega (A and Ω), the first and last letters of the Greek alphabet, to show God's omnipotence. There was also a word square which hid the words *Pater Noster* ('Our Father') twice, while the 'chi-rho' symbol spelt out the first two letters (XP) of the word 'Christ' in Greek.

This mosaic from Hinton St Mary shows the chi-rho symbol behind Christ's head.

However, it would be wrong to say that Christians were continuously persecuted throughout the centuries until their religion became officially recognised early in the 4th century. A good insight into how the Christians were treated by the authorities can been seen in correspondence in 111 CE between Pliny the Younger (see p. 263), the governor of Bithynia-Pontus (a province in what is now northern Turkey), and the emperor Trajan. Pliny wrote to Trajan to clarify what policy he should adopt regarding Christians. Trajan replied that the principle which Pliny had already been following was the right one:

'You have followed the right course of procedure, my dear Pliny ... for it is impossible to lay down a general rule to a fixed formula. These people must not be hunted out; if they are brought before you and the charge against them is proved, they must be punished, but in the case of anyone who denies that he is a Christian, and makes it clear that he is not by offering prayers to our gods, he is to be pardoned as a result of his repentance however suspect his past conduct may be. But pamphlets circulated anonymously must play no part in any accusation. They create the worst sort of precedent and are quite out of keeping with the spirit of our age.'   Pliny, *Letters* 10, 96-7

On one level, Trajan's policy was relatively enlightened, insisting that Christians should neither be hunted out nor convicted on the basis of anonymous accusations, while they should also be given an opportunity to recant. However, the emperor does also set down the basic legal position that Christianity should be treated as a crime to be punished.

His policy prevailed for nearly 150 years, during which time Christianity was never formally persecuted by the Roman authorities, although the door had been left open for local communities to prosecute Christians if they so wished. Consequently, there may have been persecutions at a local level, but while later Christian writers found inspiration in the stories of those who became martyrs for the faith (from the Greek *martus*, meaning 'witness'), the numbers in this period were relatively small – the notion that Christians were being routinely fed to the lions or beheaded is simply not true.

However, the situation changed for the worse under the emperorship of Decius (249-251), a period of great instability in the empire (see p. 54). Decius wanted to restore order and traditional values to the Roman world, and he saw the growing popularity of Christianity as a threat to peace and harmony; consequently, the persecution of Christians became government policy. In the years which followed, there were further persecutions under Valerian (253-260) and Aurelian (270-275), but the worst came under Diocletian, who in 303 instigated a purge of Christians which was to last for eight years.

Official recognition

These 3rd-century persecutions perhaps indicate that Christianity was a growing force which had to be taken seriously by the Roman state. It had never simply been a religion of marginalised groups, such as the poor, women and slaves, as there had always been wealthy and influential figures who at least sympathised with the Christians – for example, Marcia, the concubine of the emperor Commodus, used her influence to achieve the release of Christian prisoners from the mines.

One such aristocratic Christian was Helena, the mother of the emperor Constantine (see p. 56), who had a close relationship with her son and must have influenced his own promotion of Christianity. In October 312, Constantine defeated his rival Maxentius at the battle of the Milvian Bridge outside Rome. According to the Christian chroniclers Eusebius (*c.* 263-339) and Lactantius (*c.* 240-320), the battle marked the beginning of the emperor's conversion to Christianity.

What was Constantine's vision?

The two main sources – Lactantius and Eusebius – give differing accounts of visions which Constantine was supposed to have seen before the battle. Lactantius, writing a few years later, claims that on the night before the battle the emperor had a dream in which he was commanded to 'inscribe the heavenly sign of God' on his soldiers' shields. The next day, they went into battle with a Christian symbol on their shields – either the cross or the chi-rho symbol – and duly won.

By contrast, Eusebius tells a different story, which he claims the emperor himself had told him on oath many years after the battle. Constantine had apparently seen a vision of a cross in the sky before the battle, along with the Greek words which translate as 'you will conquer in this'. According to Eusebius, Constantine regarded the battle as a Christian victory and put up in Rome a statue of himself holding a cross.

Many scholars have dismissed the stories of Constantine's visions as Christian propaganda, pointing out that Constantine himself continued to promote the state cult and only converted to Christianity on his death-bed in 337. Nonetheless, within a month or two of the battle, Constantine and Licinius, his co-emperor in the east, signed the **Edict of Milan**, which made Christianity a legal religion of the empire.

In fact, Constantine soon went much further. In the following year, he started actively favouring Christianity: he restored Church property in Africa (and presumably other provinces), he made enormous donations to the Church from imperial funds and also allowed the clergy exemption from compulsory civic duties (a rare privilege). Moreover, he personally paid for the building of five or six new churches in Rome, including the

The Church of the Holy Sepulchre in Jerusalem.

original Basilica of St Peter, the church now at the heart of Vatican City. The profile of the Christian community in the city was fundamentally changed – far from being an outlawed sect, Christians could now own property, build churches, worship freely and take part in public life. Moreover, the architectural revolution went far beyond Rome – one of Christianity's holiest places, the Church of the Holy Sepulchre in Jerusalem, was first constructed in 326 under the personal supervision of Helena.

The rest of the 4th century saw an intellectual and political power struggle between Christians and pagans. The former quickly gained the ascendancy, and their victory was finally completed in the reign of Theodosius I (379-395) who, in 380, declared Christianity to be the only legitimate religion of the empire; after this, he stamped out many pagan practices. In the years which followed, pagans found themselves in the galling position of having to plead for tolerance and the right to worship. One of their leading spokesmen was the Roman statesman Symmachus, who appealed with these famous words:

> 'We ask, then, for peace for the gods of our fathers and of our country. It is just that all worship should be considered as one. We look on the same stars, the sky is common, the same world surrounds us. What difference does it make by what pains each seeks the truth? We cannot attain to so great a secret by one road alone.'   Symmachus, *Relatio* 3.10

2. Roman Religion

Yet Symmachus' appeal was too late – his tragedy was that although the Romans had often been accepting of other religions, they had never extended the same tolerance to Christianity. Perhaps if they had done, history may have been different. As it was, the new religion survived the sack of Rome by Alaric the Goth in 410 (who was himself a Christian), and went on to become the predominant religion of Europe for centuries to come.

Review 7

1. Describe or draw the following Christian symbols and explain their significance: the cross, the chi-rho, the fish, the alpha/omega.
2. Why do you think that Nero saw Christians as an 'easy target'?
3. Why do you think Christianity appealed so much to people despite the threat of persecution and death?
4. Find out about the Arch of Constantine in Rome. What event does it celebrate?
5. Do you agree with Symmachus that all religions are equally valid?
R. Read Eusebius' description of the persecution of Christians in Gaul in 177 (*Ecclesiastical History* 5.1.6-16). What can we learn about early Christians and their persecution from this passage?
E. Imagine you are a Christian living in the early empire. Describe why you follow your faith, the dangers you face, and how you manage these.

3

Roman Society

What do we mean by 'Roman society'? As we have seen in Chapter 1, the term could relate to over a thousand years of history, during which time Roman culture spread across three continents. There would clearly be a world of difference between the way people lived in Rome in the 6th century BCE and the 4th century CE; likewise, there were probably significant variations in distant parts of the empire at any one point in time: today, we would not expect people in Britain, Portugal and Syria to live according to exactly the same customs, and we should not expect it of those living in those regions during Roman times.

This chapter will focus predominantly on life at Rome in the late republic and early empire, the 1st centuries BCE and CE (although other places and times will also be referred to), since this is the period for which we have the greatest wealth of literary evidence. In addition to the material in this chapter, further insights into Roman society are given in the final two chapters on Pompeii and Herculaneum.

Sources

There is a wide range of sources which reveal something of everyday life in the Roman world; it is important to be aware that they all have their own points of view and prejudices, and so what they say should not always be taken as the whole picture.

In this chapter, we often read about Roman life from the perspective of satirists, who were aiming to make fun of the customs and people among whom they lived. In particular, Petronius, Juvenal and Martial, who were all writing during the 1st and early 2nd centuries CE, offer us witty and at times cynical views into their world. We should be careful how we treat them as sources, since they were writing to make people laugh rather than to record exactly how society worked. Despite this, however, it is unlikely that their work would have been considered amusing if it had not been based in everyday truths, and so it is likely that they do offer us an insight – albeit exaggerated – into the society in which they lived.

---

1. Housing and households

The Roman term *familia* refers to more than the English translation 'family' would imply. For in Roman terms, a *familia* incorporated all the people and property attached to the male head of the family – who was known as the *paterfamilias* ('father of the family') – including blood relatives, slaves, houses, farms and land. The base of this *familia* was clearly the home – the physical space where the household lived.

i. Living space

When people think of Roman houses, they are most likely to think of a *domus* – a well-designed large house with an internal garden, decorated with beautiful art, and containing plenty of living space and rooms for entertaining guests. However, the number of Romans who lived in such luxurious homes was tiny; in fact, the vast majority lived in cramped and dangerous apartment blocks known as *insulae* ('islands'). A thorough survey of Rome made in the 4th century CE records 1,797 houses as opposed to 46,602 *insulae*. To understand the living conditions of the average Roman, therefore, we need first to examine what it was like to live in an *insula*.

Insulae

As the Romans conquered progressively more of the Mediterranean world from the 3rd century BCE, so the city of Rome grew – upwards as well as outwards. Even by this time, *insulae* commonly consisted of three storeys; by the beginning of the empire, these buildings had become so dangerous and liable to collapse that the emperor Augustus was forced to pass a law forbidding them to be built higher than 18 metres; it is unlikely that this law was obeyed very closely, since we hear of *insulae* six or seven storeys high after the passing of the law.

As might be expected, the quality of these *insulae* (and of the apartments in them) varied; the best evidence comes from the Roman port town of Ostia, since hardly any *insulae* have survived in Rome itself. An *insula* typically had at least three storeys, with access to the upper floors from a staircase leading off the street. Sometimes the building would surround a central courtyard which might contain a cistern providing water – the apartments (*cenacula*) themselves rarely had running water or heating facilities. It seems that the lower storeys were safer, while rooms at the top were smaller, darker and flimsier. Therefore, those on the lower floors were more highly priced; some lower storey apartments in Ostia were quite large and elegant, and could fetch a significant rental price.

However, if the satirist Juvenal is to believed, many of the *cenacula* in Rome were places of great squalor:

'We live in a city which is, to a great extent, propped up by flimsy boards. The manager of your apartment building stands in front of the collapsing structure and, while he conceals a gaping crack (a crack many years old),

The remains of an insula on the side of the Capitoline Hill in Rome.

he tells you to "sleep well" – even though a total cave-in is imminent! It's best, of course, to live where there are no fires and no panics in the dead of night. Here, one neighbour discovers a fire and shouts for water, another neighbour moves out his shabby possessions. The third floor, where you live, is already smoking – but you don't even know! Downstairs there is panic, but you, upstairs, where the gentle pigeons nest, where only thin tiles protect you from the rain, you will be the last to burn!'

Juvenal, Satires 3.193-202

Juvenal wasn't the only writer to mention flimsy apartments. Cicero (see p. 40), writing to a friend about apartments which he rented out, joked that 'two of my buildings have fallen down, and the rest have large cracks. Not only the tenants, but even the mice have moved out!'

Juvenal also mentions the fire hazard in this passage, and there is no doubt that this was a major danger. Even though the *insulae* were often built of brick, an apartment typically had a brazier alongside wooden furniture, a recipe for disaster. Some fires, such as that of 64 CE (see p. 212), destroyed large parts of the city. We even hear of Crassus, an immensely wealthy politician of the 1st century BCE, making huge profits out of such disasters by buying up buildings which had burnt down, and those adjoining them, at a knock-down price; he would then build new *insulae* out of the burnt-out rubble and charge high rents for basic accommodation. In fact, Crassus was so keen to make a killing like this that he even bought more than 500 slaves who were skilled as architects or builders.

Some people lived in apartments which were not part of an isolated apartment block. There is evidence that the upstairs rooms of some houses were hired out to tenants, while people who worked in shops which fronted onto a street often lived in a small room above the shop – perhaps with many family members.

The price of property

As today, the price of property in large cities was far higher than in remoter regions. Juvenal again has something to say on this (albeit in exaggeration, no doubt) suggesting to a friend that, if he can remove himself from the excitement of the city, he will live far more comfortably elsewhere:

'If you can tear yourself away from the chariot races in Rome, the finest home in Sora or Fabrateria or Frusino (*small country towns around Rome*) can be bought outright for as much as you now pay in a year's rent for your dark hovel!'   Juvenal, *Satires* 3.223-5

The domus

Although the number of houses, known as *domûs* (sg: *domus*) in the city was small, they played a disproportionate role in daily life since wealthy men used their living space to work, greet friends and clients (see p. 152), and conduct politics.

This famous mosaic of a guard dog at the entrance to the house says 'cave canem' – beware of the dog!

The house of the Tragic Poet took its name from the mosaic of a set of actors preparing for performance.

Our best evidence for the *domus* comes from the preserved ruins of Pompeii and Herculaneum, and a number of their houses are described on pp. 308-24 and pp. 341-8. The layout of Roman houses was hugely variable, but as a template it is perhaps helpful to refer to Pompeii's House of the Tragic Poet, located to the north of the town's forum (see map on p. 276). Built in its present form at the end of the 1st century BCE, its space is based around three key areas – from the entrance door, one enters into the *atrium* (reception hall), at the back of which is the *tablinum* (master's study); behind this, at the back of the house, is the *peristylium* (colonnaded garden).

The plan and table on pp. 130-1 outline the layout of the house. However, we should be careful not to divide the rooms too neatly into separate functions; in fact, the activities of the house probably spilled over into a number of spaces. For example, the kitchen was too small to cope with the preparations for a large dinner party, so slaves might have used the *peristylium* to prepare food (and probably also to do the washing up afterwards). Similarly, it is unlikely that slaves had their own sleeping space, and so they probably lay down in out of the way corners. Moreover, the *atrium*, where the *paterfamilias* traditionally greeted guests and clients, was also a key area for storage, as well as for drawing water; in addition, it was quite possibly a space where women set up the loom to weave.

There are some aspects of life in a *domus* which it is especially hard for us to know about. For example, most seem to have had upper floors which have not been preserved (although Herculaneum in particular provides some exceptions). The rooms on the upper floor, which were not grand, were probably used for sleeping or storage; they may even have been rented out as living accommodation. We can also only guess at how many people lived in such a house, but it would almost certainly have included the *familia* in its widest sense – the nuclear family with some close relatives, as well as the slaves and freedmen attached to the family. Thus, one modern scholar has estimated that about 20 people may have lived in the House of the Tragic Poet.

A	**atrium**	The **atrium** was the most public part of the house, designed to impress the visitor. In its centre was usually an *impluvium* – a rectangular pool into which rain water fell from a specially designed hole (the *compluvium*) in the roof. This provided the house's main water supply.
Al	**ala**	The **alae** were alcoves where the family kept busts of their ancestors (see p. 187).
C	**cubiculum**	A Roman bedroom was small – perhaps just big enough for a bed and chair, and it wasn't considered the individual's private space as it is today. It could also double up as a general store room or family room.
Cu	**culina**	The kitchen. This was a small and poky room, with a cooking hearth. The house's toilet was located right next to it!
P	**peristylium**	The colonnaded garden was often ornately decorated with a rich variety of flowers, shrubs and trees, as well as fountains and statues.
T	**taberna**	The entrance of the house gave out onto the street and the two front rooms were turned into shops, either rented out by local tradesmen or run by the family itself. Each shop had a door linking into the house.
Ta	**tablinum**	The master's study was at the centre of the house. This might be lined with books or contain chests into which family riches or heirlooms were placed.
Tri	**triclinium**	The dining room was a key element of a *domus*: a typical Roman dinner party is described on pp. 155-8.
F	**fauces**	This was the entrance passage into the house. The House of the Tragic Poet is famous for its mosaic in the floor just inside the front door: a fierce dog is depicted above the slogan *cave canem* – 'beware of the dog'!

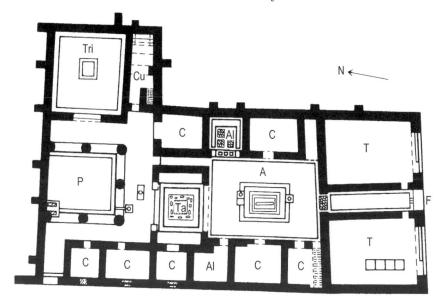

Plan of the House of the Tragic Poet.

This wardrobe has been reconstructed based on the evidence of remains buried in Pompeii. Behind it are the imprints of two chests created by Fiorelli's Process (see p. 274).

A bronze statuette of a Lar, holding a drinking horn and a dish for offerings.

How was a *domus* decorated? In the houses of Pompeii, vivid wall paintings were typically full of red, orange and blue-green colours, but there were also yellows, purples and black. Onto these were painted scenes, frequently taken from mythology (in the House of the Tragic Poet, the *atrium* was lavishly decorated with six large wall paintings of scenes from Greek mythology), but country landscapes or still-life scenes such as flowers, fruit and animals were also depicted. In many houses, painters represented architectural features such as buildings and pillars, giving the images greater perspective and suggesting that the room was more spacious than it really was.

What about furnishings? Evidence from Pompeii indicates that houses had many of the items (generally made of wood) which we might use in our homes today: tables, chairs, beds, screens, shelves, chests and cupboards were common. In the House of Venus in a Bikini (named after a statuette of the goddess found there), the contents of a large cupboard were found in the *atrium*, including bronze jugs and plates, a bronze basin and cake mould, two bronze signet rings and other pieces of jewellery, nine dice and bits of gaming equipment, as well as some coins made of gold, silver or bronze. In other words, a mixture of the sort of day-to-day items which might be stored in a home today.

ii. Family religion

The entire *familia* was bound together by the gods protecting the family – sometimes known as the household gods. These were different from the Olympian gods of state religion (see pp. 69-77), and were predominantly worshipped at a domestic level; it was thought vital to worship these gods properly in order for the family to prosper. There were two main groups of household gods: the **Lares** and the **Penates**.

The Lares were believed to be the protective spirits of the family's ancestors, who watched over the entire household, as well as its property and fields. Every house had a special shrine to the Lares, a *lararium*, which usually stood in a prominent position (in the House of the Tragic Poet, it is at the back of the *peristylium*, in full view of the *atrium*). The front of a *lararium* often took the shape of a miniature temple; it was like a small cupboard, with a shelf where statues of the Lares were kept; on its back wall, there might be paintings of the Lares, such as in the

The *lararium* in the House of the Vettii. Two dancing Lares (similar to the one pictured on the previous page) hold raised drinking horns. Between them is the Genius of the paterfamilias who is making a sacrifice. Below is a snake – snakes were often considered guardian spirits of the family.

lararium in the house of the Vettii which is shown on p. 133. Although we do not know exactly how often worship took place, one theory is that the entire *familia* would gather every morning in front of the *lararium* and say prayers to the Lares, perhaps also leaving an offering of incense, food or drink such as wine or milk.

The comic playwright Plautus (see p. 230) even begins his play *The Pot of Gold* with a Lar emerging from the home:

'So no one wonders who I am, I'll tell you briefly: I am the Lar Familiaris of this *familia* here – where you saw me come out. I have owned and looked after this house for many years now – for the present occupier's father and grandfather before him. But it was his grandfather who entrusted to me treasure in gold – secretly from everyone: he buried it in the middle of the hearth, praying to me to look after it for him.'

Plautus, *The Pot of Gold* 1-8

This passage, in which the Lar mentions his special task of protecting the family treasure (the pot of gold of the title), gives a good indication of the role of the Lares: to protect the family from generation to generation, so forming a link with their ancestors. Ancestor worship was common in many ancient societies – as it still is in some modern ones – and even in the western world today, many people are fascinated to learn about their family history and genealogy.

Home is where your Lar is

Referring to 'the Lares' was often just another way to talk about 'home'. One graffito written on a wall in Pompeii seems to have been written by a Roman homesick for his city: 'Gladly we came here, but much more gladly do we depart, eager to see again, O Rome, our own Lares.'

At times, however, the concept of the Lares could be extended to make them the protective ancestral spirits of a neighbourhood or even of a town or city – one of the temples in the forum of Pompeii may have been dedicated to the 'Public Lares' – or the town's protective ancestral spirits (see p. 291).

The second set of gods were the Penates, who were believed to be spirits protecting the larder or store-house of the family (the word Penates is derived from *penus*, the Latin for 'store-cupboard'). It might seem strange that such gods were considered so important, but it should be remembered that poverty and starvation were a constant threat for many in the Roman world, particularly in Rome's early history when the city was entirely dependent on local farmland.

Worship of the Penates particularly took place at mealtimes. They too had their own figurines which might be brought onto the table as the family ate. Servius, a 4th-century CE commentator on Virgil's *Aeneid* (see p. 3), explains the ritual of earlier days:

'Amongst the Romans, when dinner had been served and the main course taken away, the custom was for there to be silence while an offering from the meal was taken to the hearth and put in the fire, and the slave reported that the gods were favourable.'

Servius, *Commentary on Virgil's Aeneid* 1.730

In the *Aeneid*, Virgil also gives the Penates a more public role, similar to that played by the 'public Lares'. For when Aeneas escapes from the ashes of Troy, he takes with him statuettes of the city's Penates, as well as one of Vesta. These he brought to Italy and, when Rome was founded several generations later, they were placed in the temple of Vesta, the symbolic 'hearth' of Rome (see p. 92). **Vesta** herself was also a goddess who was important at both state and family level; as goddess of the hearth, she was responsible for the fireplace from which a Roman family took warmth, light and food.

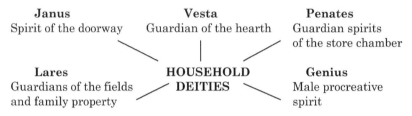

Janus	**Vesta**	**Penates**
Spirit of the doorway	Guardian of the hearth	Guardian spirits of the store chamber
Lares	**HOUSEHOLD DEITIES**	**Genius**
Guardians of the fields and family property		Male procreative spirit

The divinities worshipped in the Roman home.

There were two other divinities associated with family religion. One was the **Genius**, or the 'guardian spirit' of the *paterfamilias*. In fact, a *Genius* could be a protective spirit of anything – even a place – but in the family sense it referred to the head of the household. The *Genius* of the *paterfamilias* was represented in art by a snake, often a symbol of health and prosperity in the ancient world. Such a snake is a key part of the image painted onto the *lararium* of the House of the Vettii. The other divinity was the god **Janus**, the god of the doorway (see p. 78), who protected the entrance of the house.

A Roman house, therefore, was rich in religious symbolism. The statesman Cicero, whose own house in Rome was burnt down by his political enemies, felt particularly strongly about the importance of the home:

'What is more sacred, what is more inviolably surrounded by every kind of sanctity, than the house of every individual citizen? Within its circle are his altars, his hearths, his household gods, his religion, his observances, his ritual; it is a sanctuary so holy in the eyes of all, that it would be sacrilege to tear an owner from it.'   Cicero, *About his Home* 109

Review 1

1. Define the following terms: *domus, familia, insula, paterfamilias.*
2. Explain the significance of the following to household religion: *Genius, Janus, Lares, lararium, Penates, Vesta.*
3. How do Roman *insulae* compare to blocks of flats in cities today?
4. Imagine you are an estate agent responsible for selling a *domus* in ancient Rome. Design a pamphlet advertising the house.
5. Compare and contrast the types of religious shrines or artefacts which people have at home today with those of the Romans.
6. How well decorated was a typical Roman house in comparison with your house? How important do you think this is for a house's character?
7. Compare and contrast some of the Houses of Pompeii (pp. 308-24) and Herculaneum (pp. 341-8). What similarities and differences do they have?

---

2. Childhood and education

i. The early years

Exposure

Babies who were unwanted at birth were taken outside the city and abandoned, either to die or to be rescued and enslaved. There was a variety of reasons why a baby might have been exposed: perhaps the family couldn't afford to feed another mouth, or else it was the result of an unwanted pregnancy for a slave-girl or prostitute. It is impossible to know how many babies were exposed in this way, but the number is likely to have been significant. A letter written in 1 BCE by a Roman citizen in Egypt to his pregnant wife suggests the Romans' matter-of-fact attitude to exposing children:

> 'I am still in Alexandria. ... I beg and plead with you to take care of our little child, and as soon as we receive wages, I will send them to you. In the meantime, if (good fortune to you!) you give birth, if it is a boy, let it live; if it is a girl, expose it.' *Papyrus Oxyrhynchus* 744.G

Exposure did not automatically mean death, as some children were rescued and brought up by other people as slaves or loved children. Interestingly, a common theme in Roman literature is that of the exposed child who grows up to become great or successful. The most obvious example of this is Romulus, who was exposed with his twin Remus by the river Tiber (see p. 4), but it was also a common plotline in Roman comedies (such as Plautus' *Casina*, which is described on p. 234). Nor is this phenomenon limited to Roman folktale, as can be seen from the examples of Moses in the Jewish tradition and Oedipus in Greek mythology.

A sculpture of a sleeping child.

As soon as a baby was born (see p. 166 for childbirth), a midwife would check for any deformities and it was then laid on the ground. Hopefully, the baby's father would then lift the baby into the air, symbolically accepting it as his own. Sadly, however, this wasn't always the case – sometimes a baby was unwanted and its father would have the slaves of the house take it away from the house for exposure.

If the baby was accepted by its father, then a couch was laid in the house for Juno if it was a girl, or a table laid for Hercules if it was a boy. This was to invite these gods into the house to protect the child in its first days, when the risk of mortality was high. There was particular delight at the birth of a son, as he could inherit the family name and estate; on the other hand, daughters would have to be married off with an expensive dowry.

Children play with walnuts in a relief from Ostia, the harbour city near Rome.

The next ceremony, the 'naming day', would come on the eighth day after birth for a daughter or the ninth day for a son. It was a day of religious purification and involved a non-blood sacrifice in the home, together with a party thrown by the family for close friends and relatives, who might bring gifts. However, the most important present was the *bulla* – a lucky charm, which was believed to ward off evil spirits; the child wore it as a pendant throughout childhood.

Young children spent their first years in the home. In early Roman times, when there were fewer slaves, it was the parents who did most of the child-raising. The ultra conservative Cato the Elder (234-149 BCE), who liked to live according to the standards of the 'good old days' of the early republic, was notable for his involvement with his young child:

> 'After the birth of his son, Cato considered no business (except government business) so urgent as to prevent him from being present while his wife bathed the infant and wrapped it in swaddling clothes. And she herself nursed it with her own milk ...' Plutarch, *Cato* 20.4

This final comment is interesting since in Plutarch's time, the late 1st century CE, it was usual for mothers to have their children wet-nursed. One writer who was clearly unimpressed with the way in which this custom had developed was this conservative character in a dialogue on education:

> 'In the good old days, no children were entrusted to a hired nurse, but to their own mother's care. That was what a mother was for: to mind the house and watch over the children – what could be more commendable? ... Nowadays we hand over our new-born babies to a Greek slave-girl – sometimes she's given a helping hand by a male slave, a rogue, good for nothing as likely as not.' Tacitus, *Dialogus* 28-9

As today, it seems that there were different theories and arguments about how best to bring up a child; however, it is important to remem-

This fresco from Pompeii shows a mother breast-feeding her child.

ber that poorer families would not have been able to afford slaves, and so in their case the primary childcare role would have fallen to the mother and other female relatives.

ii. Education

In early Roman times, there were no schools as we would understand them; instead children simply learnt in their own homes, often from their fathers. They might be taught the basics of reading and writing, as well as their father's trade; however it was equally important for them to learn Roman values, such as *pietas* (see p. 2) and the *mos maiorum* (see p. 18). Once again, we can try to reconstruct how early Romans educated their children from what we know of Cato the Elder's attempts to educate his son in the old-fashioned method:

'When the child was old enough to learn, Cato himself took charge and taught him to read and write, even though he owned an accomplished slave, named Chilon, who was a teacher and who instructed many boys. But Cato did not think it proper ... for his son to be criticized by a slave ... Therefore Cato himself was his reading teacher, his law professor, his athletic coach. He taught his son not only to hurl a javelin, to fight in armour, and to ride a horse, but also to box, to endure both heat and cold, and to swim strongly through the eddies and undercurrents of a river. He also says that he wrote his book (the one titled *History*) in large letters and in his own handwriting so that his son might have the opportunity at home to become familiar with his society's ancient customs and traditions.'

Plutarch, Cato 20.5-7

Reading this, it seems hard to believe that Cato also had time to be one of the leading political figures at Rome! His example seems exceptional, even by the standards of the early republic, but the passage does give a flavour of how a father in those days might have prepared his son for adult life.

However, as Rome's power grew, society became progressively more influenced by the neighbouring Greek world, which had long established education in disciplines such as literature, history, mathematics and philosophy. Some conservative Romans, such as Cato, were appalled by this, but others adapted to it and blended in the new with the old. One such man was Aemilius Paulus, a near contemporary of Cato:

'He devoted himself to the education of his children. He brought them up both as he himself had been brought up, according to the *mos maiorum*, and also in the Greek manner. He was very keen on the Greek methods, and therefore hired masters to teach them grammar, logic and rhetoric, as well as teachers of drawing, hunting and athletics.'   Plutarch, *Aemilius* 6.8-9

From the 2nd century BCE, the school system in Rome seems to have been based on the Greek model, which consisted of three stages. The first, between the ages of seven and about eleven, was a type of primary school with a teacher known as the *litterator*; after this, pupils progressed onto a secondary education with the *grammaticus*, followed by tertiary education at the age of 16 with a rhetoric teacher, who taught them the art of public speaking.

Schools and teachers

There were no schools in the Roman world as we would recognise them – distinct buildings with classrooms, assembly halls and playgrounds. School fees were relatively cheap, and so a teacher had to find space wherever he could to teach. This would usually be a room hired in a public place – perhaps at the back of a shop (two early Roman words for 'school' were *taberna* and *pergula*, both of which really mean 'shopkeeper's booth'). The furniture would be sparse, perhaps just some wooden stools or benches, while there might be some busts of famous men, but little else in the way of display on the walls. We also hear of teachers meeting their students in public places, such as pavements and squares, where it must have been hard to compete against the surrounding noise!

Who went to school?

It is hard to know exactly what proportion of children went to school. Education wasn't compulsory and so parents only sent their children if they wanted to and could afford it. It is likely that the majority of boys attended the first stage of education (although the wealthiest families might provide a private tutor for their sons instead), while a significant number of girls probably attended at least some of this primary stage too. However, the second and third stages were predominantly reserved for the sons of the rich – by the age of 14, girls were getting married and boys from poorer families had started working. The poet Horace speaks thankfully of his father who, although only a freedman, somehow found the money to take him to Rome and send him to the school of a *grammaticus* called Orbilius:

'If my character is decent and moral ... then my father deserves all the credit. For although he was a poor man ... he was not content to send me to Flavius' school (*the local primary school*), which the burly sons of burly centurions attended ... My father had the courage to take his boy to Rome, to have him taught the same skills which any equestrian or senator would have his sons taught ... I could never be ashamed of such a father, nor do I feel any need, as many people do, to apologise for being a freedman's son.'

Horace, *Satires* 1.6.65ff.

His father's investment was richly rewarded; Horace went on to be a leading poet at the court of the emperor Augustus, and one of the most important and influential lyric poets in the history of European literature.

Teachers were badly paid, and so tended to come from the lower rungs of society – sometimes they were freedmen or foreigners. They didn't need any special qualifications, and in theory anyone could set themselves up in the role. But it seems that a teacher's life was not easy. Juvenal, once again cynically ridiculing the world around him, shows sympathy for the lot of a *grammaticus*:

'What *grammaticus*, even the most learned, ever receives the salary which his hard work deserves? ... But still the parents set impossible standards for you ... (they) insist that you mould the tender minds of their sons as a sculptor moulds a face from wax ... and then they say: "Do your job well, and when the end of the year comes, we'll pay you for the twelve-month period the same amount that a chariot driver earns in one race."'

Juvenal, *Satires* 7.215ff.

Juvenal's sarcasm at the end here is based on the fact that, as today, there was no comparison between the modest pay of a teacher and the exorbitant earnings of a top sports star (see p. 198)!

Other writers are less flattering about teachers, often portraying them as boring, strict, and with a liking for using the cane – Horace even nicknamed his teacher *Orbilius plagosus*, or 'Orbilius the flogger'! In the following passage, the satirist Martial complains about being woken up by a teacher holding an early morning class just outside his block of apartments:

> 'What do you have against us, spiteful schoolteacher? We know you are hated by all the boys and girls you teach. Before the crested cockerel has even crowed, you shatter the silence with your harsh voice and the lashes of your whip ... Would you be willing, you old windbag, to accept the same pay for being silent as you now receive for shouting out lessons?'
>
> Martial, *Epigrams* 9.68

The reason that classes started early in the morning – sometimes before daybreak as here – was so that the teacher could make the best use of daylight, and presumably also because the surrounding area was a little quieter at this time of day. Lessons lasted until at least lunchtime, with some teachers even carrying on into the afternoon. Wealthier pupils would be accompanied to school by their *paedagogus*, an educated family slave (usually a Greek) who would oversee the boy's studies – sitting in school with him, helping him with homework and perhaps even tutoring him a little, and probably also carrying his bags around.

The litterator

Lessons with the *litterator* were limited to three subjects: reading, writing and arithmetic. As he had five whole years to teach his charges to read, write and count, the teaching does not usually seem to have been at all inspiring. There was lots of repetition, with pupils endlessly having to practise writing letters of the alphabet; once this was mastered,

A relief from Gaul, showing a teacher, flanked by pupils, all in fine armchairs, while a late arrival tries to apologise. The students are reading from papyrus scrolls.

Roman writing implements.

they were forced to copy out useful phrases such as *laborare est orare* ('to work is to pray'). The following extract from the diary of a Roman school-boy gives some idea of the monotony:

> 'I copy the letters and then show the work to the teacher. He corrects it and copies it out properly. I get ready to start again by rubbing the wax smooth – that's a job, the wax is too hard. Here we go: ink and papyrus now. Up ... and down ... up and down ... and then along comes teacher and says I deserve to be whipped!' *CGL* III, p. 646

We can learn here much about the equipment used by Roman pupils. They first used wax tablets – thin sheets of wood covered with wax, on which pupils could write with a stilus, an implement with a sharp end for marking the wax and a flat end to rub the wax out and reset it. When pupils were competent writers, they would be allowed to move on to write with a pen and ink on papyrus, thick reed paper invented in ancient Egypt.

The grammaticus

Those children whose parents could afford it moved on to the *grammaticus* at the age of about 12. The basis of the studies was Greek and Roman literature; until the 1st century BCE there was little Roman literature to speak of, but this century saw the emergence of some of Rome's greatest writers, such as Cicero, Lucretius, Virgil, Horace and

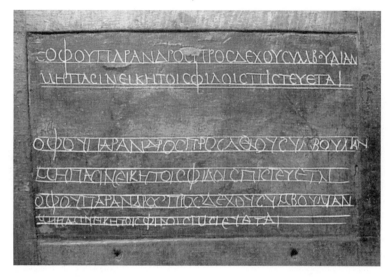

This wax tablet shows a writing exercise in Greek: the teacher has written the top two lines, which the pupil has copied below.

Ovid. From the 1st century CE, writers such as these were studied; in particular, Virgil's *Aeneid* was a standard text, much as the works of Shakespeare have been in the English-speaking world.

In addition, a Roman pupil would also learn Greek at this time. This was considered the language of educated people, partly because there had been so many great thinkers in the ancient Greek world – the epic poet Homer, philosophers such as Plato, historians such as Herodotus and Thucydides, and orators such as Demosthenes. Moreover, it was also important to learn Greek because the eastern half of the Roman empire was predominantly Greek-speaking; Greek was the language of government and law there, and a Roman provincial official would have needed to know Greek fluently.

The teaching style of the *grammaticus* seems to have been little more inspiring than that of the *litterator*. Instead of learning to appreciate the themes and stylistic sophistication of great literature, pupils were trained to focus on more mundane aspects such as grammar, figures of speech or the poet's use of mythology. A typical question might be: 'How many verbs and nouns are there in this poem?', while pupils were also expected to learn and recite passages by heart. However, since Roman culture was predominantly oral, where people listened to words much more than they read them, the development of a strong memory was essential, and it seems that this was one of the main focuses of this stage of the educational process.

The rhetor

At the age of 16, the privileged few would move on to lessons with the *rhetor*. He might educate them in many areas, including history, law, music, philosophy and geometry. However, his most important task was to train them in rhetoric, the art of public speaking. This was a crucial skill in a world without the various means of communication which today we take for granted – newspapers, radio and television, email, the internet; a successful public figure in Rome had to be able to speak well in front of a large crowd of people.

Pupils learnt to compose speeches which fell into two categories: *suasoriae* and *controversiae*. In a *suasoria*, a pupil had to argue in favour of or against a particular decision, be it historical or fictional; Seneca the Elder gives the following example of a *suasoria*:

> 'Agamemnon at Aulis has been warned by the prophet Calchas that it is against the will of the gods for him to set sail until he has slaughtered his daughter Iphigenia. Agamemnon deliberates: should he slaughter Iphigenia?'
> Seneca, *Suasoriae* 3

A Roman orator.

Pupils would have written a speech either in favour of or opposing the sacrifice of Iphigenia. This particular example shows the clear influence of the Greeks on Roman education, taken as it is from a famous moment in the story of the Trojan War. However, other *suasoriae* asked pupils to debate events in Roman history, such as 'Should Sulla have resigned his dictatorship?'

Conversely, a *controversia* required a pupil to argue about a particular legal case, which was often hypothetical and unlikely, as the following example illustrates:

> 'The law states: a priestess must be chaste and pure.
> A young woman was captured by pirates and offered for sale. She was bought by a pimp and set up as a prostitute. She persuaded men who came to her to give her the money as a gift (*i.e. without any sex act*). However, she could not persuade a soldier who came to her. When he seized her and tried to force her, she killed him. She was brought to trial, acquitted, and returned to her family and homeland. She files a petition to become a priestess. Her petition is opposed.'   Seneca the Elder, *Controversiae* 1.2

A pupil had to prepare a speech arguing either for or against the woman being admitted to the priesthood. He needed to concentrate not just on a high quality in his arguments, but also on his style of delivery, focusing on areas such as pronunciation, emphasis, facial expression and hand gestures. The training was in some ways like a barrister's training today, and it is no surprise that many of Rome's leading politicians were also accomplished lawyers.

However, if a passage from the opening of Petronius' satirical novel *Satyricon* is to be believed, not everyone approved of rhetoric training. Encolpius, the narrator, has this to say:

> 'I'm of the opinion that the rhetoric schools make idiots of our young men, because they offer nothing that relates to real life. It's all pirates standing in chains on the beach, tyrants ordering their sons to cut their fathers' heads off, oracles demanding the blood of three virgins, and so on. Improbable fairy stories to argue around – and the manner of speech required is a ridiculous mixture of honeyed words and delicate phrases which are totally at odds with the bloody subject matter!'
>
> Petronius, *Satyricon* 1

While this is clearly satirical exaggeration, it would be a surprise if it did not reflect the views of some in society. Later in the same novel, a freedman takes the argument further, claiming that all education was overrated, and that it was the 'school of life' which mattered – the lack of a formal education has not stopped him from becoming a success in life:

> 'All right, so I didn't learn geometry, didn't do essay writing and such rubbish. But I can read; I can count. And I'll bet that did me more good than

the money your father wasted on your fancy school fees with the Rhetor ...
I was taught by a real teacher: "Hold on to what you've got and mind how
you go", he said. That's what I call education. That's what made me what
I am today.'   Petronius, *Satyricon* 57

Although the reader is perhaps meant to laugh at this character, his
basic point can also be heard in our society today – some people do
indeed make great successes of themselves with little formal education.

It is hard for us to know how much progress those pupils who did pro-
ceed through school made (there were no exams, and therefore no
results for us to inspect), nor how much advantage it gave them over
those who were less educated. However, the fact that this education system survived relatively unquestioned for centuries suggests that parents felt that it was providing their children with the skills required to
make a success of adult life.

iii. Coming of age

Roman boys and girls came of age in different ways. Girls were considered to be adults from the day of their marriage – a ceremony described
on pp. 160-4. However, men tended to marry later, and so there was a
special ceremony to mark their arrival at adulthood. When a boy

A young man in a toga.

reached the age of about 16 a date was chosen, often on a public holiday; 17 March, the festival of Liber (the Roman equivalent of the Greek god Bacchus – see p. 78) was popular. Liber was an appropriate god for the occasion – according to the poet Ovid, he was represented as being both a boy and a young man.

On this day, the youth would put on the *toga virilis*, or 'toga of manhood' for the first time. For formal occasions until then, he had worn the *toga praetexta*, which had a purple border, whereas the *toga virilis* was purely white (see Appendix 4 to read about Roman clothing). He would also dedicate his *bulla* to the household gods. He next set out for the forum with his father, male relatives, and friends, where he would be enlisted as a full citizen and his name would be placed on the list of his tribe. The group then headed up to the Capitoline Hill to make a sacrifice, after which they headed home for a family party. The youth had entered public life as a young man and full citizen.

Review 2

1. Define the following: *bulla, toga virilis, litterator, grammaticus, paedagogus, rhetor.*
2. How common is infanticide in the world today? What are the reasons for it and have they changed since Roman times?
3. Why do you think teachers were not paid and valued more highly by the Romans? Do such attitudes still exist today?
4. Write an imaginary school report on a Roman boy (although such reports did not exist) for each stage of the educational system.
5. Draw a table charting the similarities and differences between Roman education and the education you are receiving today.
6. Imagine you have to compose a speech on the examples of a *suasoria* and a *controversia* given on pp. 145-6. How would you go about it?
7. What sort of coming of age ceremonies exist in society today? Do you think that it is important to mark the arrival of adulthood in some way?
E. Imagine you are a pupil at one of the three stages of Roman education. Write a diary detailing your experience at school during a typical week.
E. Imagine you are a Roman youth who has just had his coming of age ceremony. Write an account of your day and how you feel.

---

3. Working life

i. Types of work

As today, there was a huge variety in the types of work in the Roman world. The vast majority of people were either engaged in trades and manual labour, or they were unemployed. Much of our knowledge about

A marble relief showing a coppersmith's workshop. On the shelves above are the finished products – buckets, plates and bowls.

Bankers do deals in the forum.

types of trades comes from pictorial evidence such as mosaics and frescos, but we can get also an idea from Plautus' comic play, *The Pot of Gold*, in which one wealthy character bemoans the number of craftsmen and tradesmen demanding payment from him:

> 'On your doorstep stand the clothes cleaner, the clothes dyer, the goldsmith, the wool weaver, the man who sells lace and the man who sells underwear, makers of veils, sellers of purple dye, sellers of yellow dye, makers of muffs and shoemakers who add balsam scent to their shoes, linen retailers, bootmakers, squatting cobblers, slipper makers, sandal makers, and fabric strainers. They all demand payment ... and just when you think you've paid them all, they leave, but others appear, three hundred more, demanding payment – purse makers, weavers, fringe makers, manufacturers of jewellery cases – all cluttering up your atrium!'
>
> Plautus, *The Pot of Gold* 507ff.

Evidence for a similar variety of trades can be found at Pompeii (see p. 298). One feature of the passage above is how a rich man views the traders beneath him on the social scale, and many of the wealthy elite of Roman society looked down on all forms of trade and business; Senators were even forbidden to engage in these areas, which were dominated by the merchant class, the equites (see p. 361). The wealthiest men made money by owing farming estates and property in the city (as we have seen with Crassus); this allowed them time to devote themselves to law and politics, the preserve of the rich.

However, by the late 2nd century BCE, unemployment was becoming a serious problem in the city of Rome. Its population was growing beyond one million, and many newcomers were poor country folk who had been forced to come to the city to look for work. The success of the empire was in part to blame for this, since many slaves had been brought to Italy and given jobs such as farm labouring previously held by the free. In some cases, slaves might even live better lives than free men, since any slave who lived with a family would have secure board and lodging. The following witty epitaph on the tomb of a poor man highlights a plight shared by many:

> 'All a person needs. Bones resting sweetly, I am not anxious about suddenly being short of food. I do not suffer from arthritis, and I am not indebted because of being behind in my rent. In fact, my lodgings are permanent – and free!'   *CIL* VI.7193a

In addition to hunger and health problems, the text here mentions the problems of rent and accommodation. All the properties available to the poor had to be rented, and there was little sympathy shown to a tenant who fell behind on his payments. Moreover, rental contracts only covered a very short period – perhaps just a month – and so a poor family would always be wondering if their home would be taken from them.

150

3. Roman Society

Perhaps the key point to be made about the working lives of many Romans is that – apart from the corn dole (see box below) – they didn't have the safety net which exists in much of the western world today: no trade unions, no social security payments, no pension schemes, no workers' rights. As a result, there was no job security. For example, we hear in the 1st century BCE of a heavily pregnant woman working as part of a gang doing heavy agricultural digging. She gave birth while in the fields, but wrapped the baby in leaves, hid it and went straight back to work, scared of losing that day's wages. Thankfully, her supervisor found out and was kind enough to send her and the baby home with her pay straightaway. It is unlikely that many workers were treated so kindly.

The corn dole

The one way in which the state did provide assistance to the poor was with a monthly handout of grain, which could then be used to make staple food such as bread. This was known as the corn dole (or *annona*, after the Roman goddess of plenty), and almost certainly saved many poor Roman families from starvation. It was the tribune Gaius Gracchus who first legalised the provision of subsidised grain in 122 BCE (see p. 33); in 58 BCE, the tribune Publius Clodius went a step further and made the supply free, and many became dependent on it – some writers sneered that all Romans wanted was 'bread and circuses' (see p. 193). However, the amount of grain available each year depended on the weather and soil conditions in the countries producing the grain, such as Sicily and Egypt. In bad years, the shortage of corn at Rome could cause serious social unrest.

The corn dole is measured and distributed to the poor.

151

ii. Patrons and clients

Fundamental to the social structure of Roman life was the system of patrons and clients, whereby a man would attach himself as a 'client' to the service of another more wealthy than him. The latter would be known as his 'patron', a word linked to the Latin *pater* and therefore *paterfamilias*, and it was the legal duty of a patron to give his client the same protection as he would to any member of his family. In the absence of any social security system, it was a network which provided people with some sort of safety net. It had originated as a relationship between free citizens, but freedmen (see p. 180) were also automatically bound to serve their former masters as clients.

A client would be expected to come to his patron's house every morning at first light and join all the other clients for the *salutatio* ('greeting'). He was expected to arrive dressed in a toga and to wait his turn in the queue, which was determined according to his social status. When he was called forward, the patron might ask him to do some tasks for him, and in return he might promise to help him with a problem. Most of all, however, the client would hope for a handout, *sportula*, a word which originally referred to the 'little basket' in which food was given. In time, however, it came to refer to a handout of cash; by the early 2nd century CE, the typical daily amount seems to have been 6¼ sesterces per head (see Appendix 3 for currency values).

A client needed to be respectful towards his patron and address him as *Domine* ('Master'); the satirist Martial wrote an amusing poem in which he forgot to do so and paid for it:

> 'Yesterday, Caecilianus, when I came to bid you good morning, I accidently greeted you by name and forgot to call you *Domine*. How much did this liberty cost me? You knocked a hundred quadrantes off my allowance!'
>
> Martial, *Epigrams* 6.88

However, there were also rules for the patron in return. He was expected to welcome his clients to his house (Martial also complains about patrons who duck out of the back door rather than meet their clients in the morning), and to invite them to dinner from time to time. Yet while it might seem that the patron had to give away a lot of time and money, he too benefited greatly from the relationship. For a man's importance was partly measured by the size of his clientele. His clients would also do favours for him – these might range from odd-jobs and bits of business, to accompanying him to the forum in the morning or campaigning for him in an election.

It would be wrong to think simply of this relationship in terms of the poor being attached to the rich. In fact, many patrons would also be clients themselves, since the whole of Roman society was a ladder reaching up to the emperor (from the time of Augustus). In one poem, Martial complains about having made the long and wearisome walk to his patron's house, only to be told that his patron is out visiting his own patron as a client!

Review 3

1. How do the attitudes to workers in Roman times compare with those in the modern world? Are there parts of the world where workers still have few rights?

2. Why do you think that the patron/client system was so important to Roman society?

3. Is there anything like the patron/client system in society today, even at an informal level?

E. Imagine you are a Roman craftsman. Describe your typical working week, including your visits to your patron.

---

4. Food and hospitality

i. Food and diet

As today, it is very hard to make one statement about how, when and what people in the Roman world ate, since customs would have differed greatly over time and from place to place; moreover, the rich no doubt ate a far greater range of foods than the poor. As a general rule, however, it seems that the main meal of the day was the evening meal (*cena*), while breakfast (*ientaculum*) and lunch (*prandium*) were light in comparison. Martial says that he just ate a little bread and cheese for breakfast, while lunch might also include cold meat, fruit or vegetables, perhaps left over from the previous night's dinner.

For the wealthy, a dinner could be a grand event with a number of courses. However, the majority of the population would have eaten far less impressively. People living in *insulae* probably sat on chairs and stools and ate what they could afford. For the poor, this was no doubt based around boiling their grain from the *annona*, since few of them would have had an oven at home. A typical meal might therefore have been porridge or puls – a boiled wheat dish similar to couscous; we also hear of the poor eating cheap foods such as beans, leaks or sheep lips.

It is likely that eating out was also common, particularly if there was no oven at home. Many snack bars (*thermopolia* – see p. 302) have been found at Pompeii, Herculaneum and Ostia, and these would have provided people with fast food which was relatively cheap; they would also drink here – apart from the wealthy, most Romans would have had to settle for cheap wine or vinegar; *posca*, a mixture of vinegar and water believed to be healthy, was popular with soldiers.

The 'sea creatures mosaic' from the House of the Faun in Pompeii. A lobster being caught by an octopus, under the astonished gaze of a variety of sea creatures.

A Roman cookbook

We still have some Roman cookbooks. In particular, one collection dating from the late 4th or early 5th century CE lists a wide variety of recipes, such as 'sweet and sour pork', 'liver sausage', and 'rabbit with fruit sauce'. One of the most popular ingredients was a fish sauce called *garum*, or *liquamen* (see p. 302), large amounts of which were shipped all over the Roman empire. The following recipe is for 'Numidian chicken'; unfortunately, if you want to try it at home, the measurements are not given:

'Clean the chicken, poach it, and then remove it from the water. Sprinkle with asafoetida (*a spice*) and pepper, and broil it. Grind together pepper, cumin, coriander seed, asafoetida root, rue, dates, and nuts. Pour over these vinegar, honey, liquamen, and olive oil. Stir. When it boils, add starch as a binder. Pour this mixture over the chicken. Sprinkle with pepper and serve.'   Apicius, *Cookbook* 6.9.4

ii. Dinner parties

There are many myths about Roman dinner parties (*cenae*). The Romans have often been portrayed as gluttons who stuffed themselves full of every type of lavish food evening after evening. This clearly cannot have been the case. As we have already seen, most Romans did not have the means to feast lavishly, even on special occasions. Moreover, it is highly unlikely that wealthy Roman families were hosting dinner parties every evening – on most days, they must have eaten quietly at home as anyone else did. However, there is no doubt that a Roman dinner party was an important social occasion for the upper classes; it was an opportunity for the *paterfamilias* to entertain friends and impress contacts, while he would also be expected to invite his clients to dinner from time to time.

A *cena* might typically begin at about the ninth hour (some time after 3 p.m. – see Appendix 5), and could go on for hours. However, it is important to be aware that no two *cenae* were exactly the same. We hear of one which finished after three hours – this was short – while others lasted into the early hours of the morning. The meal was given in the house's *triclinium*, literally the 'three-couch-room', and the plan below shows the layout of the three couches. The host usually sat in position X, with the most important guest at Y; in fact, the seating plan was a social statement in itself, and sometimes different diners were even served different food. In the following passage, Juvenal complains that having been invited to dinner by his patron he is treated as a second-class citizen:

'So after two months you are invited as the last guest – lowest position, lowest table. You're over the moon to receive the card ... But what a din-

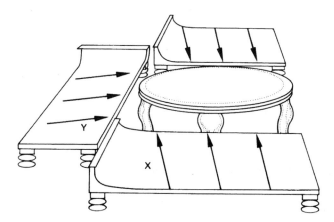

A triclinium with places for nine guests, three to each couch.

ner! The wine's worse than dishwater ... while your host Virro drinks wine that's been lying in its jar since the consuls wore long beards ... And look at that enormous lobster, spreading all over the platter, piled high with a garnish of asparagus. Reserved for his Lordship, that is: it looks down on the other guests. But *you* receive half an egg with a bit of crabmeat squashed up in it, on a tiny saucer – food for a ghost. *He* dresses his fish in the finest oil; *you* get oil reeking of the lamp, to disguise your anaemic boiled cabbage.'   Juvenal, *Satires* 5

Not all hosts were as rude as Virro. Pliny acknowledges that it would cost too much to give all his dinner guests good wine, but says: 'My freed-men do not drink my kind of wine; I drink theirs.'

The menu

A standard cena had three courses:

1. The *gustatio* (hors d'oeuvres), which consisted of light appetisers such as eggs, olives, or salad-vegetables. This was followed by *mulsum*, wine sweetened with honey.
2. The *cena* proper; in simple meals this consisted of a single meat or fish dish (or vegetables); more expensive dinners might have a variety of courses at this stage, perhaps including different meats.
3. The *secundae mensae* (dessert), which often included fruits, nuts or simply sweet cakes.

A slave announced the guests (who wore formal evening clothes – the *synthesis*) as they arrived. They were led into the *triclinium* and shown to their places, where they would lie forward on the couch, with their left arm supporting their weight. Holding their plates in their left hand, they would use their right hand to eat; they would mainly use their fin-gers, although they might have spoons and knives to help with some foods (the Romans didn't use forks). They took their food from the cen-tral table, which was kept supplied by the slaves, who would also walk

A still life showing fruit, nuts and a water jug from the House of the Stags in Herculaneum, 1st century CE.

round pouring wine and offering basins of water for diners to wash their hands in.

Menus ranged from the modest to the magnificent. Juvenal, this time the host of a *cena*, claims that the following dinner he is planning is modest:

'Here's what we're having – all home-grown; nothing from the market. First, a tender plump kid from my little country farm at Tivoli – the pick of the flock ... Then wild asparagus (my bailiff's wife cut it from the hill-side) ... Good large eggs, still warm, carefully wrapped in straw; and the hen that laid them. Grapes which after six months are as fresh as when they were picked. Baskets of pears (two varieties) and apples ranking with the best orchards.'   Juvenal, *Satires* 11.64-74

At the other end of the scale, Petronius wrote a hilarious fictional account of a wildly extravagant *cena* given by Trimalchio, a *nouveau riche* freedman who has plenty of money but little taste. He comes up with all sorts of outrageous tricks at his dinner party, including live thrushes flying out of a cooked animal, a room with flowing pools of wine, and Egyptian slaves singing for the guests while giving them pedicures at the same time!

Entertainment

Hosts would also want to put on entertainments during or after the meal. One option was the *comissatio*, a drinking session which would be led by the master of ceremonies (*rex convivii*), who would either be the host or a guest appointed by him. It was his job to decide the strength of the wine, which the Romans always watered down – perhaps by adding as much as four-fifths of water to one-fifth of wine; he would then fix the number of cups which guests had to drink, and they normally had to be downed in one. Dancers, acrobats and clowns might also entertain the guests at this stage of the meal.

These were not the only forms of entertainment. We also hear of guests playing games similar to dice and backgammon, one of which, called 'knucklebones', was even played by the emperor Augustus, as he explains in a letter recorded by Suetonius:

'Yesterday and today we gambled like old men, at dinner. We played knucklebones; anyone who threw ones or sixes put a coin in the pool. A "full house" scooped the pool.'   Suetonius, *Life of Augustus* 71

Other hosts with more highbrow and literary tastes might organise poetry recitals or philosophical discussions, as Juvenal does for his dinner party:

'If you're expecting Spanish dancing-girls with castanets, you've got the wrong address ... Such debauchery is for the rich. Gambling and adultery are quite the done thing for them, but not for us. Our dinner will have a nobler entertainment. We'll hear Homer's tale of Troy, and Virgil's fine poem, a rival even for Homer.'   Juvenal, *Satires* 11.171ff.

We should be aware that Juvenal is dealing in stereotypes here, and there is no firm evidence that the *cenae* of the wealthy were any more or less debauched than those of the middle classes. As today, behaviour probably depended a lot more on the characters of the guests than on their social and financial status. The following inscription found on the wall of one wealthy Pompeian house makes clear the high standard of behaviour expected from dinner guests:

'Do not cast lustful glances or make eyes at another man's wife. Do not be coarse in your conversation. Restrain yourself from getting angry or using offensive language. If you cannot do so, then go home!'

CIL IV.7698b-c

A wall painting from Pompeii depicting a banquet. Slaves attend to the guests, who are drinking. A man on the right is drunk and being supported by a slave.

Review 4

1. Define the following: *cena, comissatio, synthesis, triclinium.*

2. How do Roman eating habits compare with those today?

3. How does a *cena* compare to a modern dinner-party or formal social occasion?

4. How would you summarise the Roman attitude to drinking alcohol? How does it compare to attitudes to alcohol consumption today?

E. Imagine you are a slave who has to organise a *cena* for your master. Describe all the arrangements you make.

5. Women

It is much harder for us to know about the lives of women in the Roman world than it is about those of men, since the overwhelming written evidence comes from men. This means that we usually learn about women from a male perspective – be it in plays, poems, histories, or court cases; as a result, our evidence about Roman women is based on how men chose to see the women in their lives. Moreover, we generally hear about wealthier women who married into families of a high social status. The majority of women must have lived simple, hard lives of poverty – either in the city or in the country – but these were not the sort of women to interest educated writers.

A further problem is that it is very hard to generalise about the lives of women in a civilisation which spanned both centuries and continents. However, if there is one statement which can be made, it is that Roman women were regarded as inferior to men, just as they have been in the vast majority of societies throughout history. It was accepted without question that a woman's main purpose in life was to marry and have children, while her other main task was to run the household and manage domestic chores such as childcare, cooking, cleaning and sewing. At no stage in Roman history did women have any political rights, while every woman lived under the power of a *paterfamilias* – usually either her father or her husband.

i. Childhood

As we have seen, baby girls were at more risk of being exposed by their parents than baby boys. If a girl was accepted, then a different path lay ahead of her than that of a boy. Although some girls did receive basic education in reading, writing and arithmetic from the *litterator*, they were also taught 'women's work' at home – learning how to spin and to weave, to cook and to manage the house. Moreover, it seems that some young girls were forced into a life of work outside the house, if these two epitaphs are anything to go by:

> 'In memory of Viccentia, a very sweet girl, a worker in gold. She lived nine years.'

> 'In memory of Pieris, a hairdresser. She lived nine years. Her mother Hilaria put up this tombstone.'
>
> *CIL* VI.9213 & VI.9731

However, even when girls learnt trades as these two did, the most important aspect of their upbringing would have been learning how to be a good wife. Marriage for a young woman was her 'coming of age' ceremony, in the same way as a boy put on the *toga virilis* for the first time.

ii. Marriage

From early Roman times, there were three distinct types of marriage. The *confarreatio* was reserved for wealthier families and involved the solemn offering of a cake of spelt (*farreus panis*) in the presence of the Pontifex Maximus; more common among the plebs was the *co-emptio*, in which a father sold his daughter to a groom for a nominal (and symbolic) price; finally the *usus* was similar to a modern common law marriage – if a couple had lived together for a year, then they could be declared married.

Cum manu or sine manu?

In the first two types of marriage mentioned here, the legal power over the bride passed from the father to the groom; she was said to come under his 'hand', and so the marriage was described as *cum manu* ('with the hand'). Such marriages came with a dowry payment to the groom, which he had to return if he wanted a divorce. However, by late republican times, the alternative type of marriage, *sine manu* ('without the hand'), had become the norm. In this case, the wife remained under the legal power of her father (or, if he had died, a guardian usually appointed from within her family), and she did not have to hand over a dowry to her husband. The advantage of this was that she would probably have a far greater say in managing her property and affairs; on the other hand, it made divorce much less financially punishing for her husband.

Surprisingly, it was not necessary to register a marriage with the state or religious authorities; all that was needed was for a man and a woman to acknowledge that they wished to be married, and they could then just go and live together as husband and wife. However, in most cases there was ceremony and celebration, the extent of which depend-

160

ed mainly on the circumstances; poor families could not afford lavish ceremonies, while people getting married for the second time (or more) might opt for modest affairs.

Betrothal

The Roman institution of marriage was essentially a practical and economic affair. Today, western society has generally adopted the practice of 'love marriages', but 'being in love' wasn't usually on the list of requirements for a Roman match. Marriages were arranged between a bride's father (perhaps with the help of his wife) and the groom's family, and parents were always keen to find a match which would maintain or improve their daughter's social status. It is hard to know how much say a daughter might have had – the following lines from a poem by Catullus suggest that sometimes her influence was small:

'Little girl, it is not right to reject the man to whom your father and mother gave you. You must obey them. Your virginity is not entirely yours. One-third of it belongs to your father, one-third to your mother, and only one-third to you yourself. Don't fight against your parents who have surrendered to your husband a dowry and their rights over you.'

Catullus, *Poems* 62.59-65

While these lines might seem shocking to a modern reader, a wise father would have wanted to ensure that his daughter was in favour of the match – but how many fathers were wise in this way we cannot tell. The total lack of evidence from women themselves means that we can only guess at how many women might have been fearful or unhappy at the prospect ahead of them.

Some women were betrothed very young – perhaps even at the age of six or seven – although they would not get married until their teens, usually between the ages of 14 and 18. A high price was put on the virginity of a bride, and so families would be keen to marry off their daughters relatively soon after they had reached physical maturity. By contrast, a groom might typically be in his mid-twenties, and we even hear of men in their 40s marrying teenage girls.

Once a betrothal had been agreed, an engagement party, the *sponsalia*, might be held. Friends and relatives were invited and the husband-to-be might present his wife with gifts, most notably a ring which his future bride would wear on the fourth finger of her left hand. In fact, the modern tradition of this being the 'wedding finger' comes from the Romans; one Roman writer explains why the tradition had been adopted:

'When the human body is cut open as the Egyptians do ... a very delicate nerve is found which starts from the annular finger and travels to the heart. It is therefore thought fitting to give to this finger in preference of all others the honour of the ring.'   Aulus Gellius, *Attic Nights* 10.10

Even the name 'annular finger' is derived from the Latin *anulus*, meaning 'ring'. It is interesting that the Romans associated the heart with marriage, even though people didn't normally marry after falling in love. In an arranged Roman marriage, love was supposed to grow with time and the link between the ring and the heart symbolised this.

The wedding ceremony

There was a 'traditional' wedding ceremony in Roman times although, as has already been observed, we should not imagine that every wedding conformed to this type. The same is true in our society – while a 'white wedding' in church is perhaps considered traditional in Christian communities, there are many types of ceremony, religious and civil, and couples like to add their own touches to the occasion. What follows is an account of the 'traditional' Roman wedding ceremony.

The superstitious Romans took great care over picking a well-omened date: the second half of June was particularly popular (since Juno was the goddess of marriage). The ceremonies started the night before the wedding, when a bride dedicated her childhood toys to the Lares. That night, she also wore a special dress, the white *tunica recta* ('straight tunic' – so called because it was woven on an upright loom), and a yellow hairnet, both of which she had woven herself. She slept in these

The bride and groom join hands under the watchful eyes of the *Pronuba*.

A Roman bride preparing for her wedding.

clothes, and in the morning girdled the tunic with a belt made of ewe's wool (which symbolised fertility); this was tied in a tight knot, the 'knot of Hercules', which her husband was to untie that night. This knot was meant to suggest fertility as well, since in Greek mythology Hercules was credited with fathering seventy children!

The dressing process then continued with the help of the bride's friends, who no doubt provided advice and moral support too. They made up her hair, arranging it in six tresses and parting by a spear (although even the Romans seem to have forgotten the origin of this tradition). On her head the bride then placed a garland of flowers which she had picked herself, followed by the bright yellow wedding veil, which symbolised her new status as an adult woman who was expected to cover her head in public.

It was now time for the main ceremony to begin. When the groom arrived at the bride's house, which had been decorated with garlands, the main religious element took place – to ensure the favour of the gods, the auspices were taken (see p. 90). Either a pig or a sheep was sacrificed, and an *auspex* inspected its insides to look for omens. If they were declared to be good, the marriage contract was signed in the presence of ten witnesses, who ensured that the union had legal validity. A married woman, called a *Pronuba*, would join the couple's right hands (this was a common sign of good faith in the Roman world, especially in business dealings). After this, a feast was often held in the bride's house.

The procession

After this came the procession of the bride to her new home, an event full of symbolism. She would act out being torn from the arms of her mother (to commemorate the seizing of the Sabine women – see p. 7), and was then led by torchlight through the streets by three boys with living parents – one of these would carry a torch lit from the bride's hearth, the other two would lead the way; the bride herself carried a distaff and spindle to signify her new domestic role, while a noisy crowd would also shout *fortuna* or *talassio* ('good luck') and tell rude jokes or sing obscene songs.

The groom had gone on ahead to his own house, which was also decorated with flowers. Upon arriving there, the bride anointed the doorway with oil and wool, and was then carried over the threshold by attendants; this was to ensure that she did not trip, which would have been a terrible omen for her first entrance to her new house. Inside, her new husband presented her with water and fire (in the form of a torch), two of the essential elements of a Roman home. The bride greeted her husband with the words: *ubi tu Gaius, ego Gaia* ('where you go as husband, I go as wife'), and was then presented with the keys to the house. The final stage of the wedding ritual was for the couple to head to their bedroom and consummate the marriage.

iii. The matrona

The bride now became a *matrona* – a married woman who was expected to run the household. In wealthier families, she was sometimes also called the *materfamilias*, signifying her authority over the slaves and children of the household. Roman men had a clear idea of how they thought a *matrona* should behave – and once again, it was based on examples from early Roman history such as Lucretia (see p. 9). In the following passage, written in the early 2nd century CE, the biographer Plutarch discusses the ideal relationship between husband and wife:

> 'When two voices sing in unison, the melody of the deeper voice prevails. So, too, in a temperate household every activity is carried out with both parties in agreement, but every activity also makes clear the sovereignty and choice of the husband ... That wife is worthless and unfit who has a sad expression when her husband is eager to make jokes and be cheerful, or who makes jokes and laughs when he is serious. The first behaviour reveals an unpleasant character, the second an inconsiderate one ... A wife should have no emotion of her own, but should share in the seriousness and playfulness and melancholy and laughter of her husband.'
>
> Plutarch, *Moralia* 139D-140A

The idea that a wife should 'have no emotion of her own' seems absurd to us today, but sadly it has been a common view in many cultures throughout history. That said, there was almost certainly a gap between the ideal and the reality of married life in Roman times. An alternative viewpoint is given in Plautus' comic play *Casina* (see p. 234), which revolves around a husband (Lysidamus) trying to cheat on his wife (Cleostrata) with their slave-girl Casina. Cleostrata usually proves to have the measure of her man, as the following lines suggest:

> '*Cleostrata*: What low dive have you been skulking in?
> *Lysidamus*: A dive? Me?
> *Cleostrata*: I know more than you think!
> *Lysidamus*: What do you mean? What do you know?
> *Cleostrata*: That you are the most useless creature alive. Where are you going, you good-for-nothing? Where have you been? Where have you been drinking? Good heavens, you're drunk! Look at the state your clothes are in!
> *Lysidamus*: God strike me dead – and you too – if a drop of wine has passed my lips.
> *Cleostrata*: Go on! Do what you like! Drink! Eat your head off! Ruin us all!'
> Plautus, Casina 243-7

Although this is a scene from a comic play, the audience would surely not have found it funny if it was not based to some extent on patterns recognisable to them from their everyday lives.

Duties
A woman's lifestyle depended on her social position. Wealthy women could be in charge of a large household of slaves, and responsible for

A woman sells game to a customer.

A woman giving
birth.

overseeing social events such as dinner parties. Most women, however,
lived humbler and harder lives, having to manage childcare, domestic
chores, such as cooking, cleaning and weaving as much cloth as possible
for the family. Poorer women often also had to work in order to make
ends meet – perhaps as nurses, shopkeepers or seamstresses.

However, perhaps the most important duty for all women was childbirth. This was a much riskier business in the ancient world than it is
today, since healthcare was rudimentary; as a result, there were many
miscarriages and stillbirths, while women themselves were in serious
danger of dying owing to complications (as Cicero's daughter Tullia did
– see p. 185). On top of this, women had to endure the pains of labour
without modern anaesthetic drugs. In the following passage, Pliny the
Younger writes to his young wife's grandfather to tell him of her miscarriage:

'Because you are so very anxious for us to produce a great-grandson for
you, you will be very sad to hear that your granddaughter has had a miscarriage. She's a young girl and didn't even realise that she was pregnant;
consequently, she failed to take certain precautions necessary for pregnant
women, and she did things she did not have to. She has paid for her ignorance, and her lesson has been costly; she was herself gravely ill.'

Pliny the Younger, *Letters* 8.10

Pliny's wife was clearly ill-informed about her sexual health and how to
recognise the signs of pregnancy. Her miscarriage must been even sad-
der for the fact that there is obvious family pressure for her to produce

166

family heirs, a common preoccupation of Roman families. However, on another level Pliny's wife was lucky – many women would not have survived the experience.

Politics

Woman had no political rights at any stage in Roman history – they could neither stand for office nor vote (indeed, the only women with any formal position in public life were the Vestal Virgins, whom you can read about on pp. 92-4). Therefore, the only way in which women could hope to have influence was through their male relatives. Nevertheless, the following amusing anecdote suggests that women were often interested in knowing what was happening in Roman politics, particularly if it involved their own rights:

'It used to be the custom of senators in Rome to take their young sons into the senate with them. When any important business under discussion was postponed until the following day, it was voted that no one should reveal the subject of the debate until a decision had been reached. The mother of the young Papirius, who had been in the senate with his father, asked her son what the senators had been discussing. The boy replied that it was a secret and he was not allowed to say. This made his mother all the more eager to know; the secrecy and the boy's silence provoked her curiosity and she questioned him still more insistently. Then under pressure from his mother the boy had the idea of telling a witty and amusing tale.

He said the senate had debated whether it would be better for the state if one man had two wives or one woman had two husbands. When his mother heard this, she was thrown into panic, rushed excitedly out of the house and told all the other married women. The next day a great crowd of them came to the senate. Weeping, they begged that one woman might have two husbands rather than a man have two wives. The senators were amazed at the women's outrageous behaviour and wondered whatever this demand meant. The boy Papirius came forward and explained his mother's insistence and what he had told her.'

Aulus Gellius, *Attic Nights* 1.23

This passage is interesting since it suggests that, although women had no formal rights, they were still prepared to go and protest when times became desperate.

Influential women

In the 2nd century BCE, some women of the upper class started to escape from the shackles which had held back their ancestors. For one thing, the increased number of slaves in Roman cities meant that wealthy women now had their household work done for them, giving them time for education and leisure. A second factor was the increase of *sine manu* marriage, providing women greater freedom from their husbands in their financial affairs.

One famous early example of this new type of woman was Cornelia

A sculpture of Cornelia
with her two sons.

(*c.* 190-100 BCE), the mother of the Gracchi brothers (see p. 33), although she also remained true to traditional values and was often held up as an example of how a *matrona* should behave. As well as running a large household, Cornelia oversaw the upbringing of her sons – Quintilian, a leading writer on rhetoric, claims that they both owed their eloquence to her. In fact, they respected their mother so much that on one occasion she even managed to persuade them to spare an opponent's life. After both her sons had been assassinated, Cornelia drew much admiration for her dignity in the face of grief, as Plutarch describes:

'She bore all her misfortunes with great nobility and said of the shrines where her sons were buried that they had the tombs they deserved. She spent her time at Misenum and did not change her way of life. She had many friends and, being hospitable, she entertained them lavishly. She had a circle of Greeks and other literary men about her and was on friendly terms with foreign kings. She was very pleasant to her visitors and used to tell them about the life of her father, Scipio Africanus. They admired her most when she spoke of her sons without tears or emotion and related their achievements and fate as though they were noble Romans of old.'

Plutarch, C. Gracchus 19

We can see here Cornelia mixing the old with the new – on the one hand showing traditional restraint in the face of grief, on the other entertaining important and educated foreigners and enjoying reading and discussing literature with them.

Educated women

By the 1st century BCE, it had become fashionable for noble women to receive an education in music, poetry and philosophy. Indeed, there are a number of portraits of young women with a pen to their lips, while we also hear of women forming literary circles; the poets Catullus and Propertius both praise the lovers they write about partly for their intelligence and wit. Sadly, there is very little evidence of female writing, but we do have the following fragment from a poet called Sulpicia, who wrote in the time of the emperor Augustus:

> 'I hate my birthday but it's coming soon.
> I hate the country too –
> But I'll have to go there,
> Sad as it makes me.
> And without Cerinthus!
> What could be nicer than staying in a town?
> Is a farmhouse a fit place for a girl?'
>
> Sulpicia, *Fragments* 4.8.1-3

With education came some liberation, which gave women more social confidence and provoked a mixed reaction from men. Juvenal wrote a satire of more than 600 lines complaining about the women of his day, including such lines as: 'If you're looking for a woman with decent old-fashioned moral standards, you must be out of your mind ... you'd be pushed to find a girl who'd keep off sex for nine days.' As ever with Juvenal, however, it is hard to know how seriously to take him. An alternative view is offered by Ovid, who wrote a poem, *Ars Amatoria*, advising men how to chase women: 'Others can praise the good old days; I'm only glad I'm a modern man; this is the time for me!'

Over the following centuries numerous aristocratic women had a significant impact on Roman public life. For example, in 63 BCE,

This famous fresco from Pompeii shows a young woman of the
1st century CE thoughtfully holding her stylus to her lips while
she holds the wood-backed wax tablets on which she is writing.

Sempronia, the wife of a senator, was involved in the conspiracy of
Catiline (see p. 36) without the knowledge of her husband. The historian
Sallust, a critic of hers, paints a picture of a passionate woman who 'was
well read in Greek and Latin literature and could play the lyre and dance
far better than a respectable woman needs to'. Sempronia avoided the fate
of many of the conspirators, who were put to death; her rebellious streak
may have had a further influence on Roman history, since her son,
Decimus Junius Brutus, was one of Julius Caesar's assassins (see p. 37).

With the onset of empire, women close to the emperors often had
great power and influence. The first significant 'imperial lady' was Livia,
the third wife of the emperor Augustus. She had no children by him but,
if her critic the historian Tacitus is to be believed, managed to manipulate the emperor into adopting her own son Tiberius as his successor.
Tacitus dryly comments that:

'He was adopted as son ... not as earlier by his mother's secret plotting, but
at her open insistence. For she had the elderly Augustus so firmly under her
thumb that he banished his last surviving grandson.'   Tacitus, *Annals* 1.3

However, some modern scholars feel that Tacitus' portrayal of Livia as a manipulative schemer was unfair. In her defence, they point out that after Augustus' death and deification, she became his priestess and was attended by a lictor, just as magistrates were (see p. 359). Such honours and privileges were unprecedented for a woman at that time.

Nevertheless, after Livia, Tacitus gives various other examples of scheming imperial women, including Messalina, the young wife of Claudius, as well as Agrippina the Younger and Poppaea, respectively the mother and wife of Nero. Yet all of them paid the ultimate price for their proximity to power – Claudius had Messalina executed for treason, a fate shared by Agrippina at the hands of Nero, who some years later also kicked his pregnant wife Poppaea to death in a fit of rage.

However it would not be true to say that the portrayal of the imperial court was only ever one full of deceitful and manipulative women; some wives and mothers are portrayed far more positively. One example was Agrippina the Elder, the grand-daughter of Augustus and wife of the popular general Germanicus. She was the first to accompany her husband on campaign, breaking the tradition that a wife stayed at home; moreover, she did so while raising six children! During a campaign on the Rhine, when rumour came of an impending attack by barbarian tribes, she even ensured that the troops in the base camp held their nerve:

Agrippina the Elder.

171

'If Agrippina had not prevented them, some soldiers would even have gone so far as to break down the bridge over the Rhine. But that great-hearted woman performed the role of general and distributed food and medicine to any needy or wounded soldier. According to Pliny in his *History of the German War* she stood at the bridge and thanked the returning army ... Tiberius took it to heart that ... Agrippina had more power over the army than the officers and generals.'   Tacitus, *Annals* 1.69

While Tacitus' portrayal of Agrippina the Elder might be somewhat idealised (he was trying to present Germanicus in the best possible light), she was the first of an impressive line of noble imperial women, including Faustina, the wife of Antoninus Pius (see p. 51), Julia Mamaea, the mother of Alexander (see p. 54), and Helena, the mother of Constantine, who clearly had a huge influence on her son's decision to adopt Christianity as a legal religion (see p. 121).

Nor is it only at the imperial level that we meet influential women: for example, St Augustine, one of the most important figures in the early Church, describes in his autobiographical *Confessions* how his mother Monica inspired him to convert to Christianity (she and Helena are just two of a number of women who were prominent in early Christianity), while the example of the priestess Eumachia at Pompeii (see p. 293) suggests that upper-class women could have an impact on public life in the towns and cities of the empire.

Divorce

As with marriage, divorce was a private matter between individuals and did not need to be approved by the state or religious authorities. All that was required was for one party to walk away from the marriage – although in practice it was easier for the husband to do this, especially if there were children involved, since they automatically stayed with their father. One common cause of divorce was infertility, and it was always assumed that this was the fault of the woman.

Divorce was quite common among the upper classes, for whom marriage was mainly about making political alliances. Sometimes, husbands and fathers forced women to divorce and remarry to suit them – for example, the dictator Sulla had his pregnant daughter divorce her husband and remarry Pompey, his new political ally. Pompey himself had first been married to the daughter of his trial judge (when he was accused of stealing military booty), who agreed to acquit him if he married his daughter. The bystanders are supposed to have sung the wedding hymn when he was acquitted! Pompey eventually married five times, including his match with Julia, the daughter of Julius Caesar.

There is little evidence on how divorce impacted on family life since the Romans did not seem to reflect on this much, although Cicero does write to his friend Atticus about the distress of his nephew, Quintus, after he learns the news of his parents' divorce:

Family values

There was generally a double standard regarding adultery: it was accepted that men would commit it with slaves or prostitutes of either sex (although not with another man's wife), while there was revulsion at the idea of a woman sleeping with anyone other than her husband.

At the end of the 1st century BCE, the emperor Augustus was concerned both by the decline in moral standards and in the falling birth rate. He therefore passed a series of laws in 18 and 9 BCE to make sure that all men and women between 25-60 were married. Childless widows were expected to remarry within twelve months and divorcees within six, while the unmarried and childless were penalised by the loss of inheritance rights. On the other hand, women who produced three children were given the legal freedom to manage their own affairs without a male guardian. However, Augustus was undermined in these laws by his own daughter, Julia, who had a reputation for taking numerous lovers!

'I saw that the boy was remarkably upset. He was in tears as he cried to me about it. I saw in him a remarkable affection and sweetness and kindness, and I therefore have more hope that things will be as they should. I just wanted you to know this.'   Cicero, *Letters to Atticus* 6.3.8

Like Pompey and Sulla, Cicero came from an upper-class family; it is unlikely that divorce was as common at other levels of society, where there was not the need to make political alliances.

However, we should not think that arranged marriages prevented couples from experiencing true love. Many inscriptions on tombstones testify to the strength of love between husband and wife, such as the following left by a husband:

'To Urbana, the sweetest, chastest, and rarest of wives, who certainly has never been surpassed, and deserves to be honoured for living with me to her last day in the greatest pleasantness and simplicity, with equal conjugal affection and hard work. I added these words so that readers should understand how much we loved each other.'   *CIL* VI.29580

There was no doubt a great range in the quality of marriages at every level of society. Many sources give evidence of marriages which were as happy as that of Urbana and her husband; at the other end of the spectrum, there are plenty of stories of cheating spouses and violent and abusive husbands. In other words, as today, it is impossible to make one statement about the quality of Roman marriages. Ultimately, the success of each depended on the character and commitment of the two people involved.

Review 5

1. Define the following: *auspex, cum manu, pronuba, sine manu.*
2. Which aspects of a traditional Roman wedding also feature at weddings today? Which aspects seem strange to you?
3. Draw up a table listing the similarities and differences between the ancient and modern attitudes to marriage and divorce.
4. To what extent can male attitudes towards women in ancient Rome still be seen in your society and other parts of the world today?
R. i. Read Livy's account (34.1-6) of the repeal of the Oppian Law in 195 BCE. What does it tell us about the political and social role of women at this time?
R. ii. Read Catullus' Poem 61, which celebrates the wedding of two noble Romans. What can we learn from it about wedding ceremonies?

---

6. Slaves and freedmen

Slavery was a fact of life in the Roman world. Although it is impossible to know exactly how many slaves there were, estimates suggest that by the early imperial period about 30% of the population of Rome were slaves. Cities such as Rome had a higher percentage of slaves than the rural parts of the empire, but it is likely that this figure of 30% was about the same throughout the cities of the empire.

Today, slavery is rightly thought of as barbaric and inhuman, and we are horrified by the notion of so many people enslaved and by the ways in which they were treated. However, in judging the Romans on this issue, it is important to bear in mind that slavery was a fact of life in every ancient society, and also in our world until very recently: indeed, only in the last two centuries have serious campaigns of abolition been waged (slavery was only abolished in the British empire in 1833 and in the USA in 1863), while there are still practices in every part of the world today which should rightly be described as 'enslavement'.

In fact, it should be acknowledged that the Romans were rare amongst ancient peoples in offering the prospect of freedom to many of their slaves. Freed slaves held the status of freedmen and had many of the rights of Roman citizens. Thus, to be born or captured as a slave in the Roman world did not necessarily mean that you would end your life in slavery; indeed, by imperial times, a large proportion of the citizen population must have had ancestors who had been slaves or freedmen. This made Roman society more aspirational and progressive than many others in the ancient world.

i. Routes into slavery

The Roman slave population increased dramatically from the 3rd century BCE, when Rome started to conquer many new territories. During the next two or three centuries, the most common route into slavery was to be captured in war. For example, during the Second Punic War with Carthage (218-202 BCE), it is reported that the Romans enslaved around 180,000 captives of war; later, in 25 BCE, one relatively minor military assault – the comprehensive defeat of the Alpine tribe of the Salassi – saw the entire surviving population of 44,000 sold into slavery. Captives of war therefore represented big business for the slave dealers, who usually followed closely behind an army ready to jump into action.

There were various other routes into slavery, especially after Roman expansion had reached its limits in the early 2nd century CE. As we have seen, exposed children could be rescued and brought up as slaves, while in a few desperate cases, parents might even sell their children into slavery. Travellers in the Roman world were also in danger from kidnappers or pirates, who would sell their captives on to slave traders, while we also hear of Romans trading wine for slaves with foreign tribes such as the Gauls – some Gallic chiefs were so fond of Italian wine that they would apparently exchange one slave for a single jar. Convicted

This slave chain for six people was found in Cambridge. The large holes are for the slaves' necks.

These captives of war sit among the weapons also captured in battle.
They are waiting to be taken to a slave market and sold.

criminals could also be enslaved – and perhaps condemned to fight in
the games as gladiators (see p. 206).

The final route into slavery was to be born a slave. Any child of a
slave mother was automatically classified as a slave, and for many
Romans this was the cheapest way of obtaining a new slave – even if it
meant feeding an extra mouth with no return for the first few years.
Such slaves were known as *vernae*, and evidence suggests that they
often held a higher status in the family than purchased slaves, since
they were felt to be easier to manage. Some Romans made a lot of money
out of raising *vernae* and then selling them on – they might spot their
talents as young children, then train them up in a specific craft and
skill, allowing them to be sold at a considerable profit.

ii. The slave trade

Slave markets could be found all over the Roman world; the largest were
in big cities such as Rome and Ephesus, although the tiny Greek island
of Delos was also famous for its slave market, which could apparently
handle 10,000 slaves in one day. However, not all slaves were bought at
these large markets – some dealers could set up their own impromptu
sales in public places such as a forum, while others might rely equally
on private deals.

At the slave market, the slaves were displayed on platforms and
could be undressed for closer inspection. New arrivals were marked with
chalked feet. Slaves wore placards around their necks to advertise their
qualities (including their origin, state of health, and likelihood of running away), and the whole trade was overseen by the aediles, since they
were responsible for all public markets and for ensuring that buyers
were not cheated (see p. 357). We have no firm evidence for the prices

fetched, but it is clear that they ranged greatly depending on the age, health and skill level of the slaves.

iii. Types of slave

Slave labour was used to do many of the things which machines can be used for today, and so slaves were employed in a wide variety of ways; there were three main types of slave in the Roman world:

- **Domestic slaves** lived in the household with the family and performed all the tasks related to it. Having a large number of slaves in your house was a major status symbol, and the wealthiest houses were able to employ individual slaves in roles such as nurses, *paedagogi*, cooks, gardeners, hair-dressers, secretaries and cleaners. However, most households had to make do with their slaves taking on a variety of tasks.
- **Industrial slaves** were employed in mines, factories, in the galleys, and on large farming estates known as *latifundia*. These slaves often lived and worked in the harshest conditions; slaves on the *latifundia* would be overseen by an overseer (*vilicus*) who was probably also a slave, but who might be very harsh on them since he himself would fear demotion or punishment if the farm was not productive enough.
- **Public slaves** were owned by the state and performed many roles in a city. Some might work on construction projects of roads or public buildings, while others might be employed to clean public buildings such as temples and baths. Other public slaves had more specific roles, such as maintaining the public aqueducts.

These three types do not cover every type of slave – for example, some men were forced to become gladiators, while, as still sadly happens today, women might be forced to work as prostitutes for the profit of their masters.

iv. Rights and treatment

In Roman law, slaves were considered to be the property of their owner. They had no legal rights, and their families were not recognised – any children they had would automatically be regarded as the property of their owners. A newly enslaved individual was stripped of his or her former identity and usually given a new name. Even when slaves were involved in law – as witnesses to legal cases – their evidence was only admitted if they had given it under torture, since this was felt to make them more afraid of the law than of their master.

However, the way in which a slave was treated depended almost entirely on his or her circumstances. Household slaves who lived with a sympathetic master might hope to have a good relationship with his family, while they were also guaranteed food and a place to live – more than many of the poorest Roman citizens. However, slaves set to work on the *latifundia* or in the mines usually lived and worked in terrible conditions, nor did they have any personal relationship with their master. Indeed, they were treated little better than animals – the agricultural writer Varro even divides the 'instruments' by which the soil is worked into three: 'articulate instruments' (i.e. slaves), 'inarticulate instruments' (e.g. oxen), and 'mute instruments' (e.g. carts). In the following passage, a historian describes the conditions of mine slaves in Spain:

> 'The slaves engaged in the operation of the mines secure for their masters profits in amounts which are almost beyond belief. They themselves, however, are physically destroyed, their bodies worn down from working in the mine shafts both day and night. Many die because of the excessive maltreatment they suffer. They are given no rest or break from their toil, but rather are forced by the whiplashes of their overseers to endure the most dreadful of hardships; thus do they wear out their lives in misery ... although they often pray more for death than for life because of the terrible scale of their suffering.'   Diodorus Siculus, *History* 5.38.1

Such was the awful fate of hundreds of thousands of slaves in the Roman world. This passage is in fact unusual since writers rarely talk about industrial slaves, usually referring instead to the household slaves who are part of their everyday lives.

The treatment of domestic slaves varied widely too. Many were repeated victims of domestic abuse – flogging was common, while sources also speak of branding and mutilations such as leg-breaking and eye-gouging; moreover, many would have been sexually assaulted on a regular basis. In fact, physically harming the body was a particularly Roman way of distinguishing slave from free; it was considered disgraceful to attack a free man, but slaves were fair game – as the rhetorician Quintilian put it 'flogging is disgraceful and therefore suitable only for slaves'. It seems that some masters actually took a sadistic pleasure in watching their slaves suffer, as this famous story suggests:

> 'Vedius Pollio, a Roman equestrian, a friend of the emperor Augustus, found that lamprey eels offered him an opportunity to display his cruelty. He used to toss slaves sentenced to death into ponds of lampreys, not because wild animals on land were not capable of killing a slave, but because with any other type of animal he was not able to enjoy the sight of a man being torn to pieces, completely, in one moment.'
>   Pliny the Elder, *Natural History* 9.39.77

Elsewhere, Juvenal speaks of slave-girls forced to sleep with their mas-

This relief from the theatre of Sabratha in Libya depicts a scene
of a slave being rebuked by his master.

ters arousing the jealousy of wives, so that they are whipped and punished persistently. Yet it was not just physical pain which many slaves
must have suffered; they must also often have been tortured by fears –
for example, a master might threaten to sell on a slave's child to another owner.

Against this depressing picture we can also set examples of good and
appreciative relationships between masters and slaves. Cicero had a
close and trusting friendship with his secretary Tiro, whom he eventually freed, while Pliny the Younger admits to feeling grief-struck at the
death of loyal slaves. Moreover, those who followed the philosophy of the
stoics (see p. 103) believed that all people – slave or free – had a soul and
should be treated as fellow human beings. The 1st-century CE stoic
Seneca endorses this view in the following letter to his friend Lucilius:

'I was happy to learn from people who had just visited you that you live on
friendly terms with your slaves. This attitude is quite in keeping with your
good sense and liberal education. Some people say: "They are just slaves."
But they are fellow human beings! "They're just slaves." In fact, they are

our fellow slaves, if you stop to consider that fate has as much control over us as it has over them.'   Seneca the Younger, *Letters* 47.1ff.

Perhaps influenced by these ideas, laws about the treatment of slaves became progressively more humane during the imperial period. Early in the 2nd century CE, the emperor Hadrian passed a series of laws which forbade masters to kill their slaves or to sell them as prostitutes or glad-iators, without first going through the courts, while in the late 4th cen-tury a law was even passed forbidding owners to separate slave children from their parents.

Runaways and rebellions

Masters were always wary of slaves trying to run away. To discourage this, the penalty if caught was harsh. Recaptured runaways might be crucified, burned alive or sent to face wild beasts in the arena. Some masters even had their slaves branded, often on their faces, while others fitted their slaves with metal identification collars, some of which have survived; the inscription on one collar reads as follows: 'I have run away. Capture me. When you have returned me to my master, Zoninus, you will receive a reward.'

In addition, Romans always lived in fear of a slave revolt. At a domestic level, we occasionally hear of slaves who rebel against their master, such as the murder of the ex-praetor Larcius Macedo by some of his slaves. Following Roman law, all the slaves in his household were executed, including those who had had nothing to do with the plot. Three large-scale slave revolts have also been recorded in Roman history, the most famous of which was led by Spartacus in the 70s BCE. When the Roman army finally defeated his army of slaves which had held out for over a year, 6,000 of them were captured and crucified along the Appian Way, the main road south between Rome and Capua.

---

v. Freedmen

The act of freeing a slave was known as manumission, from the Latin *manus* ('hand') and *mittere* ('to send'), so that the word literally meant 'to send out of one's hands'. There were two common ways in which a slave might be legally freed: either the slave and master might appear before a magistrate who would touch the slave with a rod or wand to sig-nal that he was now free, or a master would state in his will that he wished to free some or all of his slaves.

One of the main purposes of manumission was to offer an incentive to slaves to work hard, in the hope of ending their lives free. During their years of service, some slaves were allowed to earn a small sum of money, the *peculium*, with which they could eventually buy their free-

Two freedmen, one a blacksmith, the other a carpenter. The tools of their trade are above and to the sides.

A slave being freed, showing his progress from the lowly stoop of a slave to shaking his ex-master's hand as a freedman.

dom from their master. In other cases, masters were more generous and would free their slaves for long service or an outstanding act. Masters who fell in love with slave-girls might free them to marry them, while if they had children by a slave-girl, they might free them so as to make them heirs. In a similar vein, a newly freed slave might save up the money to purchase a female slave 'partner', so that he could then free her.

Some masters had more selfish reasons for manumission. For some, freeing slaves was a way to impress friends, since any man who could afford to free slaves and buy others would appear very affluent. There were also cases of masters who were facing serious court proceedings freeing all their slaves, so preventing them from being tortured and revealing any incriminating evidence. Some heartless masters also freed elderly slaves who were too weak or sick to work any more – they had no resale value, and so it was cheaper to free them than look after them in old age. Such slaves usually had no means to support themselves and many must have starved to death.

Rights and status

Upon being freed, a freedman was permitted to wear the *pileus*, a felt cap symbolising liberty. Freedmen were Roman citizens, but they were not allowed to run for public office or to become members of the senatorial or equestrian classes, even if they made enough money (however, the same was not the case for their descendants, who had the full rights of citizenship). However, in imperial times, one college of priests, the *Augustales* (see pp. 80-1), was set up and generally comprised freedmen; this gave them an opportunity to hold public office and show their loyalty to the emperor.

A freedman was still tied to his former master as a client, and required to work for him for a number of days each year. In fact, many freedmen continued to work full time for their former masters – although they were now paid, a master no longer had to provide them with accommodation, clothes and food. Other freedmen went on to work in a variety of fields, such as teaching, construction or slaughtering. A few became highly successful businessmen, who were among the wealthiest in their community, as with the Vettii brothers in Pompeii (see p. 312).

Such cases were the exception rather than the rule, yet they tended to breed the resentment of some Romans offended by their success and influence; they in turn imagined a time in the past when the city hadn't been populated by so many people of foreign origin, and longed for it. Such views were famously voiced in a satire of Juvenal, in which a xenophobe is disgusted by the influence of the Greek culture from the eastern Mediterranean:

'Citizens, I cannot bear a Rome that has become a Greek city. And yet, what portion of the dregs in our city is Greek? For a long time, Syrian

3. Roman Society

A sculpture of a freedman wearing the *pileus*.

Orontes (*a river in Syria*) has poured its sewage into the Tiber – its language, its customs ... and the prostitutes who are sent to hang out at the race track.'   Juvenal, *Satires* 3.60ff.

It is hard to know how common such views were. By the time that Juvenal was writing in the late 1st century CE, it is likely that the overwhelming majority of the citizen population of Rome had some ancestors who had been slaves or freedmen. It was in fact one of the triumphs of Roman society that it was able to give opportunity and hope to so many foreigners (and their descendants) who came to Rome in the lowest social category possible.

Review 6

1. How many different jobs might each type of slave have done in Rome?
2. How would you define 'slavery'?
3. Why do you think slavery has been such an accepted part of life until fairly recently? Why has this attitude changed in the last two centuries? What aspects of our society do you think might horrify people in future?
R. i) Read letters 3.14 and 8.16 of Pliny the Younger. What can we learn about the varied treatment of slaves from these letters?
R. ii) Read the 'Slavery Today' section at www.anti-slavery.org. How many modern forms of slavery are listed? How do they compare to what you have read about slavery in ancient Rome?
E. To what extent do you think that a Roman's lifestyle and prosperity depended on his slaves?

An allegory of death. Death, represented by the skull, is suspended from the plumb-line of a builder's level, above a butterfly (symbolising the spirit) and a wheel (symbolising fortune). The arms of the level portray wealth and poverty: on the right, the beggar's sack, on the left, the royal sceptre and cloth dyed royal purple. The whole image suggests the fragility and unpredictability of life.

7. Death and funerals

Death was far more visibly present in the ancient world than it is in modern western society, where medical knowledge has advanced hugely. In the Roman world, as today, death could come at any time, but there was a much heavier concentration of deaths at certain life stages: in childhood and early adulthood, during childbirth for women, and after the age of 50 (which was considered to be old). Some estimates suggest that more than half of children born didn't live until their fifth birthday, and so most parents would have expected to lose at least one child. It is worth considering how all this impacted on society – for example, there would have been many more orphans but fewer grandparents, while people would have been much more aware of the shortness of life.

Although Romans were therefore much more used to death, this is not to say that they that they did not feel their grief every bit as keenly as people do today. One famous example of a bereaved parent was the leading statesman Cicero, whose daughter Tullia died in childbirth in 45 BCE, aged in her early thirties. Cicero was transfixed by grief, being unable even to return to his country villa where she grew up because the memories were too painful for him. Instead, he took himself off to another part of the Italian countryside, from where he wrote to his great friend Atticus:

> 'I have isolated myself in this lonely region from all human conversation. In the morning, I hide myself in the dense, impenetrable forest and don't emerge until nightfall. Next to you, solitude is my best friend. My only form of communication now is through books, but even my reading is interrupted by fits of weeping. I resist as best I can these urges to cry, but I am not yet strong enough.'   Cicero, *Letters to Atticus* 12.15

Such emotions must have been shared by parents at every level of society, and vast numbers of inscriptions on tombs testify to the grief and love of the bereaved. Cicero himself was in his early 50s when he wrote this, by which time he had seen and experienced many hardships in both his personal and his professional life. Yet the death of his daughter still tears his heart.

i. Funerals

The information left to us about funerals mainly refers to those of the rich and important, and these were certainly grand affairs – even in death, social status and wealth determined how you were treated. However, most funerals were probably much simpler, taking place at night within a day or so of death (the funeral of a child was always held at night and with little ceremony, perhaps so as not to draw attention to a family's loss). There would probably be a simple procession from the home to a cemetery, where the corpse was cremated or buried.

A relief from a sarcophagus showing a grand funeral procession. The body of the deceased is carried on a bier, while musicians lead the way and mourners follow behind.

185

Traditionally, when a Roman was at the point of death, a close relative tried to catch his dying breath with a kiss, and he would then close his eyes and mouth. All present shouted the dead man's name, and the preparations for the funeral began. The body was washed and anointed to prevent decay, and then dressed in the deceased's best clothes. A small coin was then placed in the corpse's mouth; this was thought necessary in order to pay Charon, the ferryman in Graeco-Roman myth who escorted the dead over River Styx in the Underworld.

In the case of a rich man, his body would be placed for eight days on a couch in his atrium, feet facing towards the door, and surrounded by flowers, wreaths and candles. During this period, women kept up a lament, beating their breasts and tearing their hair and clothes, while visitors came to pay their respects. Cypress or pine branches were hung outside the house to signify the loss.

Funeral clubs

Romans felt that it was very important to have a proper burial, inheriting the Greek belief that, if a body was not disposed of properly, the soul would not be able to pass into the Underworld and so would never find rest. For this reason, many poorer Romans joined a 'funeral club' – a sort of funeral insurance policy. Members of these clubs paid a joining fee and then a monthly membership subscription. When they died, the club paid their funeral expenses and fellow members attended their funerals. The clubs also served a social purpose for the living, since they held monthly meals, where poorer people could make friends and connections.

However, the very poorest citizens and most slaves could not afford membership of these clubs; upon death, their corpses would normally have been removed from the city and placed in unmarked communal graves.

For the wealthy, the funeral itself would take place on the eighth day after death. Central to the ceremony was the procession either to a public crematorium or to a private burial ground (which had a space for cremations), both of which would be outside the city. As in most ancient societies, it was forbidden to bury or burn corpses inside the city walls to avoid the spread of disease. This meant that tombs and cemeteries tended to develop around the streets just outside the city walls, such as by the Appian Way outside Rome, and by the 'Street of the Tombs' in Pompeii (see pp. 277-8).

The procession itself could be a lively affair. Flute and horn players might lead the way playing solemn tunes, to be followed by hired mourning women, who lamented and praised the dead man in song; then might come actors and jokers, including one called the *Archimimus* (a mime actor – see p. 236), who represented the character of the deceased, and imitated his words and actions. Next walked any slaves whom the

A Roman nobleman carrying the busts of his ancestors.

dead man had liberated, wearing their caps of freedom, followed by the corpse on an open coffin, usually carried on the shoulders of his slaves or freedmen.

The dead man's relatives walked behind the corpse in mourning; sons with their heads veiled, and daughters with their heads bare and their hair dishevelled. These relatives carried or wore masks representing the ancestors of the family; these were to symbolise the ancestors honouring the deceased and welcoming him into company of the dead. A particularly prominent man might have a public funeral, in which case his body would be carried in procession via the forum, where his son (or another close relative) would deliver a speech recording his achievements and praising his character. During the republic, such honours were limited to prominent men, but from early imperial times distinguished women could also be given extravagant public funerals.

The procession then headed outside the city to the burial ground. In early Roman times burial was common, but by the end of the 1st century BCE most people were cremated; the corpse was placed on a funeral

The emperor Hadrian giving the funeral oration of his
wife Sabina in the Roman Forum.

pyre and the nearest relative opened and closed the eyes for the final
time and kissed the forehead. He then lit the pyre and allowed it to burn.
Once the fire had died down (wine was often used to calm the flames),
the ashes were gathered in an urn and placed in the family tomb.

Tombs

A wealthy family could afford a large and showy tomb – in Pompeii there
was a whole range of styles, from altars to semi-circular seats and
benches, and sometimes even walled enclosures. These would house the
funerary urns of every member of the family, perhaps including some
freedmen or even slaves to whom a surviving *paterfamilias* was well-dis-
posed. Many other families would just do with a gravestone, as today, on
which a short epitaph was often left. In fact, epitaphs are a vital source
of evidence for life in the Roman world – of the 750,000 inscriptions
recorded in Latin, about three quarters are epitaphs. Many of these offer
a window into private lives, such as the following dedication by a widower to his wife:

188

'Friends, I have not much to say – stop and read it. This is the grave, not beautiful, but of a beautiful woman. Her parents named her Claudia. She loved her husband from all her heart. She had two sons – one she leaves on earth, the other she has placed beneath the earth. Her speech was charming, her conduct was fitting. She kept house, she spun wool. I've finished. Go now!'   *CIL* I.2.1211

The widower here emphasises his wife's goodness and duty – and seems a little apologetic that he cannot afford a grander tomb. Such epitaphs were normally left by close relatives; however, in the following example, a patron pays tribute to a loyal freedman:

'To the spirits of the departed. Marcus Canuleius Zosimus lived twenty-eight years. A patron erected this for his well-deserving freedman. While he lived he spoke badly of no one; he did nothing without his patron's consent. He had much gold and silver in his trust, but he never wished to possess it. At his craft, engraving silver plate, he had no equal.'
                                                                         CIL VI.9.222

Once again, the honest and dutiful character of the deceased shines through, and it is interesting that a patron should have developed such respect and fondness for his freedman.

ii. Commemoration

After burial or cremation, a dead person's spirit was believed to go down to the Underworld where it joined the other spirits of the dead, who were known collectively as the *Manes* (literally: 'the good'); the spirit was also now worshipped as a member of the family's Lares, and in wealthy families a bust of the deceased would be made and displayed in the house, perhaps in the *alae* off the atrium. Eight days after death, the house was purified and a sacrifice made to the Lares; men were now expected to stop their mourning (hence perhaps Cicero's sense of shame that he cannot stop crying a month after Tullia's death), while women were allowed to be in mourning for the period of a year.

However, even after this, the family still had a responsibility to attend to their dead. Romans believed that the Manes needed 'nourishing' in their graves, so that a meal was often buried alongside a corpse. Furthermore, a son was expected to leave a meal at the tomb of his dead father or mother on the anniversary of death, while wine might also poured into the earth nearby. If the Manes were not fed like this then, according to ancient belief, they might waste away into nothingness or start plaguing the living. The poet Ovid relates a legend that the early Romans had once been so busy fighting a war that they had neglected the Manes, with disastrous consequences:

'It did not go unpunished: they say from that ominous day
Rome grew hot from funeral fires near the City.
I scarcely believe it, but they say that ancestral spirits
Came moaning from their tombs in the still of night,
And misshapen spirits, a bodiless crowd, howled
Through the City streets, and through the broad fields.
Afterwards neglected honour was paid to the tombs,
And there was an end to the portents, and the funerals.'

Ovid, *Fasti* 2.549-6

Ovid is an educated poet writing of the ancient past, and he even says that he can hardly believe the story; but for many less educated Romans, a superstitious belief in the power of the Manes must surely have been a reality. Honouring one's ancestors was fundamental to the Roman mentality.

Festivals of the dead
There were two public festivals in the Roman calendar concerned with appeasing the dead: the *Parentalia*, where Romans attended to their ancestors, and the *Lemuria*, a private rite held in each household to appease restless spirits.

The Parentalia lasted from 13 to 21 February, during which time temples were closed and no marriages took place. The first eight days were given over to private remembrance, and families would head out to their ancestors' tombs, where they might decorate the graves with garlands of flowers and leave food and drink offerings such as wheat, salt, wine and milk. On the 21st there was a public festival of remembrance, while the following day families gathered for a banquet in their homes. This was traditionally the time for family quarrels to be resolved and set aside, in the same way as the family was making peace with its dead during the festival.

The focus of the Lemuria was different – it was a festival to appease

A funerary banqueting scene on the urn of a deceased woman named Julia Eleutherides.

190

restless spirits, who were collectively known as the *Lemures*. According to legend, it was instituted by Romulus to appease the spirit of Remus, the brother he had murdered. It was therefore a festival to appease all spirits who had a grievance, whether from their lives or because they had not been treated properly in death. It was celebrated in silence, in the home, on three alternate nights – 9, 11 and 13 May. As with the Parentalia, temples were closed and no marriages were held during this period. Each householder had to carry out a private ritual to persuade any spirits not to haunt the household. Ovid gives an account of this strange ritual:

> 'At midnight the *paterfamilias* gets up. He makes a sign with his thumb in between his fingers in case he happens to meet a spirit. He washes his hands in spring water and then takes some black beans which he immediately throws away, turning his face as he does so, and saying: "I cast these away. With these beans I restore me and my family." He says this nine times, without looking back. People think the spirits gather the beans and follow behind the *paterfamilias* unseen. He puts his hands in water again and clashes bronze gongs together. He asks the spirits to leave his house and says, nine times, "Spirits of my ancestors, depart!" Then he looks back and is convinced he has carried out the ritual correctly.'
>
> Ovid, *Fasti* 5.429ff.

Again, it is hard to know if educated Romans really carried out this ritual or, if they did, whether they took it at all seriously. However, for the superstitious majority, the warding off of restless spirits must have been deadly serious – just as it still is in many cultures of the world today.

Review 7

1. Define the following: *Lemures, Manes*
2. Why do you think the Romans placed so much importance on burial?
3. What similarities and what differences can you find between Roman funerals and those of other societies with which you are familiar?
4. Why do you think it was important for Romans to remember and respect their dead?
5. Does modern society have any ceremonies like the Parentalia and Lemuria?
R. Read Polybius' account of a typical funeral of a famous man (6.53-4). How does such an occasion compare to a state funeral today?
E. 'The Roman ceremonies of death were all designed to give proper honour and respect to the deceased.' Do you agree?

4

Roman Entertainment

A visitor only has to travel through central Rome today to see the prominent position given to theatres, baths and arenas in the ancient city. Chariot racing, gladiatorial shows, plays and baths were all forms of entertainment and relaxation at the heart of Roman society. Taken together, they reveal the full spectrum of Roman life, both public and private, for all its good and for all its evil.

The politics of entertainment
Entertainment in Rome was intensely political. Chariot racing, gladiatorial shows and plays were all funded for the people's enjoyment by Rome's ruling class. In the republican period, ambitious politicians, usually aediles or praetors (see Appendix 2 to read about the structure of Roman politics), competed with each other to offer ever more spectacular shows, and this often involved putting forward vast sums of their own money to win the support of the masses. The magistrate in charge of a show was known as the *editor* ('presenter').

With the coming of the empire, however, the dynamic changed. Where once the people had voted for their political leaders, this right was now taken away from them (see p. 364). The satirist Juvenal (who, along with other satirists, should always be treated with caution as a factual source – see p. 125) complained about the change in attitudes among the masses in the following famous lines:

> 'There was a time when the people gave every honour – the governance of provinces, civic leadership, military command – but now they hold themselves back, now two things only do they ardently desire: bread and circuses.'   Juvenal, *Satires* 10.77-81

The 'bread' here refers to the corn dole (see p. 151). As for the circuses, it is hard to know if Juvenal is putting forward his own view, or merely satirising the views of traditionalist Romans who longed for the republican past and were disappointed in the people's lack of political engagement. In fact, it seems that the arenas of the games – the theatre, amphitheatre and circus – now offered the masses their best opportunity to make their voices heard.

Equally, these arenas provided the emperors with a valuable platform to appear in public. When an emperor was present at a spectacle, he could be seen to be taking his place among his people, and even to be listening to their will. There are many stories of crowds showing pleasure or displeasure to public figures (provincial games were typically put on by local rulers or politicians), and these games became an important environment for Rome's rulers to take the temperature of the public mood.

Further reading

A number of passages from Roman authors describe the relationship between the emperor and his people at public games: Josephus (*Jewish Antiquities* 19.24-7) relates how Caligula's ignoring of the people's wishes helped bring about his assassination; Pliny the Younger (*Panegyric* 33) contrasts the attitudes of the emperors Trajan and Domitian; Suetonius (*Claudius* 21) describes how Claudius aims to please his people at all costs, while Fronto (*To the Caesar Marcus* 1.8) suggests to Marcus Aurelius that he is utterly at the mercy of the people at such events.

Of the four topics covered in this chapter – chariot racing, gladiatorial shows, plays and baths – the baths stand slightly apart, since they did not involve crowds coming to watch a spectacle and politicians vying to please them. Nonetheless, they were a fundamental part of Roman life, and were also publicly subsidised for the people. Moreover, in the luxury and benefit which they offered, they too represented an important form of public entertainment.

I. CHARIOT RACING

Chariot racing had long been popular in the Mediterranean world – it is recorded on pottery fragments from the Mycenaean Greek world of the second millennium BCE. It continued to develop in Greece, where it was one of the earliest events in the Olympic Games from 680. In Italy, there are records of it taking place amongst both the Etruscans and the Lucanians of Sicily. It also seems to have been popular in Rome from its earliest days – according to Roman legend, Romulus used the occasion of a chariot racing event to try to distract the Sabine men (see p. 7).

1. The Circus Maximus

A stadium for chariot racing was known as a *circus* (a word linked to 'circuit' and 'circle'). The Romans therefore called their chariot racing games the *ludi circenses* ('circus games'). There were a number of circuses in Rome, but the largest and greatest was without doubt the Circus Maximus ('The Greatest Circus') in the valley between the

A reconstruction of
the Circus Maximus.

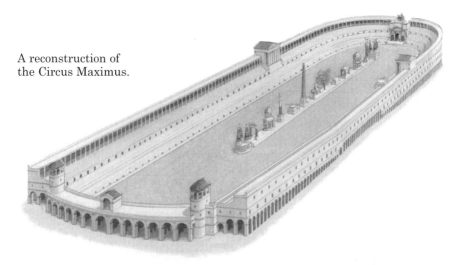

A view of the Circus Maximus today. The outline of the *spina* can still be seen.

Palatine and Aventine hills near the centre of the city (see map on p. 352). In Rome's early days, people had marked out the natural lie of the land as a chariot racing circuit, with spectators sitting on the surrounding slopes.

As the centuries passed, the stadium developed into the largest sporting arena in recorded history. It was often badly damaged by fire, but on each occasion Rome's leaders simply took the opportunity to enlarge and modernise it. In 46 BCE, Julius Caesar had it upgraded extensively, developing the seating area (*cavea*) to give a capacity of 150,000. In the following century, it had grown further to a capacity of about 250,000 – about twice the size of the largest sports arenas in the

195

world today (later, a 4th-century source even claimed that the capacity had reached 385,000, but this was surely an exaggeration).

The stadium itself was typical of a Roman circus. Down the middle of the sandy track (which was 600 metres in length and 150 metres across) was a narrow dividing embankment which the Romans called the *spina* ('backbone'). At either end of the *spina* was a turning point (*meta*), marked by a post originally made of wood; however, early in the 1st century CE the emperor Claudius had each post replaced with three of gilded bronze.

Along the *spina* between the *metae* were various monuments and symbols of the gods: for example, the emperor Augustus set up an obelisk from the time of Rameses II to mark his conquest of Egypt, while there were also statues of gods such as Neptune, the god of horses (see p. 72), as well as seven large wooden eggs (*ova*), which were lowered to indicate how many of the seven laps of a race had been completed (in imperial times, seven bronze dolphins were also added to do the same job). However, one drawback of such monuments was that they eventually became so numerous that spectators on the lower seats could not see the action on the other side of the track!

The starting cages

One important feature of the Circus Maximus was the starting cages, known as *carceres* ('cells'), which were similar to starting gates used in horse racing today. They were originally built in wood, but were refashioned first in stone in 46 BCE and then, a few decades later under the emperor Claudius, in marble. They were constructed at the curved end of the track to allow a staggered start for chariots (since some cages had a more advantageous starting position than others). There were twelve cages, each one with a spring-loaded starting gate; when the signal was given to start the race, all were released at the same time and the chariots flew out.

The seating wrapped round three sides of the stadium (with the fourth for the starting cages) and contained three tiers. The lowest was made of marble and reserved for VIPs: state priests (including the Vestal Virgins – see p. 92), senators and wealthy *equites*. The next tier, of stone, was

A relief showing the *carceres*, with attendants closing the gates.

This terracotta plaque shows a wild beast show taking place in the circus. In the background are the seven eggs used during racing to indicate the number of laps completed.

available for anyone – unlike at the amphitheatre, there seems to have been little segregation at the circus, which meant that men, women and children from different sections of society might all sit together; the top tier may have been standing room only. The final aspect of the seating area was the royal box, or *pulvinar*, which was located on the top tier of the Palatine side of the stadium, from where the emperor could be seen by all the spectators. The *pulvinar* also contained a shrine to the gods.

The Circus Maximus was designed with numerous stairways and exits (as was the Colosseum), so that the whole crowd could come and go quickly and safely. Outside the stadium, the arches underneath the seating area played host to numerous shops and taverns (it was in one of these *tabernae* in 64 CE that a fire broke out which was to devastate the whole city). According to the sources, this area was frequented by a lively range of people, including cooks, astrologers and prostitutes.

Wild animals

The Circus Maximus could also play host to events which eventually became more common in the amphitheatre. In particular, wild beast shows were often put on until 64 CE, when a moat surrounding the track was filled in as part of the stadium's redesign after the great fire. This moat had been constructed in 46 BCE, soon after the general Pompey had put on a near-disastrous wild beast show: he sent in armed captives from Gaetulia in north Africa to fight against twenty elephants, but the iron fence surrounding the track buckled in various places from the impact of the charging beasts, causing terror and chaos in the crowd!

---

2. Preparing for the games

As with professional sport today, a huge amount of time and money was invested in preparing the horses and charioteers for the races. There were only four teams (known as *factiones*) who competed in the *ludi circenses* at Rome – the Reds and the Whites are the earliest recorded *factiones*, soon to be followed by the Blues and the Greens (the emperor Domitian unsuccessfully tried to introduce two new teams, Gold and Purple). Since as many as twelve chariots could compete in a race, each team might field up to three chariots. There is therefore a natural comparison with Formula One races today, where teams often put out two cars in a Grand Prix, whose drivers might try to help one another (or not!).

Each team was overseen by an owner (*dominus factionis*), who could be compared to a modern football chairman. He supervised his team's set of stables and employed a wide variety of staff, such as stable-boys, trainers, veterinary surgeons, grooms, guards, saddlers, dressers, and waterers. His most important employees, however, were without doubt the charioteers (*agitatores* or *aurigae*). They could switch teams and, as with top sports stars today, owners often paid extraordinary sums of money to sign up the very best.

The charioteers

Charioteers were usually of low-born origin – either freedmen or slaves who might be able to pay for their freedom after a few victories. However, as with famous sports stars today, a good charioteer would be able to win great wealth and fame – the prize money for one race could be as much as 60,000 sesterces (see Appendix 3 for currency values), and the satirist Juvenal complained that one Lacerta, a Red charioteer, could earn one hundred times a lawyer's fee. Against this, it should be remembered that chariot racing was a dangerous sport and these men risked their lives every time they entered a race.

Perhaps the most famous and successful charioteer in Roman history was Diocles from Lusitania (modern Portugal), who lived in the 2nd century CE, first competing in 122. By the end of his 24-year career, he had recorded 1,462 wins in 4,257 races. He died at the age of 42, having amassed prize-money of more than 35 million sesterces! Others did not live so long; the brilliant Scorpus died during a race at the age of 26 having won 2,048 victories. Martial wrote him a poetic farewell, something normally reserved for emperors and generals:

'Let sad Victory break the palms of Idumaea. Favour, beat your breast with merciless hand. Let Honour put on mourning. Grieving Glory, cast your crowned locks on the unkind flames. Ah villainy! Scorpus, cheated of your first youth, you die. So soon you yoke the black horses of death. The goal, always quickly gained by your speedy chariot – your life's goal too, why was it so close?' Martial, *Epigrams* 10.50

A mosaic depicting a charioteer wearing his team colours.

Elsewhere, Martial relates that gilded busts of Scorpus could be found all over the city of Rome; this rings true, since many images of charioteers have been found on the walls of streets and buildings of excavated cities such as Pompeii and Ostia. Another indication of the popularity of these men comes from a comment made by Suetonius, who says that, before the reign of Nero, charioteers were able to get away with mugging people unpunished.

Nero the charioteer

The psychologically disturbed emperor Nero fancied himself as a charioteer, something which appalled the Roman upper classes. In 65 CE, he had the Olympic Games postponed for a year (which had never happened before in their 800-year history) so that he could compete during his forthcoming tour of Greece. He entered in a ten-horse chariot and was declared the winner even though he was thrown from his chariot and failed to complete the race – the judges justified their decision by saying that he would have won if he had managed to finish! He later paid them one million sesterces for their trouble. After Nero's death, the Olympic council deleted the results of that year's games from the records.

Sadly, this wasn't the only story involving Nero and the races. According to Suetonius, he kicked to death his pregnant wife Poppaea in a fit of rage after she scolded him for coming home late from the *ludi circenses*.

The horses

Great care was taken over breeding horses, just as it is in the horse-racing industry today. The animals (usually stallions) were purchased from stud farms all over the empire, and especially from north Africa and Spain. Horses would start their training at the age of three and be ready to race at five, when they would be transported to Rome on special ships. Supporters kept statistics of the names, breeds, pedigrees, and victories of famous horses, and the most successful ones were known throughout the empire – Martial (10.9) complains that, even though he is well-known as a poet throughout the Roman world, he is less famous than Andraemon, one of Scorpus' horses! The popularity of horses can be seen today from the many inscriptions surviving on pottery and mosaics; for example, one describes a horse called Victor (appropriately enough), which won 429 times, while another records the 386 victories of a horse named Tuscus.

Incitatus

Nero wasn't the only emperor to have an unhealthy passion for the races. Caligula, a fanatical supporter of the Greens, was obsessed with a horse called *Incitatus* ('Spurred on'). According to Suetonius, he gave it gifts such as a marble stall, purple blankets, a collar of diamonds and a troupe of slaves. On the night before the races, he would even send out soldiers into the streets near *Incitatus'* stables to enforce silence so that the animal's sleep wouldn't be disturbed. Suetonius even claims that the emperor wanted to appoint the horse consul; however, this may simply have been Caligula's way of insulting the political classes – suggesting that even a horse could do the job better than they could!

---

3. A day at the races

Once the crowds had packed into the stadium, the day would begin with an entry parade (*pompa*) led by the *editor* of the games. Behind him would come the charioteers and horses, as well as musicians and soldiers, who carried images of the gods and goddesses believed to be present at the races. These images were carried to the shrine in the *pulvinar*.

The races would follow. Each one consisted of seven laps of the track anti-clockwise (a distance of about 6.5 km, or 4 miles), and in imperial times there were normally 24 races in a day, with each race lasting for about ten to fifteen minutes. Four-horse chariots (*quadrigae*) were the most common type, but there were also races of two-horse chariots (*bigae*); occasionally we hear of chariots being drawn by teams of six, eight or even ten horses! As the race approached, the charioteers drew

The *editor* prepares to drop the *mappa* to signal the start of the race.

lots for their position in the *carceres*; once the horses were ready, the *editor* prepared to give the starting signal. He did this by dropping a white cloth (*mappa*), at which point the gates sprung open.

Once the race had begun, tactics were all important. Charioteers would wear a tunic, colour-coded according to their faction, and a leather helmet, while they would also carry a whip. They raced differently from their Greek counterparts in that they wrapped the reins around their bodies, steering by transferring their weight from one side to another. If they crashed, they were in real danger of being dragged along by the reins and so they carried a knife to cut themselves free. The horses of a *quadriga* were also arranged carefully; the two in the middle would be yoked together, but the outside two were simply be joined by a rope to give them more flexibility. The most important horse of the team (and the source of most inscriptions) was the one on the left-hand side, since it acted as the pivot when the horses rounded the *metae*.

A charioteer would not necessarily want to start at break-neck speed, since he needed to pace his horses for the race ahead. While he had to keep an eye on the other chariots at all times, the most difficult bit of the course was rounding the *metae*: on the one hand, he would not want to go too wide, since this might let in rivals; on the other hand, if he went too close, he risked crashing or being barged into the *spina* by a team outside him. Most accidents (known as *naufragia*, or 'shipwrecks') happened around the *metae*.

201

A relief showing a crash near the *metae*.

Injuries

If they survived a crash, charioteers might suffer appalling injuries. In the following passage, Pliny the Elder describes a treatment for injured drivers which perhaps made them wish they hadn't survived after all!

> 'Sprains and injuries caused by a blow they treat with the dung of wild boars, collected in the spring and dried. The same remedy is applied to charioteers who have been dragged or injured by a wheel, or severely bruised in any other way; in an emergency it can be used fresh. Some think that it is more effective if it is boiled in vinegar. They say too that powdered and taken with a drink it is a good cure for fractures and strained muscles, while for those injured in a crash it is better taken in vinegar ... If you cannot get wild boar's dung, the next best is that of the domestic pig.'
>
> Pliny the Elder, *Natural History 28.237*

Horses were just as prone to injury during the races. Sources speak of concussions and broken bones, blows to the eye from an opponent's whip, tongues cut from snapping on the bit too hard, as well as wounds from flying chariot wheels.

A mosaic showing a victorious charioteer approaching the prize-giver to receive his palm branch of victory while a trumpeter plays alongside.

When the race was over, the *editor* presented the winning charioteer with a palm branch, with the payments to him and his team made at the end of the day.

The supporters

Supporters of chariot racing in the Roman world were every bit as fanatical as the most ardent sports fans today. Dio Chrysostom, writing in the 2nd century CE, makes the following comments about supporters at a *ludi circenses* in Alexandria:

> 'When they enter a stadium, they lose all consciousness of their former state and are not ashamed to say or do anything that occurs to them ... constantly leaping and raving and beating one another and using abominable language and often reviling even the gods themselves and flinging their clothing at the charioteers and sometimes even departing naked from the show. The disease continued throughout the city for several days.'   *Orationes* XXXII, LXXVII

For some fans it was quite literally a matter of life and death: Pliny the Elder, writing in the previous century, records that at the funeral of a Red charioteer, one supporter was so devastated that he threw himself onto the funeral pyre! As today, many fans would have worn clothing in the colour of their team and there were surely many arguments between rival supporters.

A further cause of the supporters' intense passion was the massive betting which took place, meaning that the result mattered much more to many supporters than the quality of the spectacle. Pliny the Younger, no fan of the races, includes this as one of his criticisms of obsessed fans:

> 'It surprises me ... that so many thousands of adult men should have such a childish passion for watching galloping horses and drivers

standing in chariots, over and over again. If they were attracted by the speed of the horses or the drivers' skill, one could account for it, but in fact it is the racing colours they really support and care about and if the colours were to be exchanged in mid-course during a race, they would transfer their favour and enthusiasm and rapidly desert the famous drivers and horses whose names they shout as they recognise from afar ... When I think how this futile, tedious, monotonous business can keep them sitting endlessly in their seats, I congratulate myself that I do not share their pleasure.'   Pliny the Younger, *Letters* 9.6

Pliny's words, although written two thousand years ago, would surely ring true to those today who find sports fanaticism hard to understand!

Some fans would do anything they could to try to help their team – even to the extent of putting curses on opposing charioteers! Various such curse tablets have been found, of which the following two are typical:

'I appeal to you, spirit (whoever you are), and I demand of you from this hour, from this day, from this moment, that you torture and kill the horses of the Greens and Whites and that you kill their drivers in a crash ... and leave not a breath in their bodies.'   *ILS* 8753

'Help me in the circus on 8 November. Bind every limb, every sinew, the shoulders, the ankles and the elbows of ... the charioteers of the Reds. Torment their minds, their intelligence and their senses so that they may not know what they are doing, and knock out their eyes so that they may not see where they are going – neither they nor the horses they are going to drive.'   Text from R. Wünsch, *Antike Fluchtafeln*

Romance?

However, it seems that not all supporters went to the circus purely for the races. In his poem *Ars Amatoria* ('The Art of Love'), written at the beginning of the 1st century CE to advise men on how to pursue women, Ovid suggests that the mixed seating plan at the circus gave them the perfect opportunity to chat up and flirt with women. He advises potential Romeos as follows:

'Don't forget the races, those noble stallions:
the circus holds room for a vast obliging crowd.
No need here for fingers to give secret messages,
nor a nod of the head to tell you she accepts:
You can sit by your lady: nothing's forbidden,
press your thigh to hers, as you can do, all the time:
and it's good the rows force you close, even if you don't like it,
since the girl is touched through the rules of the place.
Now find your reason for friendly conversation,
and first of all engage in casual talk.
Make earnest enquiry whose those horses are:
and rush to back her favourite, whatever it is.

When the crowded procession of ivory gods goes by,
you clap fervently for Lady Venus:
if by chance a speck of dust falls in the girl's lap,
as it may, let it be flicked away by your fingers:
and if there's nothing, flick away the nothing:
let anything be a reason for you to serve her.
If her skirt is trailing too near the ground,
lift it, and raise it carefully from the dusty earth:
Straightaway, the prize for service, if she allows it,
is that your eyes catch a glimpse of her legs.
Don't forget to look at who's sitting behind you,
that he doesn't press her sweet back with his knee.
Small things please light minds: it's very helpful
to puff up her cushion with a dextrous touch.
And it's good to raise a breeze with a light fan,
and set a hollow stool beneath her tender feet.'

Ovid, *Ars Amatoria* 1.135-62

As well as enlightening us on the possible flirting techniques used by visitors to the circus, this passage is interesting since it confirms various details about a typical day at the races, including the *pompa*, the crowded and mixed seating arrangements, and the support for the *factiones*.

Review 1

1. Define the following: *carceres, cavea, editor, ludi circenses, mappa, meta, ova, pompa, pulvinar, spina.*
2. How might you compare Roman charioteers with modern sports stars?
3. How does the Circus Maximus compare to modern sporting stadia?
4. Which modern sports might chariot racing be compared to and why?
R. Read Ovid's *Amores* 3.2 – another entertaining passage by this poet – and summarise what we can learn about the races from the poem.
E. Imagine that you spend a day at the *ludi circenses* in Rome. Write an account of your experience.

II. GLADIATORIAL GAMES

It is not clear exactly where gladiatorial combat originated: some sources suggest that it was with the Etruscans, while others believe that it emerged in Campania, a region to the south of Rome. In either case, it seems that it emerged out of the custom of honouring a dead nobleman with two of his slaves fighting to the death at his funeral. In Rome, the first recorded gladiatorial games took place in 264 BCE, when a certain Junius Brutus had three pairs of gladiators fight to the death in Rome's Forum Boarium (the city's main cattle market) in honour of his dead father. This was described as a *munus* (pl: *munera*): a 'duty' of remembrance owed to a dead man by his relatives. Long after the gladiatorial games ceased to be associated with funerals, the word *munera* was still used to describe them.

The games quickly grew in popularity. We hear of a *munus* in 183 BCE involving 120 gladiators during three days of funeral games. By the turn of the same century, the ruling consuls held the first gladiatorial games to be paid for by the state: Roman politicians began to realise that they could win votes and support by funding impressive *munera*. This trend continued: in 65 BCE, Julius Caesar, newly elected as an aedile, promised the people the greatest games yet: he provided 320 gladiators and actually wanted to have more; however, the Senate, scared of his growing power and popularity, passed a law saying that a citizen could keep no more than 320 gladiators in Rome.

With the onset of empire, the *munera* became closely associated with the power of the emperor – successive emperors passed laws ensuring that they were able to give far more spectacular shows than any of the magistrates. Augustus forbade the praetors to hold more than two *munera* per year, while they were only allowed to use a maximum of 120 gladiators and could spend no more than 25,000 denarii each time. By contrast, Augustus himself boasted that he put on eight shows per year, with each perhaps costing as much as 180,000 denarii. By 108-109 CE, the emperor Trajan celebrated his victories in Dacia by holding games over a 123-day period, during which 10,000 gladiators and 11,000 animals were apparently used.

1. Gladiators

Gladiators were drawn from a variety of sources, the most common of which were as follows:

- Soldiers taken as prisoners of war; for them, the life of a gladiator was perhaps preferable to being sent to the mines or put to death.
- Slaves who had committed specific crimes such as running away.
- Free men who had been convicted of serious crimes.
- Some free men who actually volunteered to sign up; in such cases, they were probably very short of money and the gladiator schools offered attractions: a job, food and shelter, and the chance to win fame and fortune – free gladiators were paid and could keep their prize money and any gifts they received.

All gladiators had to train in a gladiator school (*ludus gladiatorius*), which was run by a trainer known as a *lanista* (a word linked to the verb *lanio*, 'I tear to pieces', so that *lanista* describes someone who 'incites violence'). He would hire out his fighters to a magistrate wishing to fund a gladiatorial show as its *editor*.

This mosaic shows two trainee gladiators in a mock fight. One uses a blunted wooden sword, the other a whip, while both have wicker shields.

Lanistae had the power of life and death over their charges, who automatically took on the status of being *infamis* ('disgraceful') – meaning that they were beneath the law. According to one source, all new trainees had to swear the following oath: 'I will endure to be burned, to be bound, to be beaten, and to be killed by the sword.' Training was intensely tough; the men would spend hours practising fighting drills with blunted wooden swords, while they would also be taught how to show nobility at the moment of death.

Spartacus

The most famous gladiator in Roman history was undoubtedly a Thracian known as Spartacus; in 73 BCE, he led a break-out from his gladiator school in Capua and soon had a large following of thousands of runaway slaves. He turned them into a rebel army which fought against the Roman army for over a year with amazing success until it was finally routed in the far south of Italy.

This whole episode shook the Roman state deeply, and legislation soon followed specifying the location, organisation and ownership of the larger gladiator schools. By imperial times, Rome had four schools, all of which were owned by the state and run by agents of the emperor known as *procuratores*.

Life in a gladiator school was a mixture of harshness and privilege. The gladiator barracks which have been excavated in Pompeii (see p. 286) could have housed about 100 men; included in the complex was a punishment cell whose low ceiling would have made it impossible for a man to stand up. However, gladiators were an expensive commodity for their *lanista*, and so they needed to be looked after well. They had access to high quality medical care, received regular massage, and were fed on a high-energy diet of food such as barley, beans, oatmeal, fruit, and ash (which was believed to strengthen the body). Gladiators were probably plumper than modern athletes, as extra layers of fat gave them more protection from the slashes of a sword.

Sex symbols

Although gladiators were *infames* and often treated as the lowest of the low – despised as slaves, socially marginalised, and buried in separate cemeteries – sources suggest that they were also sex symbols for many women in the Roman world. Graffiti from Pompeii include slogans such as 'Celadus the Thracian is all the girls' heart-throb'; Juvenal satirises this phenomenon with the fictional tale of Eppia, a senator's wife, who is infatuated with a fighter called Sergius:

> 'What was the youthful charm that so fired Eppia? What hooked her? ... his (Sergius') face looked a proper mess, helmet-scarred, a great wart on his nose, an unpleasant discharge always trickling from one eye. But he was a gladiator. That word makes the whole breed seem handsome, and made her prefer him to her children and country, her sister, her husband. Steel is what they fall in love with.'
>
> Juvenal, *Satires* 6.102-12

In the story, Sergius and Eppia eloped to Egypt together (where he deserted her). In real life, other women were content to buy a jar of a gladiator's sweat mixed with sand and dust from the arena – a mixture thought to be an aphrodisiac!

Types of gladiator

The name 'gladiator' comes from the Latin *gladius*, meaning a sword. However, gladiators did not all use the same equipment: there were various types who were distinguished by their armour, their weapons, and their fighting style. The crowds loved to see different fighters pitted against one another, each one using his distinct skills and weapons. Most types of gladiators can be divided into one of two categories: heavily armed and therefore hard to wound, or lightly armed and nimble. Some of the most common were as follows:

- *Murmillo*: A heavily armed gladiator, who was armed rather like a Roman legionary soldier. He had a fish-crested helmet

Gladiatorial scenes: on the far left, a *retiarius* has been disarmed by a *secutor* and holds up a finger in a plea for mercy. In the centre a contest is taking place between two unspecified heavily armed gladiators. Beside them is a Thracian with a small shield; to his right his opponent holds up his finger and appeals to the *lanista*.

('*murmillo*' is a Greek name for a type of fish), short greaves, the curved rectangular shield of a Roman legionary, and also the legionary's short sword (*gladius*).

- **Hoplomachus**: A heavily armed fighter who was armed like a Greek hoplite – with heavy armour and helmet, carrying a round shield. He was often pitted against a *murmillo* in a re-enaction of Rome's wars against the Greeks.
- **Secutor**: A heavily armed fighter who was specifically trained to fight the *retiarius*. He had a distinctive helmet with only two small eye-holes, so that his face would be protected from a trident thrust. He also had a greave on his left leg, an arm protector, a legionary-style shield and a *gladius*. *Secutor* meant 'chaser', probably because the *retiarius* used running as one of his tactics; this meant that a *secutor* had to win quickly as he would easily tire in his heavy armour and with the shortage of oxygen under his helmet.
- **Thracian**: A lightly armed fighter who wore a crested helmet with a visor, armoured greaves on both legs, a protector on his sword arm and shoulder, a small shield, and a curved short sword designed to slash the opponent's flesh.
- **Retiarius**: The name meant 'net-fighter', and the *retiarius* was armed with a large net, a trident, an arm guard, a shoulder guard and a dagger. The *retiarius* was the lightest armed of the gladiators, and the only one whose head and face were uncovered. He was therefore more mobile than most gladiators but was also more vulnerable to serious wounds. He had to avoid fighting at close quarters, trying instead to wait for the opportunity to thrust his trident or cast his net.
- **Bestiarius**: A special type of fighter trained to handle and fight all sorts of animal. In fact, technically he wasn't a gladiator at all, since he didn't carry a sword, and perhaps for this reason the

bestiarii were not as popular as the conventional gladiators. They did not usually wear armour, but carried weapons such as firebrands, whips, spears, or even bows and lances; they were sometimes also accompanied by a team of hounds.

A helmet, shield and sword found in the gladiator barracks in Pompeii.

A *retiarius* carrying his trident and net.

Originally, the names of some of the gladiators – such as *Thracian*, *Gaul*, *Samnite* and *hoplomachus* – indicated peoples whom the Romans had conquered in war (although the gladiators themselves need not have come from these parts of the world). However, as the empire grew, and these peoples became integrated into the Roman world, the gladiator names were sometimes changed to reflect this. For example, the emperor Augustus passed a decree that the *Samnite* should be renamed as a *secutor*, since by his time the Samnites of southern Italy were loyal members of the Roman empire. Soon afterwards, the gladiator known as a *Gaul* was renamed a *murmillo*.

A last supper

The night before they were due to fight, a lavish banquet was laid on for the gladiators, which the public was allowed to come and watch. According to our sources, some gladiators consumed moderately, trying to keep themselves in the best condition possible for the following day; others ate and drank as if there was no tomorrow – which they probably believed; the most desperate of them all, however, loudly bewailed their fate, drew up their wills and asked passers-by to look after their families after they had gone.

The description of the gladiators' last supper is one of very few occasions when ancient writers try to see events from the gladiators' perspective. In another passage, Seneca the Younger tells of one man who was so desperate that he tricked his guards and took his own life:

'There was lately in a *ludus* for *bestiarii* a German, who was preparing for the morning exhibition; he withdrew in order to go to the toilet – the only thing he was allowed to do in secret and without the presence of a guard. While so engaged, he seized the stick of wood, tipped with a sponge, which was used for the vilest purposes (*i.e. to wipe the bottom*), and stuffed it, just as it was, down his throat; thus he blocked up his windpipe and choked the breath from his body.'

Seneca, *Letters* 70, 20-7

Although the stoic Seneca is full of admiration for this man's resolution to face death, it surely leaves us with a sense of horror. Elsewhere, Seneca speaks of a fighter who, while being transported on a cart to the arena, allowed his neck to get caught in the spokes as it was moving, so ending his life. We cannot know how many such tales went unreported, nor how representative they are of the gladiators' experience in general. Yet despair must have been a common emotion for many.

2. The amphitheatre

The early gladiator fights were staged in public places such as the forum or a circus. However, in the 1st century BCE, a new type of stadium was introduced specifically to hold *munera* – the amphitheatre. The oldest amphitheatre discovered in the Roman world is that of Pompeii (see p. 285), which was probably constructed in the 70s BCE. In Rome, the first permanent amphitheatre was built in 29 BCE; eventually, there were well over 250 amphitheatres in the Roman empire.

The name 'amphitheatre' came from the fact the stadium was a doubled up version of a semi-circular theatre (*amphi* meant 'both', so that 'amphitheatre' really meant 'a theatre on both sides'). In fact, in one exceptional case in 53 BCE, a candidate for tribune called Curio the Younger did exactly this. Wishing to put on theatrical entertainment (*ludi scaenici* – see p. 224) followed by *munera* and to hold both events in one place, he ordered that not one but two wooden theatres should be set up back to back, with each one mounted on a swivel. In the morning, plays were put on separately, but in the afternoon each theatre was rolled round to create one amphitheatre.

The Colosseum
The most famous Roman amphitheatre was of course the Colosseum; in fact, it was, and is, the iconic building of the entire Roman world. It was constructed during the 70s CE on the orders of the emperor Vespasian, although he was to die a few months before its opening in the spring of 80.

The story behind its construction illustrates the political nature of the *munera*. In 64 CE, Rome suffered the worst fire in its history – much of the city was gutted, including the area where the Colosseum would later be built; however, at this time, it was a densely populated and

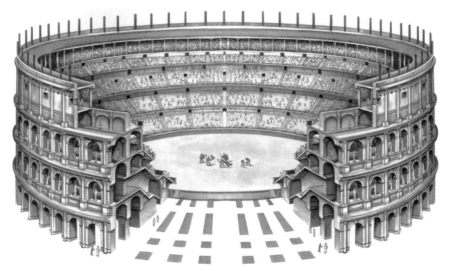

A reconstruction of the Colosseum.

impoverished part of the city. The emperor Nero, instead of organising the reconstruction of housing for his people, took all the land in that area for himself and ordered the building of a magnificent palace, his 'Golden House', which was to be surrounded by beautiful gardens. The ground now occupied by the Colosseum was turned into a magnificent artificial lake.

By 68 CE, Nero had become so unpopular that he was outlawed by the senate; he fled and took his own life. The following year, when the general Vespasian became emperor, he lost no time in trying to win the support of the people. One of his earliest acts was to have much of the Golden House demolished. The lake was filled in, and in its place Vespasian ordered that a magnificent amphitheatre should be built for the people – and so he was seen to be giving back the land which his predecessor had robbed from them, a stunning piece of public relations. He was able to fund much of the construction with the booty gained from his sack of Jerusalem in 70 CE (see p. 117).

What's in a name?

It is unlikely that the Romans ever called the Colosseum by that name. Roman sources refer to it as the *Amphitheatrum Flavium* – or Flavian Amphitheatre – since Flavius was Vespasian's family name. The word 'Colosseum' is most likely derived from the 'colossal' bronze statue of Nero (about 35 metres in height) which stood nearby and had been left untouched after the demolition of the Golden House (Vespasian renamed the statue after the sun god). The statue remained standing until well into the Middle Ages; by the time that it finally fell, the name 'colossus' was also being used to describe the amphitheatre beside it.

The stadium was the largest amphitheatre in the Roman empire. Built from blocks of hard travertine rock from nearby Tibur, its oval shape had a circumference of 545 metres, while its four-storey walls rose to a height of 57 metres. There were 80 entrances, four of which were reserved for VIPs. Although no tickets survive, evidence from elsewhere suggests that spectators were given tickets directing them to the appropriate section and row; they accessed their seats via *vomitoria* (a word linked to the Latin for 'to spew out'), entrance passages which opened out into the tiers of seats, just as one would find at a sports stadium today. The *vomitoria* meant that people could enter or leave quickly, while they also allowed the amphitheatre to be evacuated quickly in case of an emergency.

The seating capacity was approximately 50,000, and it seems that spectators were seated according to social class (although it is hard to know how strictly the rules were adhered to): the more status you held, the nearer to the action you were. The seating began 4 metres above the arena, with a terrace (*podium*) where the senators sat; also on this level were special boxes (*pulvinares*) at the north and south ends for the emperor and Vestal Virgins respectively. Behind the *podium* there were three main seating tiers; the equites (see p. 361) sat in the first, while behind them were the ordinary citizens; on the very top tier were those from the marginalised elements of society – women, slaves and the poor.

Keeping cool

Another spectacular feature of the Colosseum was its huge retractable awning which could be pulled out to protect two-thirds of the spectators from sun or rain. It was supported on poles fixed to the top of the building and hoisted into position with ropes tied to posts outside the stadium.

The arena itself was 86 metres by 54 metres in diameter; the ground was covered in sand, which was used to soak up the blood of victims (in fact, *arena* in Latin meant 'sand', and this is the origin of our modern word). A metal fence ran round the outer limit of the arena, while archers also stood by in case any animals escaped. Beneath the arena floor was a *hypogeum* (literally: 'underground area'), a subterranean network of tunnels, cages and lifts, where criminals and animals were held before being sent into the arena. Slaves worked down there to provide special effects and send up animals through trapdoors in the arena floor; the conditions for all those trapped in this artificial cavern must have been appalling. The *hypogeum* was also linked by tunnels to various points outside the stadium, so that the animals were not seen by the spectators before they made their appearance in the arena.

Sea battles

It is likely that in its earliest days the Colosseum didn't have a *hypogeum*, since Martial's account of the opening games in 80 CE includes a description of mock 'sea battles'. To achieve this, the arena must have been flooded (which would have been unworkable with tunnels below).

These mock sea battles, known as *naumachiae* (sing: *naumachia*), were another popular form of combat entertainment, and some Roman rulers, such as Julius Caesar, Claudius and Domitian, even created separate venues to host them. In these battles, condemned criminals were often forced to fight from small boats, perhaps reenacting a historical or mythical sea battle. We even hear of crocodiles being released into the water to catch any who fell in.

---

3. A day at the amphitheatre

There is a variety of written sources on the *munera*, and so it is possible for us to construct with some accuracy the events of a day at the amphitheatre. The games would be advertised on billboards in the city beforehand; on the day itself, a match programme (*libellus*) was provided for spectators, which might include profiles of the gladiators and a list of matches.

The action would have started early in the morning and ended at dusk, so it was vital for the *editor* to make sure that he provided plenty of variety. The day typically seems to have been divided into three parts – the morning primarily involved animals, at midday executions of prisoners took place, while the main event – the gladiator show – was held back until the afternoon.

The morning

The morning's show might begin with a mimic gladiatorial battle, where combatants fought with blunted weapons (similar to a fencing match today); this would give the crowd a foretaste of the real gladiatorial events to come later. However, the main action would have been based around shows involving wild animals. *Editores* prided themselves on being able to bring the most exotic and dangerous beasts from all over the Roman empire and beyond. It was clearly a way to impress the spectators, who would never have seen such animals.

These animals were used in various ways. Some were trained to perform tricks, just as circus animals do today. Sources speak of teams of panthers drawing chariots, of a tigress tearing a lion to pieces and then going to lick its trainer's hand, and of elephants bowing in front of the emperor's *pulvinar*. Another form of entertainment was to set two different types of animal against one another, such as a bear and a buffalo, or an elephant and a rhinoceros. One such fight is related by Martial, where trainers with spears are trying to goad a rhinoceros into fighting:

> '... at length the fury we once knew returned. For with his double horn he tossed a heavy bear as a bull tosses dummies from his head to the stars. (With how sure a stroke does the strong hand of Carpophorus, still a youth, aim the Norcian spears!) He lifted two steers with his mobile neck, to him yielded the fierce buffalo and the bison. A panther fleeing before him ran headlong upon the spears.'   Martial, *De Spectaculis* 26

The animals

The range of animals captured for the amphitheatre was extraordinary – we hear of elephants, lions, leopards, tigers, bulls, bears, wild boars, rhinoceroses, hippopotami, buffalo, bison, crocodiles, giraffes, ostriches, camels, and many others. These animals had to be captured unharmed (normally in North Africa or the Near East) and then brought back to Rome in cages by sea. In some regions, species were hunted to extinction; one such species was the North African elephant, which Hannibal had famously used in his march across the Alps against Rome.

A scene from a mosaic showing African animals being loaded onto a ship.

After this would have come the wild beast hunts (*venationes*) involving the *bestiarius*. Although the animals were very dangerous, his weapons gave him a significant advantage. Sometimes, the amphitheatre might have been decked out to look like a forest, with animals being gradually released from below. At other times the arena was turned into a slaughterhouse, as hundreds of animals were killed in one short period: at the opening games of the Colosseum in 80 CE, 9,000 animals are said to have been killed over 100 days. A century later, the emperor Commodus even took part in the slaughter himself: he had ostriches released into the arena and took great pleasure in decapitating them by firing arrows – the heads of which had been widened especially for the purpose.

Such slaughter was more than mere entertainment, although the crowds clearly loved what they saw. By introducing all these animals into the arena, a Roman ruler was making two political points – first, that the empire had power over nature, just as it did over human beings; secondly, by introducing animals from all over the known world, an emperor was demonstrating how far the empire had reached.

216

In these mosaic scenes, a condemned man is attacked by a wild animal; elsewhere, a bear and a bull fight chained together, while another prisoner is thrown to a lion.

Midday executions

The events at noon were among the most gruesome of the day: the execution of convicted criminals (of all ages and both sexes). Those who had been sentenced to death this way were known as *damnati ad bestias* ('condemned to the beasts'). Such executions were set up to provide entertainment, although Seneca the Younger points out that they also had the benefit of making a public example of wrong-doers:

> 'The purpose of executing criminals in public ... is that they serve as a warning to all, and because in life they did not wish to be useful citizens, certainly the state benefits by their death.'   Seneca, *On Anger* 1.6.4

The style of execution was varied in order to please the crowds. Some criminals were simply let loose into the arena to face wild beasts; they might be daubed with blood beforehand to give the animals a scent for the kill. Some mosaics show people tied to stakes and facing animals such as lions (this was how many Christians were martyred); others show men forced to perform dangerous tasks with the animals, such as using a hook to undo a chain tying a bear to a bull.

Other forms of execution tried to amuse the crowd by re-enacting famous myths, albeit with the climax of the 'myth' being the death of the 'main character' (i.e. the criminal). So, for example, the tale of Orpheus

A condemned prisoner is mauled by a wild animal.

was once played out in the Colosseum: a man was sent out into the arena, which was decked out as a forest, carrying a musical instrument; like Orpheus, he tried to play some music to calm the animals; however, unlike the mythical hero, the criminal was torn to death by an 'ungrateful bear'. There is another story of a convict who was forced to act out the death of Hercules (by being burnt on a funeral pyre), while others were forced to re-enact the myth of the eastern vegetation god Attis, who castrated himself (see p. 107).

Seneca also tells us about the *gladiatores meridiani* ('midday gladiators'), who were criminals forced to fight one another as gladiators. However, there was a twist: one fighter was armed as a gladiator, while the other was sent into the arena wearing just a tunic. When the armed man had easily killed the other, he in turn had to remove his weapons and was sent back out to face another armed convict; the process went on like this until all the criminals had been killed. Seneca, a cultured and educated man, was clearly disgusted by the sight, even if the same could not be said of the rest of the crowd:

'I happened to go to the games one midday hoping for some light and witty entertainment. I was bitterly disappointed. It was really mere butchery. The morning's show was merciful compared to it. Then men were thrown to lions and to bears: but at midday to the audience. There was no escape for them. The slayer was kept fighting until he could be slain. 'Kill him! Flog him! Burn him alive!' was the cry: 'Why is he such a coward? Why won't he rush on the steel? Why does he fall so meekly? Why won't he die willingly?' Unhappy that I am, how have I deserved that I must look on such a scene as this?'   Seneca, *Letters* 7.3ff.

The afternoon

Things then moved on to the highlight of the day: the gladiators. The event might begin with a parade, where the fighters would arrive and march, to the accompaniment of an orchestra (consisting of brass and wind instruments, and even a water organ), around the arena dressed in purple and gold cloaks, before saluting the emperor.

A funerary relief from Pompeii showing the procession with which the gladiatorial games began.

A scene from a mosaic depicting the arena; it shows the orchestra, a woman playing the water organ, two horn-blowers and a trumpeter.

Modern myth no. 1

It is commonly believed that when the gladiators arrived at the emperor's *pulvinar*, they saluted him with the words '*Ave Imperator, morituri te salutant!*' ('Hail, Emperor, those who are about to die salute you!'). However, scholars doubt whether this line was ever used, since the only source for it (Suetonius, *Claudius* 21.6) actually refers to the greeting made to the emperor by criminals condemned to fight to the death in a *naumachia*.

A *lanista* restrains a gladiator who wants to kill his defeated opponent.

These terracotta
figurines of glad-
iators were
found at
Pompeii.

When the parade was over, weapons were examined, blunt swords
were weeded out, and the fighters moved off to prepare for their bouts.
The excitement of the crowd now reached fever pitch, particularly since
many of them had probably betted heavily on the results. Most bouts
were overseen by a referee who also had an assistant on hand; they
carried long staffs to separate the fighters if necessary. A fight between
two gladiators might last for as long as 15 or 20 minutes, but when one
man could go on no longer, he signalled defeat by raising a finger. At this

point, his opponent stood over him and looked for a signal from the *editor* – to kill or to spare. The *editor* would listen to the noise of the crowd and make his decision.

Modern myth no. 2

Another common belief about gladiatorial combat is that the *editor* decided whether a defeated gladiator should live or die by putting his thumb down to indicate 'kill', or his thumb up for 'save'. However, there is no evidence that this was so; the single reference to the use of the thumb in Roman sources comes from Juvenal, who speaks of *pollice verso* ('with thumb turned'). It is left for us to guess how to interpret this; some believe that the *editor* might have stuck out his thumb to indicate a sword (and therefore 'kill'), and kept his thumb hidden to tell the victor to put away his sword and spare his opponent's life.

A gladiator was trained not to flinch in the face of death – he was expected neither to ask for mercy nor to cry out. The stoic Seneca admired such nobility at the moment of death, echoing views voiced by Cicero more than a century beforehand:

'Even when they have been felled, let alone when they are standing and fighting, they never disgrace themselves. And suppose a gladiator has been brought to the ground, when do you ever see one twist his neck away after he has been ordered to extend it for the death blow?'

Cicero, *Tusculan Disputations* 2.41

A mosaic scene of a defeated *retiarius*. The symbol beside him, Θ (theta), stands for the first letter of *thanatos*, the Greek word for death.

By a strange irony, Cicero later behaved in exactly this way when assassins were sent to kill him.

Once a defeated gladiator was slain, an attendant dressed as Charon (the ferryman of the River Styx) came out and hit his head with a mallet, while another dressed as Mercury in his guise of escorter of dead souls (see p. 74) prodded the corpse with a hot rod; it was then removed from the arena and the throat was cut to make sure that the man was really dead. In the arena, other attendants raked over the bloody sand.

In reality, defeated gladiators were probably not killed that often – evidence from the early empire suggests that it may only have been one in five. As we have seen, they were an expensive commodity, and a *lanista* would not have wanted to lose a good gladiator.

4. Conclusion

What are we to make of such horror? The events of the amphitheatre are surely the mark of a nightmarish society, where thousands derive pleasure and enjoyment from watching the humiliation, torture and murder both of their fellow human beings and of scores of animals. All the written evidence suggests that the crowds loved what they saw, and even the enlightened Seneca was repelled by only one aspect of the slaughter.

It is certainly true that the amphitheatre must be put in its cultural context. Death was ever-present in the ancient world, and it is likely that half the children born didn't survive to their fifth birthday. Moreover, the Romans were a warfaring society which was accustomed to the brutality of battle. The price of human life was very cheap and so people were far less perturbed by death.

Against this, however, must be set the fact that the Romans made torture and death a form of public entertainment on a scale unseen in most other ancient societies. The addictive nature of the spectacle is illustrated in a famous story related by St Augustine, a Christian bishop who spoke out against the amphitheatre in the 4th century CE. He describes how a Christian friend Alypius was talked by friends into attending the games, despite disapproving of them. Before they all arrived, Alypius confidently tells them:

'You can drag my body there, but don't imagine that you can make me turn my eyes or give my mind to the show. Though there, I shall not be there, and so I shall have the better both of you and of the show.'

Alypius' friends took these words as a challenge, and were even keener to introduce him to the arena. In the end, he was unable to resist the excitement of the slaughter:

'The whole place was seething with savage enthusiasm, but he (Alypius) shut the doors of his eyes and forbade his soul to go out into a scene of such evil. If only he could have blocked up his ears too! For in the course of the fight some man fell; there was a great roar from the whole mass of spectators which fell upon his ears; he was overcome by curiosity and opened his eyes, feeling perfectly prepared to treat whatever he might see with scorn and rise above it. But he then received in his soul a worse wound than that man, whom he had wanted to see, had received in his body ... He saw the blood and he gulped down savagery. Far from turning away, he fixed his eyes on it. Without knowing what was happening, he drank in madness, he was delighted with the guilty contest, drunk with the lust of blood. He was no longer the man who had come there but was one of the crowd to which he had come, a true companion to those who had brought him. There is no more to be said. He looked, he shouted, he raved with excitement; he took away with him a madness which would goad him to come back again, and he would not only come with those who first got him there; he would go ahead of them and he would drag others with him.'   St Augustine, *Confessions* 7.8

We see here at work a group psychology which overcomes Alypius and leads him to behave in ways which he would never normally countenance. Sadly, there is a part of human nature which, unchecked, will delight in the suffering of others, and this was clearly developed to the full in the seats of the Roman amphitheatre.

Review 2

1. Define the following: *arena, hypogeum, gladius, lanista, munus, podium, pulvinar, vomitoria.*
2. Explain the origin of the English words *arena, amphitheatre.*
3. Summarise the ways in which politics was involved in the events of the amphitheatre.
4. Why do you feel that spectators enjoyed watching so much brutality?
5. Are there any modern public events (sporting or non-sporting) in the world today which could be compared to the events of the amphitheatre?
E. Imagine you are a gladiator. Write about your training and your daily life.
E. Imagine you are a slave working in the *hypogeum* at the Colosseum to put on a show. Describe the experience.
E. Imagine you are a spectator at the amphitheatre. Describe your day and explain what you did and did not enjoy watching.

III. ROMAN DRAMA

The Romans were unsure as to the exact origins of their theatrical tradition, but it seems certain that it evolved from the ancient Greek world, where European drama (particularly tragedy and comedy) was born in the 6th century BCE. The Greek cities of Magna Graecia were home to many theatres which presented the great plays of Greek civilisation.

A key moment in the development of Roman drama came in the 3rd century, when a Greek writer from southern Italy, **Livius Andronicus** (*c.* 270-*c.* 200 BCE), started to translate some of the most famous works of Greek literature into Latin, including a version of Homer's *Odyssey*. In *c.* 240, he presented a Latin version of a Greek play for the first time at a Roman religious festival (Greek plays had always been performed at religious festivals, in honour of Dionysus, the god of acting); the innovation clearly caught the public imagination, since two years later another religious festival created space for dramatic shows.

It seems that once the Greeks had brought drama to the Italian peninsula, local communities developed their own versions. Livy records that, as early as 363 BCE, the Etruscans (see p. 13) provided dancing clowns at scenic games designed to appease Jupiter during a plague. Moreover, in southern Italy another popular dramatic form emerged, known as the **Atellan Farce** (after the town of Atella in Campania where it originated). This seems to have been a type of travelling street theatre presenting unscripted country entertainments. It made fun of everyday life, relying heavily on slapstick and buffoonery, with the actors wearing exaggerated masks typically portraying recurring characters. Atellan farces continued to be performed at Rome well into the imperial age.

1. Organisation

Plays were usually put on in the Roman world as part of religious festivals, and they took the name of *ludi scaenici* ('scenic games'). After Livius Andronicus' introduction of the first play, the number of festivals with a theatrical content quickly grew: by about 200 BCE, there were six *ludi scaenici* attached to major Roman festivals, all of which took place between April and November. After that, the number of days given over each year to *ludi scaenici* steadily increased: in 180 BCE, there were about 24 festival days for drama, which had increased to 42 by 44 BCE.

The *ludi scaenici* were paid for in part by the Roman state, and in part by those magistrates responsible for running them (usually the aediles, although one festival was funded by the praetors). Therefore, as with the *ludi circenses* and *munera*, the games offered politicians the opportunity to win popularity; from about 200 BCE, there seems to have been no limit to the amount of money which an aspiring politician could spend. Martial even satirises a woman called Proculeia who wants a divorce from her husband in order to protect her dowry when it looks like he will be bankrupted by funding the *ludi scaenici*:

'He was a praetor. The purple robe (*the symbol of the sponsor*) of the Megalensian festival was going to cost 100,000 sesterces, even if you gave a pretty thin show, and the Plebeian festival would have run off with 20,000. That's not divorce, Proculeia, just good business.'

Martial, *Epigrams* 10.41

The 'good business' here is Proculeia's decision to divorce her husband before he could ruin them both financially in his quest to win votes.

2. The theatre

The first major stone theatre in Rome wasn't built until the general and statesman Pompey (see p. 35) commissioned a theatre in 55 BCE (although permanent theatres had appeared in cities of southern Italy, such as Pompeii – see p. 283). Before this, theatres were temporary wooden structures which stood for the period of the festival only; this way, the ruling elite could keep political control of the theatre – without permanent theatres there could be no performances unless they funded and provided the theatrical space. However, by the 1st century BCE, even the temporary theatres had become elaborate: linen awnings protected the spectators from the sun, the stage-buildings were lavishly decorated and there were seats tiered on scaffolding for the spectators.

The new permanent Roman theatres which followed on from Pompey's original were designed on the Greek model, but with some

The extensive remains of the Roman theatre in Sabratha, Libya.

notable adaptations. For example, a Roman theatre was normally free-standing (rather than being built on a hillside) and enclosed on all sides. The back wall of the stage set (*scaenae frons*) usually consisted of three storeys (although some theatres only had two) and many columns. It matched the height of the seating area (*cavea*) and attached to it on both sides. The *scaenae frons* usually had three doors set into an elaborate facade. Each of the doors led onto the stage by a small set of steps.

The stage itself (*pulpitum*) was made of wood and set on pillars; the area below it would be used to manoeuvre stage machinery and props. In imperial times, a stage was about 50 by 8 metres, although in the theatre of Pompey it must have been about 90 metres wide. The front wall of the stage was normally a little over a metre high and made of elaborate stone. The semi-circular area at the front of the *cavea*, known as the *orchestra*, was normally a seating area reserved for VIPs (such as senators in Rome). Most theatres had awnings to provide shade for spectators.

The Theatre of Pompey

In 55 BCE, the leading Roman general and politician Pompey financed the building of a theatre on the Campus Martius (see map on p. 352) in the hope of winning support for his campaign for the consulship. In fact, it was a much larger complex than merely a theatre, including arcades, a temple to Venus and a large portico. It was even used as a meeting place for the Senate in 44 BCE after the Senate House in the forum had burnt down; it was at the entrance to the complex that Julius Caesar was assassinated, in front of a statue of Pompey, his great rival.

The theatre itself was massive, with a diameter of about 150 metres. Pliny the Elder thought that it could seat 40,000 spectators, although modern commentators now think that this is exaggerated and estimate a figure nearer to 20,000 – still significantly more than any theatre in the world today (for example, both the Royal Opera House in London and La Scala in Milan have a seating capacity of less than 2,500). One of the main legacies of the theatre was that it became a model for many stone theatres built throughout the Roman world during imperial times.

The audience

Since admission to the Roman theatre was free, the audience tended to be drawn from all social classes, and it seems that in most theatres there was a hierarchy of seating: the senators and VIPs would sit in the orchestra, a number of rows behind them were reserved for the equites; beyond this, the further back you sat, the lower your social status.

Sources suggest that audiences could be either wildly supportive or brutal in their condemnation. On the one hand, we hear of spectators learning the songs of the theatre and then singing them by heart; on the

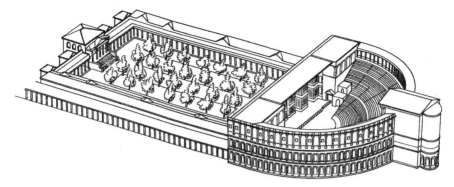

A reconstruction of Pompey's theatre and temple complex.

other hand, there are stories of actors making mistakes and being hissed or booed off stage. In the prologue to Plautus' *Poenulus*, the playwright's plea for good behaviour from the audience suggests that there was often room for improvement:

> 'Let no elegant tart take a seat on the edge of the stage; let neither lictor (*see p. 359*) – nor his rods – speak at the wrong time, nor the usher wander in front of people's faces, or show them to their seat while an actor is on stage. Those who have stayed too long at home in idle slumber should now stand and wait patiently, or else refrain from sleeping in. Let no slaves crowd in but leave room here for free men, or else pay cash for manumission (*see p. 180*); ... let nurses attend to their pretty brats at home, let no one bring them to this play ... married women are to view this play in silence, laugh in silence, temper here and there their tuneful chirping, (and) take their prattle home.'　　Plautus, *Poenulus* 15ff.

It is interesting to note here that the jokes only work if audiences are normally made up of a wide variety of spectators: lictors, free men, married women, and perhaps also slaves and nurses.

Actors
It seems that in the earliest days of Roman theatre actors were respected – Livius Andronicus and his contemporaries even acted in their own plays. However, by the 1st century BCE they had come to be disdained and held a very low social status. Writing in 34 BCE, Cornelius Nepos compares Rome with Greece, where acting was still seen as a noble calling:

> '(In Greece) to go on the stage and be a spectacle for the people was not a dishonour; all these activities with us are considered to bring *infamia*, or to be alien or vulgar to decent behaviour.'
> 　　　　　　　　　　　　　　　　　Cornelius Nepos, *Preface* 5

Two statuettes of
actors in mask and
costume.

By this time, actors (like gladiators) were indeed legally *infamis* and
subject to severe restrictions: they were denied Roman citizenship, their
descendants were banned from marrying into the senatorial class for
four generations; they could be killed with impunity if caught
committing adultery, and there was even a law allowing magistrates to
beat them if they had not acted well.

Actors, called *histriones*, were typically organised into a troupe under
the charge of a troupe leader (*dominus*). By imperial times, they were
either drawn from the ranks of slaves or from the lower classes,
although they had to be skilled enough to act and sing in a variety of
different roles. Competition between the troupes seems to have been
fierce – prizes were awarded to troupes or individual actors, and sources
tell of how they stationed their supporters throughout the theatre with
instructions to applaud at the right moment.

Roscius

Despite their low social status, successful actors could gain both fame and wealth. The most famous comic actor in late republican times was Roscius, who earned so much money that the dictator Sulla elevated him to membership of the Equites (see p. 361). After this, he acted without taking a salary, so as to avoid acquiring *infamis* status. Meanwhile, a contemporary of his, the tragic actor Aesopus, left a fortune of twenty million sesterces.

3. Comedy and tragedy

Livius Andronicus and the early Roman playwrights who followed him tried to write both comedies and tragedies, many of which were direct translations or close adaptations of Greek originals. Two other important writers in this period were **Gnaeus Naevius**, who wrote between about 235 and 204 BCE, and **Quintus Ennius** (239-169 BCE). After them, however, writers tended to focus on either comedy or tragedy.

Roman tragedy

It is very hard to evaluate Roman tragedy since so little of it survives – we can only really rely on fragments and what other Roman writers have said about it. However, it is clear that Andronicus, Naevius and

A Roman tragedy portrayed on a terracotta relief. Behind the actors is the typical Roman stage, with a *scaenae frons* and a roof above.

229

Ennius all took their tragic writing very seriously and drew heavily on the fine example of Greek tragedy – for example, more than half of Ennius' plays are set in the Greek mythological world of the Trojan War.

In addition to the tragedies modelled on the Greek tradition, these same writers also developed another form of serious play, with its subject centred on Roman history. These plays were known as *fabulae praetextae* after the type of toga worn in them (see Appendix 4 to read about Roman clothing); only one of them has survived (*Octavia*, attributed to Seneca), but we do know the titles of some others, including Naevius' *Romulus*, Ennius' *Sabines*, and Accius' *Brutus*. These titles suggest that playwrights were keen to explore themes from early Roman history, which you can read about in Chapter 1.

The first Roman playwright to concentrate solely on tragedy was Ennius' nephew, **Marcus Pacuvius** (220-*c.* 130 BCE). He was far more innovative in his choice of subject matter, fond of complex plots (often drawing on specific Athenian tragedies), which often raised deep moral or philosophical issues. His plays were produced on stage long after his death, and he was admired for the quality of his language; writing over a century later, Cicero praised his 'finely styled and elegant verses' and claimed that he was the greatest Roman tragedian.

Following on from Pacuvius was **Lucius Accius**, the son of a freedman born in Umbria in 170 BCE. He was Rome's most prolific tragic playwright, and we still have the titles of 40 plays. He seems to have based most of them upon well known Greek myths, and to have enjoyed writing passages with violent and bloody description: for example, Thyestes dining on his own sons, or Medea murdering her children.

However, as time wore on tragedy came to appeal less and less to the public, and few tragedies were composed after the time of Accius. There are references to tragedies in imperial times – most notably those of **Seneca the Younger** (eight of which survive) – but it is less likely that these were intended for public performance; instead, they were probably composed for intimate, courtly performances or readings.

Cantica

Despite tragedy's decline, songs sung by tragic singers, which were known as *cantica*, remained popular among Roman audiences (perhaps as songs from popular musicals are today); at the funeral of Julius Caesar, the crowd started singing a *canticum* from a tragedy of Pacuvius which included a particularly poignant line: 'Have I saved them only to perish at their hands?'

Roman comedy

Much more is known about Roman comedy, which took on a whole life of its own. The two greatest writers of the genre were **Plautus**, who came from Umbria in central Italy and was writing between 205 and 184 BCE,

A father is held back from attacking his son, who has come back late from a party. In this comic scene, a slave props up the young man, while a musician plays the pipes in the middle.

This mosaic of comic actors was found in modern Tunisia, showing that comedies were popular throughout the Roman world.

A tragic actor with his mask. Roman tragic masks always had a raised hair-style similar to that worn by Roman ladies.

and **Terence**, who is said to have come from north Africa and was writing in the 160s BCE. Both men wrote plays translated from or based on Greek New Comedy – a style developed in Athens in the late 4th century BCE by writers such as Menander. These plays were really the forerunners to modern sit-coms – their plots were often based around everyday social situations and they could be described as 'comedies of manners'.

Since Plautus and Terence relied so heavily on Greek material, their plays were described as *fabulae palliatae*, or 'plays in Greek costume', and all the characters did indeed wear costumes based on the Greek model. This consisted of a tunic, over which men usually wore a Greek style cloak (in Latin, *pallium*), while women wore the female version, a *palla*. Dress and props could also indicate more about a character to the audience: for example, old men often wore white and carried sticks, pimps were dressed in garish, multi-coloured *pallia*, a cook held a knife, spoon, or some sort of dish, a slave-dealer carried a money-bag, while characters who had travelled long distances (or were about to do so) often wore a wide-brimmed hat, the *petasus*, which was associated with Mercury, the god of travellers.

To complete the Greek style of costume, actors wore masks (as did actors in Roman tragedy), and they too were designed to indicate a specific type of character. One ancient writer lists 44 different types comic mask: eleven for young men, seven for slaves, three for old women, five for young women, seven for prostitutes, two for slave-girls, as well as several others. All masks were designed to cover the entire front of the head, and were usually light in weight; this meant that they were comfortable to wear, and also enabled actors playing more than one part to remove them quickly off-stage. Hair was also attached to denote character: for old men, it was white or grey (or they were bald), younger characters were typically given dark hair, while for slave characters the colour was red.

Plautus
All of Plautus' plays are known or believed to be adapted from Greek originals, and this in itself presented the playwright with an opportunity – he was able to retain the play's setting in Greece, but to add specifically Roman characteristics. His plays have a variety of plots, but many similar features: love affairs, confusions of identity, conflicts between father and son, or clever slaves who outwit their masters (this

A scene of masked comic actors found in Pompeii. A girl looks on in horror and is held by a youth, while an old slave makes the sign of the horns to ward off evil.

233

theme has long been used of comic writers – more recent examples are Mozart's Figaro and P.G. Wodehouse's Jeeves).

However, Plautus developed these plots to appeal to a Roman audience: there are plenty of jokes and puns on Latin words (he was known for his verbal brilliance), as well as references to the audience themselves and the progress of the play, while he made extensive use of stock characters such as the parasite or the lecherous old man. Music was also a particular feature of Plautus' plays – he wrote many *cantica*, operatic arias or duets, which often do little to develop the plot, but clearly added great colour to the action.

Casina

Casina is one of Plautus' best known plays, and its plot gives a good idea of the playwright's style. It was set in Athens, where the abandoned infant Casina had been found by Lysidamus and his wife Cleostrata, and the couple had raised her as their slave-girl. When the play starts, their son, Euthynicus, has fallen in love with Casina and wants to marry her. However, Lysidamus has designs on Casina himself, and so comes up with elaborate plans both to get his son out of the city, and to have Casina marry his own slave, Olympio (that way, the old man will be able to have Casina for himself). But Cleostrata is suspicious and wants Casina to marry her slave Chalinus so that she can keep an eye on things. The husband and wife draw lots, and Lysidamus wins. Yet Cleostrata finds out about her husband's plan to sleep with Casina before the wedding. By way of revenge, she dresses up Chalinus as Casina on the appointed night, and 'she' waits in Casina's darkened bedroom. When Lysidamus makes his move, he soon realises that he has been rumbled:

> 'I put my hands on a ... a ... handle. But now that I think about it, she didn't have a sword: that would have been cold ... It's so embarrassing!!'
> Plautus, *Casina* 796-7

Cleostrata has won, Lysidamus has been humiliated, and life returns to normal. There follows a brief epilogue in which the audience are told that Euthynicus will indeed marry Casina, who was really a free-born Athenian when she was discovered as a baby by her adoptive family. One final irony of the play is that the character Casina never actually appears – only Chalinus dressed up as her.

Terence

All six of Terence's plays have survived. He was more faithful to his Greek models than Plautus, with fewer references to Roman society. He is known for his sympathetic portrayal of human relationships, but also used stock characters and boisterous scenes just as Plautus did.

One innovation of Terence was his use of the prologue. Whereas other playwrights had used the prologue to give an outline of the plot, Terence perhaps preferred to leave the events as a surprise for his audience. Instead, Terence often used his prologue to feud with his critics, and on one occasion complains about how difficult it is to keep an audience's attention in the face of other attractions: it seems that he had three attempts at presenting a play called *The Mother-in-Law* (*Hecyra*), as his producer Turpio explains in the third prologue:

'Once again I bring you *The Mother-in-Law*. I have never been allowed to present this play in silence; it has been overwhelmed by disasters. If you show your appreciation of our efforts this time, we shall undo the damage. The first time I began to act, there was a rumour that some famous boxers, and perhaps a tight-rope walker too, were arriving. Friends started talking to each other, and the women were shouting – so I made a premature exit ... Well, I tried again, and everyone enjoyed the opening. But then someone said that there were gladiators on the programme, and people started flooding in, rioting and fighting for seats, with an almighty din. That was the end of *my* little performance.'

Terence, *Hecyra* 29ff.

This gives a clue as to how the theatre was to progress in later centuries, as it struggled to compete with other attractions; more than a century later, the poet Horace writes with contempt of the audiences of his day:

'Often even the brave playwright is frightened and routed, when those less in worth and rank, but greater in number – stupid illiterates always ready for a fight ... shout for bears or boxing right in the middle of the play: that's what the rabble love.'   Horace, *Epistles* 2.1.182-6

In such a culture, very few new comedies seem to have been written after the 2nd century BCE, although the plays of writers such as Plautus and Terence were still performed well into imperial times. By then, however, the popularity of both comedy and tragedy had been overtaken by that of mime and pantomime.

4. Mime and pantomime

As tragedy and comedy declined in popularity in the late republic and early empire, two younger dramatic genres – both of them originating from the Greek east – soon became the staple diet of Roman theatres from that time onwards. These were **mime** and **pantomime**. Both names can be confusing to a modern reader – the mime involved actors speaking (unlike modern mime performances), while it was actually the pantomime actor who performed silently; moreover, the Roman pantomime is not remotely connected to the modern pantomimes which grace the British stage at Christmas time!

Mime

The mime originated in Greece and initially wasn't even dramatic: many different types of entertainment, including acrobatics, song and dance, jokes, conjuring, were built around a slender plot to create a kind of variety show of sketches and short plays (in some ways, therefore, the mime can be compared to TV sketch shows today). It is first recorded in the Roman world in about 170 BCE, and eventually came to take the place of comedy during the imperial period.

It is very hard to describe exactly what was presented in the mimes – the form changed over the centuries, while productions seem to have come in many shapes and sizes. The subject matter was often coarse and obscene, with the emphasis on sex, parody of town and city life, and general buffoonery; some mimes were political, others presented scenes from everyday life. We hear of plots involving kidnappings, cuckolds and lovers hidden in convenient chests. Early mimes were unscripted, but from the 1st century BCE there was a move to script them – **Decimus Laberius** (a knight born in 106 BCE) and **Publilius Syrus** (a freedman from Syria) were the first writers to make mime a literary genre.

The mime could be presented in a number of settings: on its own, as an interlude to another play, or as part of another public or private form of entertainment (by the imperial period, some wealthy Romans were presenting mimes at their dinner parties, and the richest even kept their own troupe of actors). A mime did not need a stage – merely a few props and a curtain for a set, and so it could be put on almost anywhere. Even if mimes were scripted, it seems that the whole genre was given over to improvisation and creative input – one writer even says that dogs could appear on stage!

A mime might be accompanied by acrobats, singers and dancers. The following passage from one modern writer gives a sense of the atmosphere of the production:

> 'We can picture these small companies of strolling players, men, women and children, travelling from town to town like gypsies, setting up their show. Chief among them was the leading actor or actress (*known as the 'Archimimus'*) ... to whom the rest were little more than foils. Improvisation was probably the rule.'
>
> W. Beare, *The Roman Stage*, pp. 152-3

As we read here, women could perform in the mime alongside men – a great contrast to all other forms of drama. The actors do not seem to have worn special costumes: one source suggests that their clothing is indistinguishable from that of the spectators, while another speaks of a multi-coloured jacket. They performed barefoot and without masks, meaning that facial expression was central to the act (unlike other dramatic genres). The actor would use his face to mimic a range of emotions and perhaps even a variety of characters. The epitaph for a certain Vitalis, a mime actor of the imperial period, gives a sense of his art:

> 'At the sight of me, wild frenzy met relief;
> My entrance changed to laughter poignant grief ...
> An hour with me was ever happiness,
> In tragic role my word and act could please,
> Cheering in a thousand ways hearts ill at ease:
> Through change in look, manner, voice I so could run
> That many seemed to use the lips of one.
> The man whose double on the stage I seemed
> Shrank, as my looks in his very own he deemed.
> How often a woman whom my gestures played
> Saw herself, blushed, and held her peace dismayed!
> So parts which I made live by mimicry
> Dark death has hurried to the grave with me.' *PLM* III, p. 245

As this passage suggests, the mime drew in its audience, and it was clearly very popular throughout all levels of Roman society. Indeed, as he lay on his deathbed, the emperor Augustus is said to have asked: 'Have I played the mime of life believably?'

The politics of the mime
The mime often reflected the political mood of the politics of the day. During the republic, mimes were often critical of the government; for example, in 46 BCE Julius Caesar compelled Decimus Laberius to act out his own mime on stage – a source of shame for a man of his rank. He got his own back by including the line: 'he whom many fear has many to fear' – a clear warning to Caesar about the dangers of his power. When Caesar was indeed assassinated two years later, Cicero aimed to judge the public reaction to the event by political references in the mimes.

However, the arrival of imperial rule muzzled freedom of speech, and so mimes after that tended only to criticise opponents of the emperor. It is telling that the mime most often played between 30 and 200 CE was the story of Laureolus, a real-life bandit leader who, after a successful career, was captured and crucified. The moral of the story here was clear: under a good government, the wicked are punished and the authorities will always ultimately succeed.

Pantomime
As tragedy declined, pantomime seems to have taken its place. A pantomime was essentially a form of ballet, but one in which all of the parts were played by a single actor (in Greek, *panto* signified 'all'). A pantomime actor might be accompanied by a musician, a group of musicians or even a singer, but the actor himself, like a ballet dancer, neither spoke nor sang. As with mime, pantomime could take place in

An ivory carving of a pantomime actor holding the masks of three characters and various props.

the theatre, in other public places, or at a private performance; pantomime actors were often attached to wealthy patrons.

Pantomime was developed in the eastern Mediterranean before being introduced to Rome in 22 BCE with the support of the emperor Augustus. In its early days at Rome, the two greatest proponents were **Pylades** from Cilicia and **Bathyllus** from Alexandria, and each founded pantomime schools in their own name which survived long after their deaths. There was an important difference between the two, since Bathyllus developed comic pantomime, while Pylades (a freedman of Augustus) focused on acting scenes from Greek mythology, and Greek tragedy in particular. In time, it was the tragic pantomime of Pylades which gained most popularity at Rome.

During a performance, a pantomime actor had to show great versatility to play all the roles – male and female, young and old – in a series of solo scenes which might require him to change into and out of a variety of costumes and masks (pantomime masks differed from other theatrical masks by the fact that the mouth was always closed). This was a very demanding art, for which a pantomime actor underwent extensive training. Quintilian, a rhetorician of the 1st century CE, emphasises the skills of the pantomime actors, and in particular the importance of their hand movements:

'Their hands demand and promise, they summon and dismiss; they translate horror, fear, joy, sorrow, hesitation, confession, repentance, restraint, abandonment, time, and number. They excite and calm. They implore and they approve. They possess a power of imitation which replaces words. To suggest illness, they imitate the doctor feeling the patient's pulse; to indicate music they spread their fingers in the fashion of a lyre.'   *Quintilian XI.3, 86-8*

Theatre masks often appear in mosaics. In this one a tragic mask and a comic mask sit on a shelf with a double flute behind.

Writing in the following century, the satirist Lucian left a detailed description of a pantomime act as follows:

'In general, the dancer undertakes to present and enact characters and emotions, introducing now a lover, now an angry person, one man afflicted with madness, another with grief, and all this within fixed bounds. Indeed, the most surprising thing is that within the selfsame day, at one moment we are shown Athamas in a frenzy, at another Ino in terror; presently the same person is Atreus, and after a little Thyestes; ... yet they are all but a single man.'

Lucian, *On the Dance* 67-8

All four of the names mentioned here – Athamas, Ino, Atreus and Thyestes – are characters from Greek mythology. Indeed, a later source claimed that the pantomime was the only way in which the common people learnt the stories of Greek mythology.

Lucian then goes on to describe the musical support given to the pantomime actor:

'The dancer has everything at once, and that equipment of his is varied and comprehensive – the pipes, the panpipes, the tapping of feet, the clash of cymbals, the melodious voice of the actor (a secondary role), the harmony of the singers.'

Lucian, *On the Dance* 67-8

All in all, a good pantomime must have been a wonderful experience for both the ears and the eyes.

Pantomania

Within a few years of its introduction to Rome, pantomime had developed a passionate following. In fact, it seems that the many theatres which sprung up in the Roman world under the emperors were primarily used for pantomime performances.

Pantomime actors themselves started to have their own fan clubs, and the rivalries between these fans became so bitter that they often led to violence. In 14 and 15 CE, riots broke out between members of rival factions; they became so serious that several soldiers, a centurion and a tribune were left dead on the streets. As a result, the emperor Tiberius ordered that all pantomime acts had to take place in the theatre and that unruly spectators could be punished with exile. Some years later in 56, after similar outbreaks of violence, the emperor Nero was forced to banish the pantomimes and some of their supporters from Italy. However, Nero, an unashamed fan of the pantomimes, couldn't live without them and so called them back again in 59.

This latter story hints at another interesting aspect of the pantomimes: that although they were of a low social status, their fame and popularity often meant that they became closely associated with the imperial family, often in scandalous ways. The emperor Caligula had a close and perhaps intimate relationship with a pantomime actor called Mnester. Caligula's successor, Claudius, eventually had his adulterous wife Messalina and her various lovers executed – including Mnester (who may actually have been innocent). Indeed, some of the pantomime actors were clearly seen as sex symbols by women and men alike, something the satirist Juvenal makes fun of when describing a woman reacting to a performance:

> 'Tuccia cannot constrain herself; your Apulian maiden raises a sudden
> and longing cry of ecstasy, as though she were embraced by a man.'
>
> Juvenal, *Satires* 6.66

Pantomimes, gladiators and charioteers all apparently won the hearts of noble women, proving that the cult of celebrity was every bit as powerful in ancient Rome as it is in our society today.

5. The legacy of the Roman stage

The Roman theatre has influenced the European theatre from the time of the Renaissance, which began at the end of the 14th century CE. As the plays of Roman authors were rediscovered, they came to be performed once again; moreover, these plays influenced new works which were being produced. For example, Shakespeare would certainly have read the plays of Plautus and Terence at school (even though he was said to know 'small Latin and less Greek'). His play *The Comedy of Errors* is based largely on combining Plautus' *Menaechmi* and *Amphitryo*, while many other of his plots use ideas from comedy, such as stock characters – the most famous of these is Falstaff, who appears in three plays as the 'boastful soldier', based on the lead character in Plautus' play *Miles Gloriosus*.

Other playwrights also looked to Roman drama for inspiration. In England, famous writers such as Marlowe, Jonson and Sheridan all used Roman models, while in France the comedies of Molière owed much to Plautus and Terence – his play *L'Avare* is based on Plautus' *Pot of Gold*. It was not only comedy which cast this shadow; in Italy, the gruesome tragedies of Seneca were particularly copied in the 16th century, while a form of improvised drama involving recurring characters, the *Commedia dell'Arte*, had close similarities to Atellan farces. Like the Latin language, Roman drama never really died, but rather evolved into newer forms.

Review 3

1. Define the following parts of a Roman theatre: *cavea, orchestra, pulpitum, scaenae frons.*
2. Give a brief description of the following: *cantica, fabulae palliatae, fabulae praetextae, histriones, ludi scaenici, mime, pantomime.*
3. Which type of Roman drama would you have preferred to watch and why?
4. In what ways were politics involved with the production of Roman drama?
R. Read Horace, *Epistles* 2.1.156-213. What can we learn of Horace's views of the Roman theatre from these lines?
R. Read Tacitus, *Annals* 1.77, which tells of riots of pantomime fans in 15 CE. What can we learn about the pantomime culture from this passage?
E. Imagine you go to watch a performance of either a Roman comedy or a pantomime. Describe everything which you experience.

IV. THE BATHS

The baths of the Roman world were far more than a place where people went to keep clean. In fact, they were more like a cross between a modern sports club and a spa. The costs of the baths were low – it was actually in the interests of the state to subsidise them, since most people did not have bathing facilities at home and so public baths helped ward off disease. That said, it is hard to know exactly how hygienic the water was – it was not chlorinated, and the surviving bath houses suggest that there was poor drainage from the tubs. The Roman doctor Celsus,

241

writing in the early 1st century CE, generally considered the baths conducive to good health, but did warn against exposing open wounds to the water to avoid getting gangrene!

For much of Roman history, the baths were a fundamental part of daily life. By the 4th century CE there were many hundreds of bath houses in the city of Rome; moreover, the baths were just as popular in other parts of the empire – two centuries earlier, one writer in the city of Smyrna (modern Izmir in Turkey) claimed that there were 'so many baths that you would be at a loss to know where to bathe'.

1. Origins and development

Bathing was common in the Greek world, although the Romans took it to new heights. From the 3rd century BCE the wealthiest Romans built for themselves private bathing suites in their houses and country villas. At this time, however, the Romans were a prudish race and did not approve of public nudity (nor of the culture of the ancient Greek gymnasium, where men would exercise naked). For example, the stern Cato the Elder even disapproved of taking a bath in front of his son, while Seneca the Younger, no fan of the public baths, compares the austere republican bathing habits of Scipio Africanus (see p. 28) to the weakness (as he saw it) of his own society in the 1st century CE:

> 'In that corner ... the man who was the terror of Carthage washed his tired body from the fatigue of the country under a filthy roof and on a very poor floor ... while in our times nobody would tolerate washing themselves like that, ... today the walls are shining with rare marbles from Egypt and Numidia, ... the vault is covered with very rich gilding ... and Thasian marble, which at one time could only be admired in the rarest temples, today lines the pools which weak bodies, covered by sweat from the furnaces, dive into.' Seneca, *Letters* 86

In the same letter, Seneca claims that Romans normally had a bath only once a week in Scipio's time; on other days they just washed 'their arms and legs, which of course they dirtied working'. Seneca approves of this, arguing that, however bad the stench of a man might have been, he would really have stunk of 'hard soldiering' and 'hard work'.

Seneca's views clearly belonged to a small minority, since most Romans were in love with their baths. With the development of urban life in the Roman world (and aqueducts to support it), the urge for cleanliness won out. The first public baths began to appear in the city of Rome in the 2nd century BCE; their popularity grew with time and by the 4th century CE one source claims that there were 867 bath complexes in the city!

At first, these baths (known as *balnea*) were privately owned and run, although the entrance fee for the public was reasonable. However, by the onset of the empire, grand and lavish public baths (known as *thermae*) began to be constructed. The first of these, built on the Campus Martius, was commissioned by Marcus Agrippa early in the reign of Augustus; in the following 150 years, Nero, Titus and Trajan would also have complexes built at Rome; however, the most lavish *thermae* appeared in later imperial times: those of Caracalla (completed in 216) and of Diocletian (305). The *thermae* were so grand that there were only a few of them – only 11 of the 867 listed in the 4th century.

The baths of Caracalla

Visitors to Rome today can still see the substantial remains of the baths of Caracalla, an emperor who reigned between 211 and 217 CE (see p. 54). The massive complex occupied an area of about 13 hectares (32 acres) and could hold 1,600 bathers at any one time. Like other large *thermae*, it had a huge library, with separate rooms for Greek and Latin texts. It was also home to some of the most famous works of art to survive from the Roman world, such as the Farnese Bull and the Farnese Hercules.

Caracalla himself was one of the cruellest of Roman emperors; some modern historians have even suggested that the construction of these baths may have been his subconscious attempt to 'cleanse' himself of all the murder associated with his reign – including that of his own brother, Geta.

A reconstruction of the baths of Caracalla.

This mosaic shows girls dancing and exercising in bikinis.

2. A visit to the baths

As there were so many bath houses in the Roman world, no two of them were designed in exactly the same way. However, there were some key rooms and spaces which were common to all.

Arriving at the baths, a visitor would first have to pay the entrance fee; in early imperial times, this seems to have been a *quadrans*, the smallest coin (see Appendix 3). He (or she – women's bathing is discussed on pp. 250-1) would then head to the changing room, or *apodyterium* (from the Greek *apo* + *duo* = I take off), where he would leave his clothes in one of the niches along the walls (although he might leave on some light clothing for the exercise ground).

The visitor would then head to the exercise ground to work up a sweat. This area was known as the *palaestra*, a word borrowed from the Greeks which originally meant 'wrestling-ground' but came to refer to a place where many sports were practised. Sources speak of various

A section of the *palaestra* of the Stabian Baths, Pompeii.

The *apodyterium* of the women's section of the
Forum Baths in Herculaneum.

245

games being played there: *trigon* was played by three players, each posted at the corner of a triangle, who threw balls at each other without warning, catching in one hand and throwing with the other; *harpastum* ('snatch-ball') was another popular game, perhaps a bit like 'piggy in the middle', in which one player had to seize a ball stuffed with sand from others holding on to it and throwing it around.

Some writers speak of men fencing against a post, others of men wrestling with one another, while there even seems to have been a form of tennis played with the hand. Some expert ball players even became celebrities with the masses – the following inscription survives from a statue (dedicated in the 2nd century CE) of a famous ball player called Ursus:

'The masses loved me and loud screams resounded in the Baths of Trajan, in those of Agrippa and Titus, and many also in the Baths of Nero: believe me, it is me, come and celebrate me, ball players, and adorn, friends, my statue with flowers, violets and roses.'   *CIL* VI.9797

It is interesting to note here that the inscription mentions all of the grandest *thermae* of Rome at that time.

After exercising, the visitor would head back to the *apodyterium* and remove the rest of his clothes in preparation for the bathing process. The number and quality of bathing rooms would depend on the size and status of the bath house, but all baths had three fundamental rooms: the *tepidarium* ('warm room'), the *caldarium* ('hot room'), and the

The *caldarium* of the Forum Baths, Pompeii.

The plunge-pool in the *frigidarium* of the Forum Baths, Pompeii.

frigidarium ('cold room'). More extensive bath houses may have had other facilities, such as a *sudatorium* ('sweat-room', also known as a *laconicum*), which was similar to a modern sauna, or a swimming pool (*natatio*) – however, this would not have been used for exercise, since there was no culture of swimming lengths in the Roman world; bathers would simply have got in to relax and freshen up.

We cannot be sure about the order in which a bather typically visited these rooms – if indeed there was any norm. It is generally assumed that bathers finished in the *frigidarium* to cool off, but there doesn't seem to have been a clear rule about visiting the *caldarium* or *tepidarium* first – in some sources, we hear of people starting in the *tepidarium* and then heading to the *caldarium*, so building up a sweat slowly, while others would choose the hottest room first (perhaps even beginning in the *sudatorium* if there was one), and ease down before arriving in the *frigidarium*. It is probably true to say that there was no absolute pattern to the process, and people were free to choose the order that best suited them.

If a bather had brought his slave, then he would be entrusted with an oil flask, towel and a curved implement called a *strigil*. After heading into one of the warm rooms, the slave then rubbed olive oil all over his master's body (soap was not known to the Romans, so olive oil was used

247

A mosaic showing a wealthy Roman woman going to the baths accompanied by attendants.

Two *strigils* and an oil flask.

instead). The hot atmosphere of the room opened up the pores of his skin, allowing the oil to penetrate thoroughly; the bather might move between the *sudatorium, caldarium* and *tepidarium* at this stage. After some time, he ordered his slave to scrape the oil (and dirt) from his body with the *strigil*, and then headed for the cold plunge-pool of the *frigidarium*, where the cold water closed the pores of his skin.

248

The hypocaust

A few baths in the Roman world were heated (partially at least) by natural hot springs; the most famous example is the baths at Bath in England. However, in most baths the Romans used a system of artificial heating known as a hypocaust (in Greek, *hypo* = under, *caust* = heating), whereby the floor was raised above the ground by pillars, called *pilae*, and spaces were left inside the walls so that hot air and smoke from a nearby furnace (tended by slaves) could pass through these enclosed areas. The *caldarium* and *sudatorium* would be placed closest to the furnace, since they required the most heat.

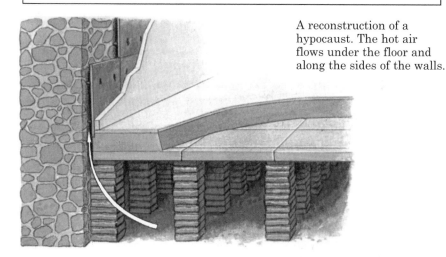

A reconstruction of a hypocaust. The hot air flows under the floor and along the sides of the walls.

The baths of Pompeii and Herculaneum

Pompeii had three large sets of baths (see map on p. 276), and its Stabian Baths give a good outline of how a bath house might have been used. They were the city's earliest baths, dating from the 2nd century BCE, and were located in the centre of the town. One interesting design feature was that they were built with separate facilities for men and women. Men would enter into a large colonnaded *palaestra*, which was bordered on one side by a *natatio*. A similar arrangement of separate facilities for men and women can be seen in the Forum Baths in Herculaneum (see p. 340).

3. The culture of the baths

The baths were part of every day life for free Romans of all classes. Men would work in the morning and then instinctively head for the baths in the early afternoon – the 8th hour seems to have been a popular time (see Appendix 5 for hours of the day). Baths typically opened at midday

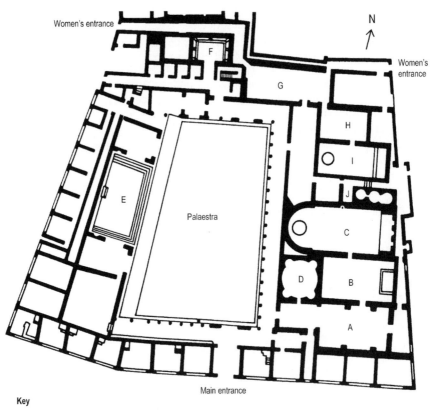

A plan of the Stabian Baths, Pompeii.

Key

A. Men's apodyterium	F. Latrine
B. Men's tepidarium	G. Women's apodyterium
C. Men's caldarium	H. Women's tepidarium
D. Men's frigidarium	I. Women's caldarium
E. Swimming pool	J. Furnace room

and closed at sunset, but presumably one could find bath houses which kept other hours. A bell would ring to signify that the baths were open for business, although the public were often allowed to use the *palaestra* before the baths themselves were available. Once in the complex, many people would stay there for the rest of the afternoon until it was time to go home for dinner.

The baths were also popular with women, but it is unclear exactly when they used the facilities. The earlier bath houses, such as the Stabian Baths, were built with separate sections for men and women. However, by imperial times this was less common, and men and women must either have bathed at different hours (with women presumably bathing in the morning when men were at work), or else there was mixed bathing. In truth, both practices were probably common at different times and in different places. However, by the early 2nd century CE mixed bathing had clearly become popular, since a series of scandals forced the emperor Hadrian to pass a decree banning men and women from bathing together!

It seems that in a large city like Rome different bath houses went in and out of fashion. According to Seneca, a popular bath house would soon lose its regulars whenever a newer complex with more impressive facilities opened up, while the 4th-century CE historian Ammianus Marcellinus tells us that it was common in his day to make polite conversation with a stranger by asking him which set of baths he used. Some writers could be damning in their views about respective baths; the satirist Martial (*Epigrams* 6.42) comments to his friend: 'if you don't bathe in the little *thermae* of Etruscus, Oppianus, you'll die unwashed!'

Seneca and the baths

One of the most famous descriptions of a bath house in full swing is given by Seneca in a letter to his friend Lucilius, while he was living above a bath house in the resort town of Baiae in the Bay of Naples. Seneca's first complaints focus on the bathers themselves:

'Here, from every direction, I hear sounds of every kind: I live right above the public bath. Now imagine all sorts of sounds that can make us hate our ears: when the strongest men exercise and shake their hands while holding large lead balls, or exert themselves or pretend to, I hear their sighs when they exhale, and their hisses and unpleasant respiration. When some lazy person is happily being oiled in the most common way, I hear the sound of the hand that hits his shoulders, different when the hand is opened or closed. Now, if a ball player comes and starts counting points, it's the end.'

He then goes on to moan about some of the other characters usually present, including the 'depilator' whose job it was to pluck hairs from bathers:

'Now add a troublemaker, and a thief caught in the act, and to that a person who enjoys hearing himself in the pool. Add those who jump in the pools, splashing. Besides these, whose voices are, at least, all the same tone, think about the depilator who speaks with a hollow and shrill voice so that it can easily be heard; and he is quiet only when he rips the hair from under the arms, forcing another to scream instead of himself. Think about the different screams of people who sell drinks, and those who sell sausages and pastries, and all the tavern owners who recommend their own products with a particular tone of voice.'

Seneca, *Letters* 56.1-2

Seneca's portrayal of the variety of life in the baths is confirmed by other sources. It seems that bathers with irritating habits such as singing in the bath were a common phenomenon. For example, we hear from Martial of a certain Fabianus, who used to go round making fun of bathers with hernias (although he got his comeuppance when he ended up with a hernia of his own!).

Seneca also mentions a thief, and they seem to have been as much a part of the baths as the bathing rooms themselves! Masters often brought slaves with them to keep watch over their valuables, while in some baths a public slave was even appointed to watch the *apodyterium*. However, these measures don't always seem to have been effective. In the baths of Aquae Sulis (modern Bath) in Britain, numerous curse tablets have been found asking the gods (and particularly Minerva, the patron goddess of the site) to avenge thefts; the following is a good example:

> 'Solinus to the goddess Minerva: I give to your divinity and majesty my bathing cloak and tunic. Do not allow sleep or health to him who has done me wrong, whether man or woman, whether slave or free, unless he reveals himself and brings these goods to the temple.' *Tab. Sulis* 32

Regrettably, we have no record of whether Solinus ever did recover his clothes, or indeed if the curse worked!

Another feature of Seneca's description is the food and drink on offer, and evidence from Pompeii and Herculaneum suggests that bars and taverns were commonly found in and near the baths. Many people would have taken a lunchtime snack while bathing; in Herculaneum a graffito on the wall of a bar near the entrance to the Suburban baths gives an idea of what was on offer (all the prices are in asses): 'Nuts, drinks: 14; hog's fat: 2, bread: 3; cutlets, for three: 12; sausage, for four: 8.' Elsewhere, we hear stories of men who used to get drunk at the baths, although most authors seem to disapprove of this. Nevertheless, the epitaph of a certain Titus Claudius Secundus famously celebrates the pleasures of life as follows:

> 'Baths, wine, and women ruin our bodies, but these things make life itself.' *CLE* 1499

It seems likely that – as here – some Romans put all three of these things together, and there is evidence that the baths could also have a seedier side; for example, a number of erotic frescoes have been discovered in the *apodyterium* of the Suburban Baths in Pompeii, while other sources record the presence of prostitutes at or near bath houses. However, we should be careful not to conclude that baths were a hotbed of sexual activity – it is clear from the sources that the primary purpose of the baths was to wash, exercise and socialise, and most people went solely for these reasons.

A dinner invitation

It seems that the baths were also seen by some as an opportunity to latch onto their social superiors, hoping to get an invitation to dinner (a dinner party would normally begin in the late afternoon – see p. 155). The satirist Martial grumbles about one such character:

> 'Whether you are in the hot room or anywhere else in the bath building, there is no way to escape from Menogenes, although you may try with all your might ... He will pick up from the dust and hand back to you the flabby inflatable ball, even if he has already bathed and has already put on his sandals. When you pick up your towel which is dirtier than a child's bib, he will exclaim that it is whiter than snow. While you are combing your hair, he will say that you are styling Achilles' locks. He will carry over to you a smoky jug of wine and wipe the sweat from your brow. He will praise everything, he will marvel at everything, until finally, having endured his thousand tedious ploys, you say, "Come and have dinner with me."'   Martial, *Epigrams* 12.82

Despite Martial's sneering attitude in this passage, he writes elsewhere of trying to procure a dinner invitation for himself, commenting that 'it is little consolation to bathe in luxury and perish in starvation'.

Review 4

1. Define the following parts of a Roman bath house: *apodyterium, caldarium, frigidarium, hypocaust, palaestra, sudatorium, tepidarium.*

2. In what ways can the Roman baths be compared to modern sports centres, spas, or Turkish baths?

3. Why do you think that baths were such a fundamental aspect of Roman society?

4. How sympathetic are you to Seneca's complaints about the baths?

E. Imagine you spend an afternoon visiting the baths. Describe everything which you see and experience.

5

Pompeii

It is a great paradox that the tragedy which struck Pompeii in 79 CE has proved such a blessing for the modern world. The city which, together with Herculaneum, was destroyed by a cataclysmic volcanic eruption, now presents for historians, students and tourists alike a treasury of information about Roman life. Indeed, had the city not been rediscovered, our knowledge of the Roman world would be infinitely poorer. Above all, the story of Pompeii is a very human one, giving us extraordinary insights into the lives – and deaths – of many ordinary people who lived during the high point of the Roman empire.

Frozen in time?

It has often been said that Pompeii is a time-capsule, capturing a moment of everyday life 'frozen in time'. However, this is not really the case. While there are certainly signs of daily life stopped in its tracks – such as the 81 loaves of bread found in a bakery oven, or the meal of fish and eggs left on a table in the Temple of Isis – there are a number of reasons why we should not think that the remains of Pompeii reflect a moment in everyday life with complete accuracy.

First, most of the city's population managed to escape from the eruption, taking many household valuables with them; secondly, the eruption itself did enormous damage, including destroying all the upper floors of buildings; thirdly, most of the organic materials – such as wooden furniture, foodstuffs and clothes – have perished; and finally, there is considerable evidence for tunnelling and looting of the site in the years after the eruption, as treasure hunters came to remove what they could for profit. Therefore, while Pompeii gives a remarkably vivid insight into life in the Roman world, we should be careful not to think of it as a city perfectly reflecting everyday life.

---

1. Location and history

It is not hard to see why Pompeii was such an attractive site for a settlement. The region of Campania was blessed with flood plains and natural harbours, and the fertility and beauty of the region were well known in ancient times. Pliny the Elder, who died during the eruption of Vesuvius in 79 CE, once described the region as 'one of the loveliest places on earth', while Florus, a well-travelled historian writing early in the following century, made this judgement:

'Of everything not just in Italy, but in the whole world, the region of Campania is the most beautiful. Nothing is more temperate than its climate: indeed, it has spring and its flowers twice a year. Nothing is more fertile than its land: consequently there is said to be a competition between Liber and Ceres. Nothing is more welcoming than its sea ... Here are the mountains that befriend the vine ...'   Florus, *Epitome* 1.16

Liber and Ceres were the deities of wine and food-produce respectively (see pp. 78 and 75), and the land around Vesuvius was indeed especially fertile owing to its volcanic soil. Fields beneath the mountain were capable of producing three or four crops per year and ancient writers tell us that spelt, wheat and millet were popular, as well as fruit and vegetables. Moreover, the slopes of the mountain provided orchards for olives and grapes; many varieties of wine were produced, some of high quality, others less so. The region was also famous for the perfume made from the roses which grew there.

There were a number of cities around Vesuvius, all of which

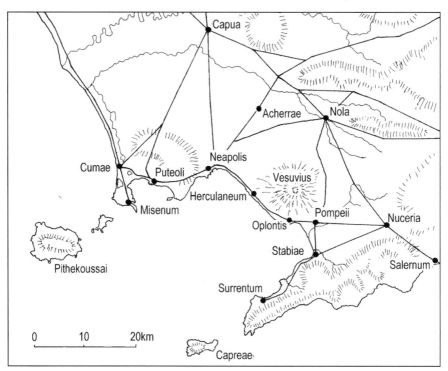

A map of the Bay of Naples showing the road network which joined the key settlements.

benefited from the natural resources of the area; they were joined by a good network of roads. Pompeii in particular benefited from its proximity to water: not only was it close enough to the sea to have its own harbour, but a river, the Sarno, also ran inland past the southern end of the city (the eruption of 79 changed the landscape to such an extent that the Sarno today flows much further to the south, while the city is much further from the sea). The Pompeians were able to control the trade up and down the river – the geographer Strabo (*c.* 64 BCE-*c.* 24 CE) tells us that:

> 'Nola, Nuceria and Acherrae have as their port Pompeii on the river Sarno, which transports goods in both directions.'
>
> Strabo, *Geography* 5.4.8

With all these natural advantages, it is no surprise that Pompeii developed into a busy and flourishing city, which benefited both from the local natural resources and from the ready access to trade routes both locally and across the Mediterranean.

An ancient view of Vesuvius

Vesuvius had not erupted for many centuries before 79 CE, and the people who lived in its shadow had no idea of its lethal threat. In fact, they seem to have felt blessed by the mountain, if we are to believe the evidence of a famous wall painting found in the House of the Centenary (see p. 258). This depicts Bacchus, the god of wine, standing by a mountain (presumably Vesuvius); all around there are symbols of fertility – grapes, a wild animal, birds, a snake, and plants growing abundantly. If this painting is anything to go by, the Pompeians seem to have associated the mountain with their god of prosperity and festivity, and were thankful for its gifts. Little did they know what awaited them.

Pompeii did not start its life as a Roman city. In fact, while a walled site existed from the 6th century BCE, it was not until 89 BCE that it came to be fully under the control of Rome. Ironically, however, the nature of Pompeii's survival makes it hard for us to know about its long history in detail – the remains of 79 CE have been considered so important that archaeologists have generally been reluctant to damage them by digging down further. Nevertheless, there are enough literary and archaeological sources for us to piece together something of Pompeii's past.

Early Pompeii

Historians have often looked to another quotation from Strabo to explain which peoples had inhabited both Pompeii and Herculaneum in early times:

The wall painting of Bacchus and Vesuvius from the House of the Centenary.

'The Oscans used to occupy both Herculaneum and Pompeii next to it, past which the River Sarno flows. Next came the Etruscans and the Pelasgians, and after that the Samnites; these peoples were also thrown out of these places.'   Strabo, *Geography* 5.4.8

Most scholars now doubt the order which Strabo gives here, although it is clear that Pompeii in its earliest days was influenced by three groups: the local Italian people, who spoke Oscan (the regional tongue and a cousin language to Latin); the Etruscans, who were the dominant power in central Italy in the 7th and 6th centuries BCE (see p. 13); and the Greeks (here called 'Pelasgians'), who set up colonies on much of the coastline of southern Italy and Sicily (see p. 22); they first moved into the Bay of Naples in the 8th century, founding a trading post on the island of Pithekoussai (later called Ischia), and two cities at the northern end of the bay: Cumae and Neapolis.

There may have been a small settlement on the site of Pompeii from the 8th century, though perhaps only a little village. The first evidence of a real 'city' dates to the first half of the 6th century, when the first walls were built – these marked out the limits beyond which Pompeii never grew. It is impossible to know whether at this time it was a Greek, Etruscan or local Italian settlement, or even a mixture, since the archaeology suggests influences of all three cultures.

It is also unclear what the settlement was like at this stage. Most agree that the focal point was the network of streets in the south-west corner which is sometimes known as the 'Old City'. There was also plenty of farming within the walls, mainly on smallholdings (in fact, there was still some farming within the walls in 79 CE), but it is not clear how developed the street and building patterns were before the 3rd century BCE.

Pompeii – what's in a name?

No one knows for certain where the name 'Pompeii' comes from. One theory is that it derives from the Greek word *pompa*, 'procession', and that the city was founded by Greeks in a grand religious procession; a variation of this idea has the Greek hero Heracles founding the city while processing back from Spain after his tenth labour (see p. 326). On the other hand, some historians have tried to link it to the Oscan word for 'five', *pumpe*, suggesting that the city was formed out of five early villages. Unless we find out much more about the early history of the city, the origin of its name is likely to remain a mystery.

Samnites and Romans

Strabo goes on to say that the 'Samnites' followed these three peoples, and this seems correct. The Samnites (whose native language was also Oscan) were tough peoples from the mountains inland who came down into the plains of Campania in the 5th century to win better land for themselves. By the end of the century they had become masters of the whole region, including Pompeii. The archaeological evidence from the 5th and 4th centuries is sparse, and it seems that Pompeii suffered a decline in trade and population.

However, towards the end of the 4th century, a new people from central Italy were starting to make their presence felt – the Romans. Now a growing power, they engaged in a series of wars with the Samnites, which they won by 290 BCE (see p. 21). Pompeii and the other cities of the region were absorbed into the Roman empire at this point, and given the status of 'allies'. This allowed them to keep power over their own local affairs, but they had to supply forces for the Roman army and follow Rome's foreign policy.

The next two centuries saw significant growth for Pompeii. The city remained loyal to Rome during the Punic wars against the

The outside city wall near the Herculaneum Gate still shows damage from the siege by Sulla's forces.

Carthaginians in the late 3rd century (see p. 24), and even seems to have prospered from the ship building industry which grew up in the Bay of Naples. Within the city, there is evidence of Roman influence, most notably in major building projects such as the Stabian Baths. Moreover, some of the most imposing houses in the city, such as the House of the Faun (see pp. 309-12), were first built in this era.

A Roman colony

In 91 BCE, many allied cities in southern Italy joined together in revolt against Rome to demand full Roman citizenship (see p. 35). Pompeii abandoned its traditional loyalty to Rome to side with the rebels in this 'Social War'. In 89, the city was besieged and bombarded by the Roman general Sulla – Oscan graffiti can still be seen in the city giving directions to locals defending the walls. However, Pompeii soon capitulated; it was fortunate not to be pillaged, as Herculaneum was.

Although Rome defeated the rebellious allies, it had little choice but to award their peoples citizenship in order to ensure long term stability in Italy. Nonetheless, the Roman state took its revenge on the Pompeians in 80 BCE by turning their city into a full Roman colony, settling at least 2,000 of Sulla's veteran Roman soldiers there, together with their families. This was a sizeable group for a city whose population perhaps numbered only around 10,000 beforehand, and records suggest that the new colonists occupied all the key political posts in the years that followed. There must have been much tension between the old and the new Pompeians.

The new status of colony brought a number of changes to the character of the city, including a new name: *Colonia Cornelia Veneria Pompeianorum* ('The Cornelian Colony of Pompeii, under the divine protection of Venus'); the words *Cornelia* and *Veneria* are both linked to Sulla: Cornelius was his family name, while Venus, who now became the protective goddess of the colony, was Sulla's patron goddess. Other key changes were as follows:

- **Language**. Latin replaced Oscan as the official language.
- **Politics**. Pompeii's political structure (described on p. 296) was changed to mirror that of Rome itself.
- **Construction**. Major new buildings were constructed, including the amphitheatre, the Forum Baths, and the covered theatre.

Despite this social upheaval, it seems that within two generations the old and the new leading families were mixing and inter-marrying. The city remained relatively unaffected by the civil wars which were played out during the middle of the 1st century; moreover, when Augustus became Rome's first emperor in 31 BCE, Pompeii benefited, like the rest of Italy, from the peace which followed: the city's walls were no longer needed for defence, and many buildings began to grow up on them; in addition, a new aqueduct was built to serve the region of the Bay of Naples, radically improving the city's water supply (see p. 280).

The city also seems to have flourished economically owing to the safe trade routes criss-crossing the Mediterranean: material excavated from the site indicates that wine was imported from as far afield as Sicily, Greece, Turkey and the Middle East, while olive oil came from Libya and Spain, and high quality pottery from France, Cyprus and northern Italy.

The earthquake
Pompeii therefore entered the 1st century CE as a city prospering from the Roman empire. We hear little about it in the historical records until 59 CE, when there was a riot in the amphitheatre (see p. 287). Four years later, in February 63 (according to Seneca the Younger, although the historian Tacitus dates it to the previous year), the whole region was hit by a terrible earthquake, described as follows by Seneca:

'We have heard, my dear Lucilius, that Pompeii, a busy town in Campania, has subsided under an earthquake ... This tremor was on 5th February in the consulship of Regulus and Verginius, and it inflicted great devastation on Campania, a region never safe from this evil, yet which has remained undamaged and has so often got off with a fright. For part of the town of Herculaneum too fell down and even the

261

structures that remain are unstable, and the colony of Nuceria, though it escaped disaster, nevertheless is not without complaint. Naples too lost many private buildings, but no public ones, being stricken lightly by the great disaster; even villas have collapsed, everywhere things shook without damage.'   Seneca, *Natural Questions* 6.1.1-3

We can know for certain that Seneca wrote this account soon after the event, since he himself died in 65. It is interesting that he chooses to describe the location and character of Pompeii to Lucilius, suggesting that the city was not well known to most Romans.

We can glean further evidence about the earthquake from a number of inscriptions and reliefs found in the town; most famous are the marble reliefs which adorned the *lararium* of the house of Lucius Caecilius Iucundus, whom you can read more about on p. 304. In one of them, the Temple of Jupiter is clearly being shaken to its foundations, while in the other the Vesuvius Gate is shown collapsing. Elsewhere in the city, an inscription which refers to an earthquake (presumably this one) was found over the main entrance to the sanctuary of Isis (see p. 112).

The earthquake did significant physical damage to Pompeii and major reconstruction was required in the years afterwards. Indeed, there are signs that much rebuilding was going on when Vesuvius erupted 17 years later; however, this was probably in response to more recent tremors, which must have hit the city as the volcano came closer to exploding. There is some evidence for these in the ancient sources; both Tacitus and Suetonius relate that in 64 CE a theatre in Naples collapsed in an earthquake as the emperor Nero was performing there; moreover Pliny the Younger, in his description of the eruption (see

The two marble reliefs from the House of Lucius Caecilius Iucundus which depict the earthquake.

below) makes the following comment:

> 'For several days past there had been earth tremors which were not
> particularly alarming because they are common in Campania.'
>
> Pliny the Younger, *Letters* 6.20.3

The people of Pompeii didn't realise that these earthquakes and tremors
were a warning sign, representing as they did an abortive attempt by
Vesuvius to blast out an open vent. In their ignorance, however,
Pompeians carried on with their lives just as they always had.

Review 1

1. What evidence is there for the way in which the Pompeians viewed the
history and geography of their city?

2. How important was Pompeii's location in its development into a
prosperous city?

3. Draw a timeline for the history of Pompeii.

R. Read Seneca's account of the earthquake (*Natural Questions* 6.1.1-3,
10). What can we learn about the event from this passage?

E. Imagine you come from a traditional Pompeian family and have seen
Sulla's army veterans settle in the city in 80. What do you feel about these
newcomers and how they are affecting the city?

---

2. The eruption

In 79 CE Vesuvius exploded back into life after centuries of dormancy.
The traditional date given for this eruption has been 24 August,
although most scholars now think that it must have happened later in
the year (see box on p. 264). What is not in doubt is that in the days,
weeks, and even months beforehand, there had been warning signs of
what was to come: as well as the earth tremors mentioned by Pliny,
wells dried up and springs stopped flowing; rumblings were heard in the
mountains and animals behaved strangely. Yet no one seems to have
realised what lay in store.

The two Plinys
The volcanic eruption of Vesuvius in 79 was the first ever to be recorded
in writing by an eyewitness – Pliny the Younger (62-113 CE). Aged just
17, he was staying at Misenum, 30 kilometres (18 miles) west of
Vesuvius, the main port of the Roman fleet in the region, where the
young man's uncle, Pliny the Elder (23-79 CE), was the fleet's
commander. The Plinys were a remarkable pair: the uncle, as well as
being an admiral in the navy, was a great scholar who wrote an

---

The date of the eruption

It has long been popular belief that Vesuvius erupted on 24 August 79 CE. The latest evidence, however, suggests that this cannot have been so. The date is taken from a medieval manuscript version of Pliny's first letter (see below); yet numerous manuscripts were copied and transmitted by monks, and no fewer than twelve dates were given for the eruption, the latest of which is 23 November 79. Archaeological evidence can be presented to support an eruption in either the summer or the late autumn.

However, a recent study of a hoard of coins found in the House of the Golden Bracelet seems to have ruled out August altogether. On one side of a silver denarius an inscription lists the titles of the emperor Titus, including 'acclaimed emperor for the 15th time' (he was 'acclaimed emperor' alongside his father Vespasian when he was still only the heir to the emperorship). Other epigraphic evidence shows that Titus had not yet been acclaimed emperor for the 15th time on 8 September 79, and so it seems that the eruption must have taken place after this date. This just goes to show that we are constantly revising our understanding of Pompeii's past, and it is exciting to think that this process will continue as time moves on.

---

encyclopaedia of the natural world in 37 books, which survive for us to read today; for his part, the nephew went on to become a Roman governor, and his volumes of letters have proved to be a valuable historical resource for later generations.

About 27 years after the event, at the request of the Roman historian Tacitus, Pliny the Younger wrote two letters about the eruption. The first tells of the death of his uncle at Stabiae (see map on p. 256), where he landed after an unsuccessful attempt to rescue people stranded around the bay; in the second letter, Pliny relates his own experiences of the eruption from his vantage point at Misenum. Reading these letters gives an insight into the bravery, panic and horror witnessed during those fateful hours.

The Plinian stage

According to Pliny, the eruption began in the middle of the day with a column of hot gas and pumice bursting into the sky to a height of up to 30 kilometres (20 miles – about three times the height an aeroplane will fly today). Pliny's description of this moment remains famous:

> 'A cloud was rising from (the) mountain ... its appearance could best be described by comparing it to an umbrella pine, for after it was carried up to a very great height as if on a tree-trunk, it began to spread out into various branches.' Pliny the Younger, *Letters* 6.16.5-6

The umbrella pine is still common in the bay of Naples area today, and the analogy makes it easy for us to imagine the sight. However, for a

An umbrella pine.

The eruption
column of Vesuvius
when it last
erupted in March
1944.

long time Pliny's account of its shape was not believed, and it was only in the 20th century that vulcanologists were able to confirm that it does indeed fit a particular type of eruption – one which they now call 'Plinian' in his honour.

At this point, it was Pompeii's misfortune to be downwind of Vesuvius. The cloud plunged the city into darkness, while pumice, ash and rock fragments began to fall, accumulating at a rate of about 15 centimetres per hour. However, these conditions did not prevent people from moving around the city, and it seems that most Pompeians chose to flee at this point – for one thing, very few skeletons of pack animals have been found, while there is also plenty of evidence of people taking belongings and valuables with them. Some Pompeians, however, chose to stay in the city in the hope that the calamity would pass. By evening, roofs were beginning to collapse under the weight of the volcanic deposit, and it must have been progressively more difficult to move through the streets. Those remaining must have faced the same dilemma which Pliny the Elder's party faced later on that night at Stabiae:

> 'By this time the courtyard giving access to his (*i.e. Pliny's*) room was full of ashes mixed with pumice so that its level had risen, and if he had stayed inside any longer he would never have got out. He was woken, came out and joined Pomponianus and the rest of the household, who had sat up all night. They debated whether to stay indoors or take their chance in the open, for the buildings were now shaking with violent shocks and seemed to be swaying to and fro as if they were torn from their foundations. Outside, on the other hand, there was the danger of falling pumice stones, even though they were light and porous; however, after comparing the risks they chose the latter ... As a protection against falling objects they put pillows on their heads, tied down with cloths.'
>
> Pliny the Younger, *Letters* 16.14-16

The Peléan stage

In the early hours of the morning there was a lull in the eruption. At this moment, some Pompeians, believing that the worst was over, tried to make their escape. In fact, it was really an indicator of a new and more awful stage to come. As the volcano lost energy, the eruption column started to collapse, bringing about two linked phenomena, known collectively as *nuées ardentes* ('burning clouds'): ground **surges** of hot gas and volcanic debris, which travel at speeds of between 100 and 300 kilometres per hour and at temperatures ranging between 100 and 400 degrees Celsius. These are swiftly followed by pyroclastic **flows**: dense flows of hot, fragmented volcanic material, lubricated by trapped gas and air; although a flow is slightly less rapid than a surge, it too can heat up to 400 degrees Celsius. This stage of a volcanic eruption is sometimes known as Peléan, after the eruption of Mt Pelée on the

Caribbean island of Martinique in 1902, during which the nearby city of Saint-Pierre was engulfed in a matter of moments, and almost all of its 28,000 inhabitants killed.

There were six *nuées ardentes* in all. The first and second hit the nearby town of Herculaneum in the middle of the night (see p. 329), but Pompeii remained untouched (these first surges might account for the shaking buildings experienced by Pliny's party at Stabiae). A few hours later, at about 6.30 a.m., the third reached and knocked down parts of Pompeii's northern wall, but the city itself remained standing. However, its luck ran out within an hour, when it was enveloped by the last three *nuées ardentes*; the sixth was particularly severe, covering the entire site and destroying the walls of the tallest buildings. The northern end of the city was buried 1.8 metres underground; in the south, the depth was only 60 centimetres and it is possible that some structures were still partially visible.

The eruption by numbers

It is difficult to imagine just how massive was the force of nature unleashed by Vesuvius in 79 CE, but these statistics might help you try: it is estimated that the initial eruption sent ash, rock and pumice stone (known collectively as tephra) into the air at a speed of 1,400 kilometres per hour, breaking the sound barrier and reaching a height of up to 30 kilometres. At this point, the volcano was sending out tephra at a rate of 150,000 tonnes per second, although this went up to 180,000 tonnes per second during the night. Perhaps most astonishingly, based on a comparison with the eruption of Mt St Helens in the USA in 1980, the size of the initial explosion has been likened to that of a ten-megaton bomb – 500 times greater than the atomic bomb which was dropped on Hiroshima in 1945.

The aftermath

The historian Suetonius tells us that in the aftermath of the eruption Titus, who had been emperor for only a few months, rushed to the Bay of Naples to organise the relief effort. A relief fund was set up and the property of those who had died without making a will was immediately donated to it. Survivors moved to nearby cities such as Nola, Naples and Capua, which were given special privileges to help resettle the survivors.

In the days and weeks after the eruption, it seems that some people tried to dig down into the buried site of Pompeii to retrieve valuables. Some of these were almost certainly looters, who were looking to make a quick profit from any valuables they could find. Soon, however, the site became overgrown and forgotten. Pompeii became a city buried in the past.

The victims

About 1,150 bodies have so far been found in the ruins of Pompeii (394 in the pumice level, 653 in the ash level, and about 100 bodies whose find-spots and condition were not documented). Even allowing for the unexcavated areas of the city, this number is not a high percentage of the city's population, which may have been around the 10,000 mark, or even more. It seems therefore that most did manage to get out of the city in the hours after the volcano exploded.

Most of those who remained had probably chosen to do so. Of the 394 bodies discovered in the pumice level, 345 were found sheltering inside buildings, the other 49 in outdoor locations. In most cases, we can only speculate at how they died: those inside were probably crushed under falling roofs, or sealed in rooms by the rising levels of ash and pumice; those outside may have been trampled to death in the crowded streets, killed by collapsing buildings, or even struck by large rocks falling from the sky. Even if people did manage to get out of the city, they were still far from safe: 48 bodies have been found near the Sarno river, and many more are likely to lie undiscovered in the area outside Pompeii. More still no doubt drowned trying to escape over the choppy sea.

Of the 653 bodies found at the levels of the *nuées ardentes*, most have been discovered in the layer between the fourth and the fifth surges; the latest research suggests that they died instantly of thermal shock from exposure to temperatures of more than 250 degrees Celsius. 319 of the 653 were discovered in outdoor areas; after the third surge, these people must have decided that they had no choice but to make a break for it. Archaeologists have been able to piece together the tragic last moments of some of the victims, as one modern scholar does here:

> 'One group of four, found in a street near the forum, was probably an entire family trying to make its escape. The father went in front, a burly man, with big bushy eyebrows (as the plaster cast reveals). He had pulled his cloak over his head, to protect himself from falling ash and debris, and carried with him some gold jewellery (a simple finger-ring and a few ear-rings), a couple of keys and, in this case, a reasonable amount of cash, at almost 400 sesterces (*see Appendix 3*). His two small daughters followed, while the mother brought up the rear. She had hitched up her dress to make the walking easier, and was carrying more household valuables in a little bag.' Mary Beard, *Pompeii*, pp. 4-5

Personal details such as these allow us to reflect on events from the family's perspective. Why had they waited so long before trying to escape? Were they worried that their daughters would not cope with the journey? Were the keys a sign that they held out some hope of returning? Where were they planning to go when they left the city?

The bodies in the Garden of the Fugitives.

This is just one poignant story for us to ponder among many. Others include the following:

- A group of 13 men, women and children whose bodies were discovered at the southern end of the city in a market garden. They were clearly trying to escape from the city, and so the garden is now known as the **Garden of the Fugitives**.
- In the house of Julius Polybius were found the remains of 12 people (six adults and six children), assumed to be the owner, his family and his slaves. One of the women, a girl in her late teens, was nine months pregnant (the bones of her foetus were also recovered). Perhaps the whole family had chosen to stay because of her heavy pregnancy.
- The bodies of a number of priests of Isis have been found in the triangular forum, crushed under falling columns.
- In one large house, a dog was left tethered in the *atrium*. As the ash and pumice level rose, it twisted and pulled on the chain to try to get itself free, but was eventually buried alive.

Perhaps the final word about the experience of escaping the disaster zone belongs to Pliny the Younger. Misenum itself was hit by the outer

The plaster cast of a dog trapped in the eruption. The outline of its collar can still be seen.

edge of the final surge, although fortunately it had lost its power and heat at that point and left only a thick deposit of ash. Nonetheless, it must have been terrifying for the inhabitants, and Pliny vividly describes the scene as people fled the city:

'You could hear women screaming, babies wailing, men shouting: some were calling out for their parents, others for their children, others for their wives or husbands, and trying to recognise their voices; some lamented their own misfortune, others that of their relatives; there were some who in their fear of dying prayed for death; many raised their hands to the gods; more still concluded that there were no gods and that this was the world's final and everlasting night.'

Pliny the Younger, *Letters* 6.20.14-15

Review 2

1. Define the following terms: *nuées ardentes, Plinian eruption, tephra.*

2. Find out about the eruptions of Mt Pelée in 1902 and Mt St Helens in 1980. How can they help us understand the eruption of Vesuvius in 79?

3. Draw up a chart listing the timetable of events during the eruption of Vesuvius, and including the story of Pliny the Elder.

R. Read the two letters of Pliny the Younger (6.16 and 6.20). What can we learn about both the nature of the eruption itself and the behaviour of people affected?

E. Imagine you are in Pompeii when Vesuvius erupts. Describe what you see and what you decide to do.

---

3. Rediscovery

i. Early excavations

The site of Pompeii was not brought to light again until the middle of the 18th century, although there were one or two near misses before then. For example, in 1592, an architect called Domenico Fontana was excavating a canal through the raised fields north of the River Sarno. The diggers came across some ancient ruins, but buried them without investigating further. Nearly a century later, in 1689, an inscription with the word *Pompei* was found in the same area by workmen digging a well; however, it was decided that this referred to the Roman general Pompey (see p. 35), and so the site was once again ignored.

In the early 18th century, there was great interest in the newly discovered site of Herculaneum (see p. 331), which intensified when the Bourbon royal family from Spain took control of Naples and Sicily in 1734. The new King, Charles VIII, was keen to fund the excavations, but merely for selfish reasons – he wanted any treasure found from the site to be removed for his own private collection. To take charge of operations, he appointed a military engineer and mining expert called Rocque Joaquin de Alcubierre, who had little experience of archaeology. In 1748, trial digs were made for the first time at the site of Pompeii.

All in all, Alcubierre was a disaster for Pompeii. He was not interested in preserving the site, but simply in looting it of treasure for his paymaster. Many of the works of art which he removed have been lost forever; in addition, when digging in the site, he knocked down walls carelessly, often destroying frescoes in the process. Further long-term damage was done to the buildings by the way in which they were filled in again – this was often done poorly, so that they were susceptible to damage from sunlight and damp. One strident critic of Alcubierre was the 18th-century art historian Johann Joachim Winckelmann, who summed up his efforts as follows:

'The incompetence of this man, who had as much to do with antiquity as the moon does with prawns, as the Italian proverb goes, has caused the loss of many beautiful things.'
Sendschreiben von den Herculanischen Entdeckungen

Fortunately, in 1750, a Swiss architect, Karl Weber, was appointed as Alcubierre's deputy. Although he had a strained relationship with his boss, he brought important innovations to the process, especially by trying to excavate the site systematically and to keep written records, including plans, maps and a list of artefacts. In 1763, an inscription was found which read *reipublicae Pompeianorum* ('to the community of the

This 18th-century drawing shows the transportation into Naples of ancient artefacts from Pompeii and Herculaneum.

Pompeians'), and at last it was known for certain that the buried city was indeed Pompeii.

Inconsistent progress was made over the following century; between 1801 and 1815, the site benefited from being under the control of Napoleonic France; Napoleon's sister, Caroline, became joint ruler of Naples, and invested heavily in the excavations from her own personal income. However, after the Bourbons regained control of the region in 1815, funding dried up again. It was not until Italy was unified as a country in 1860 that Pompeii was to get the attention it deserved.

Naming the ruins

The names used today for places in Pompeii do not date back to ancient times. As we do not know what the Pompeians called places in the city, archaeologists have made up their own names. In many cases, houses are named after a piece of art found there (e.g. the House of the Faun, after the dancing faun found in its *atrium*); in other instances, a house was called after the person or people supposed to have lived there (e.g. the House of the Vettii, after the two Vettii brothers) or after something related to the owners (e.g. a set of surgical instruments were found in the House of the Surgeon).

The same principle was used to name many public areas of the city. The main shopping street, the *Via dell'Abbondanza* ('the Street of Abundance') took its name from a fountain-head of one of its fountains, labelled *Abundantia* in Latin, while the gates were generally named after the places to which they led (e.g. the Herculaneum gate, the Sarno gate, etc.).

---

ii. Giuseppe Fiorelli

In 1860, the various regions of Italy were unified into one nation for the first time since the fall of the Roman empire. Italy's new leader, Garibaldi, wanted Pompeii to be a showcase for the new country, and to provide a direct link back to its famous past. In 1863, he appointed as the director of the excavations Giuseppe Fiorelli, a man who was to have a profound effect on the site and who remains Pompeii's most famous archaeologist. Fiorelli immediately made many important improvements to the archaeological processes at the site:

- **Digging**. He insisted that excavations were always done from above, so that excavators no longer dug sideways through walls. He also cleared away the mounds of waste which were littered around and built roofs over the excavated buildings in order to protect them from the sun and rain.
- **Recording**. To make record-keeping easier, he introduced a system of triple-numbering; the site was divided into nine regions, each of which was sub-divided into blocks (*insulae*); each individual building within an *insula* was then numbered. For example, the house of Menander is listed as I.10.4 (region I, *insula* 10, entrance 4).
- **Artefacts**. Items could no longer be removed for private collections; where possible, they were either left in situ; otherwise, they were taken to the Naples Archaeological Museum, while replicas were left in their place.
- **Funding**. He opened the site to the general public for the first time, and introduced an entrance fee which paid for caretakers.

Fiorelli's numbering system is still evident in Pompeii with signposts such as this.

A man seems to cover his face as he waits for death.

However, Fiorelli's most famous contribution to the site was his idea of the plaster casts: the way in which they were created became known as 'Fiorelli's Process'. He realised that dead bodies had been sealed in volcanic ash by the eruption. In time, these bodies rotted but cavities were left behind. Whenever a cavity was found, Fiorelli had plaster of Paris poured in and left it to set. Once it was dry, excavators could chip away around the plaster, which would reveal an exact replica of the person in the moment of death.

This discovery gave detailed information about how people died in the eruption and what they were doing in their last moments. The process could be used for any organic material which rotted to leave a cavity; as well as animals, it has been used to get replicas of wooden

The skull and teeth of this man remain as part of the plaster cast.

shutters, doors, furniture, and even root cavities to find out what plants the Pompeians grew in their gardens.

iii. Modern Pompeii

The excavation of the site continued throughout the 20th century, although there have been times of difficulty, such as during World War II (see box), the eruption of Vesuvius in 1944, and a major earthquake in 1980 which caused serious damage. As yet, about a third of the city lies unexcavated. However, the priority is to safeguard what has been brought to light – as recently as 2010, there was great publicity given to the partial collapse of two excavated houses in the site – the House of the Gladiators and the House of the Moralist.

World War II

In August and September 1943, Pompeii found itself in the middle of a war zone for the first time since 89 BCE; the allies dropped more than 150 bombs on the site, believing (incorrectly) that German soldiers were hiding in the ruins. Some key buildings in the city were hit, including the temples of Jupiter and Apollo, the gladiators' barracks, the amphitheatre, and the House of the Faun.

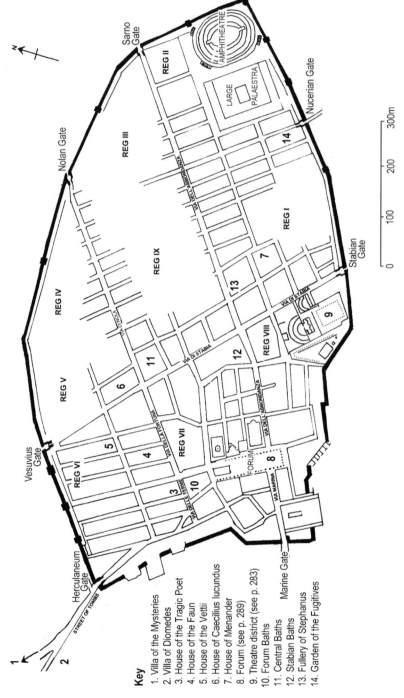

Map of Pompeii.

Key

1. Villa of the Mysteries
2. Villa of Diomedes
3. House of the Tragic Poet
4. House of the Faun
5. House of the Vettii
6. House of Caecilius Iucundus
7. House of Menander
8. Forum (see p. 289)
9. Theatre district (see p. 283)
10. Forum Baths
11. Central Baths
12. Stabian Baths
13. Fullery of Stephanus
14. Garden of the Fugitives

There are over 15,000 buildings to maintain, and more than 20,000m² of wall paintings to preserve, all of which is very expensive. One of the major threats to the site today is its popularity – more than two million visitors come each year, posing serious danger to its conservation. As a result, only about 30% of the site is fully open to the public, and unless more funding is found in the future, there may come a time when it has to be closed to general visitors. As if this is not enough cause for concern, there is also the significant threat that Vesuvius will erupt again at some point in the coming decades.

Review 3

1. Archaeologists have a saying that 'to dig is to destroy'. What do you think this means? What have been the negative consequences for Pompeii of its excavation?
2. Why is Fiorelli's process so important for our understanding of Pompeii?
3. Construct a set of arguments for and against the excavation of the untouched areas of Pompeii. Which do you think are stronger?
E. 'The site of Pompeii should be closed to the public in order to preserve its wonders for future generations'. Do you agree?

---

4. Layout

Pompeii was well designed, with gates and main roads leading to the key areas in and outside the city. Within the walls, the civic centre was the forum in the south-west, while there were also entertainment areas to the south (the 'theatre district') and the south-east (the amphitheatre and large *palaestra*). The layout of the city can be seen on the map opposite.

i. The gates

Seven gates were located strategically at different points around the city. Each one connected to key places in the surrounding region: the Sarno and Marine Gates led to the river and harbour respectively; the Vesuvius Gate to the farmland beneath the mountain; the names of the others – Herculaneum, Nolan, Nucerian, and Stabian – all indicate the cities to which roads led. Pompeii was therefore easily accessible for the many traders and travellers who came and went. Two of the gates, the Herculaneum and the Marine, were designed with separate entrances for vehicles and for pedestrians.

The cemeteries of Pompeii lay just outside the city (in common with burial practice throughout the Roman world – see p. 188), usually along the roads leading out from the gates. The most elaborate series of tombs

The outside of the Marine Gate, which had separate entrances for pedestrians and vehicles.

Some of the tombs along the Street of the Tombs.

is found just beyond the Herculaneum Gate, so that the road has been named the 'Street of the Tombs'. These tombs were usually built for the families of the wealthy, and their inscriptions can tell us a great deal about the lives of those buried there.

ii. The streets

Apart from the south-west corner, Pompeii's streets were laid out on a grid system; this made it easy for visitors to find their way around, and also allowed the maximum number of buildings to be fitted into a confined space. There were three key 'artery roads'; two are on the east-west axis (a Roman street on this axis was known as a *decumanus*) – the *Via dell'Abbondanza* (becoming the *Via Marina* to the west of the forum) and the *Via di Nola* (becoming the *Via della Fortuna* and then the *Via delle Terme* as its heads west); the other artery road is on the north-south axis (a Roman street on this axis was known as a *cardo*) – the *Via di Stabiana* (becoming the *Via Vesuvio* to the north). The *Via dell'Abbondanza* was the city's main shopping street, with numerous bars, inns, and other small shops.

The streets themselves were mostly straight and paved with blocks

Stepping stones across a Pompeian street. The ruts made by cart wheels passing between the stones are still clearly visible.

of basalt (volcanic rock). They were slightly elevated in the middle so that any water would run to the edges, while on either side were high pavements. This design was essential since the streets also acted as the city's sewers – many people just dumped their waste into them. So that people could cross the road without getting dirty, stepping stones were placed at points along the road. These were spaced so as to allow carts to pass with their wheels fitting between them (the ruts caused by these carts are still visible today). It is likely that some sort of one-way system was in force in many of the smaller streets, which were too narrow for carts to pass one another.

The pavements were typically bordered by high walls. On main streets, walls often had colourful facades, painted in reds, yellows or blues, and the wall space could be used in various ways: for electoral slogans, for marking out religious shrines, and even for painting good luck symbols such as phalluses; some people put up 'for rent' notices, or even just random graffiti, while shops and bars might advertise themselves with distinctive signs (rather like pub signs today), perhaps showing goods on sale or the gods who protected their business.

Graffiti

One feature which brings Pompeii vividly to life is all the graffiti which has survived. Like today, this was often scrawled on walls by 'the man in the street', and could refer to any aspect of everyday life. The following examples give a flavour:

'Virgula to her bloke Tertius: you're a dirty old man.'   *CIL* IV.1826

'Chios, I hope your piles irritate you so they burn like they've never burned before!'   *CIL* IV.1820

'Vilbius Restitutus slept here alone and all the time longed for his Urbana.'   *CIL* IV.2146

'Atimetus got me pregnant.'   *CIL* IV.3117

---

iii. Water supply

For much of Pompeii's history, people relied on wells or rainwater to provide them with water. The former were inefficient since they had to be dug to a great depth, while the water from them tended to contain sulphur. Rainwater offered a cleaner and easier option (when it fell), particularly in *atrium* houses where it could be stored in cisterns which drained off water which fell into the *impluvium* (see p. 130).

However, a great leap forward came towards the end of the 1st

The *castellum aquae*.

century BCE, when Marcus Agrippa (see p. 352), a leading ally of the emperor Augustus, commissioned an aqueduct in the Bay of Naples to supply the fleet at Misenum. This was fed by the springs in the hills inland, and one of its branches led off to Pompeii; it has been estimated that the daily flow of water into the city may have been 6,480,000 litres.

The branch of the aqueduct led to a water storage facility, the *castellum aquae* ('water castle'), which was located at the highest point of Pompeii, just inside the Vesuvius Gate (about 43 metres above modern sea level). Here, the water was filtered and then distributed in the city via one of three ducts, which probably supplied different areas. It has been claimed that the ducts were used to prioritise the water supply – with the public fountains first, followed by public buildings, and then finally private houses. Although the water system does seem to have had this order of priority, there is no evidence that the three ducts were used in this way; moreover, it would have been very complicated to run three parallel supply systems.

Water released from the *castellum aquae* travelled downhill into the city by force of gravity, flowing through a network of lead pipes laid at the edge of roads, just below the surface (in order to make repairs easy). These pipes led to towers dotted throughout the city (14 have been discovered); each one regulated the water pressure by storing water in a lead tank on its top; water was then released to service the local area, and in particular the public fountains. These fountains were a vital resource, since most houses did not have running water; more than 40 have been found, and it is estimated that almost all Pompeians lived within 80 metres of one.

A fountain on a street corner, with a water tower in the background.

Water hygiene

How hygienic was Pompeii's water supply system? In truth, there must have been various health hazards which people had to contend with on a daily basis. First of all, the pipes were made of lead (which the Romans did not realise was poisonous); secondly, they often leaked and the water supply could be contaminated with the dirt and waste washed away in the street; thirdly, the water stored in the *castellum aquae* or the water towers could easily become stagnant and so a breeding ground for disease; finally, the communal nature of the public fountains (used by animals as well as people) meant that bacteria and germs were easily transmitted. In other words, not exactly the ancient equivalent of bottled mineral water!

Baths

The water supply was also vital for the running of the city's bathing complexes (you can read about the bathing process on pp. 241-53). There were three main sets of public baths, although one of these, the Central Baths, was still under construction at the time of the eruption; the oldest set, dating to the 2nd century BCE, were the Stabian Baths (see p. 250); the Forum Baths were built just to the north of the forum in the middle of the 1st century BCE. In addition to these, there were a number of private baths, including the large Suburban Baths located just outside the Marine Gate; moreover, the wealthiest houses had their own small sets of baths.

iv. The theatre district

Pompeii also had its own 'theatre district', centred on two theatres at the southern end of the city. The large theatre, with an estimated capacity of 4,000 in its final form, was first built in the 2nd century BCE when the city was coming under the influence of Hellenistic culture. It was

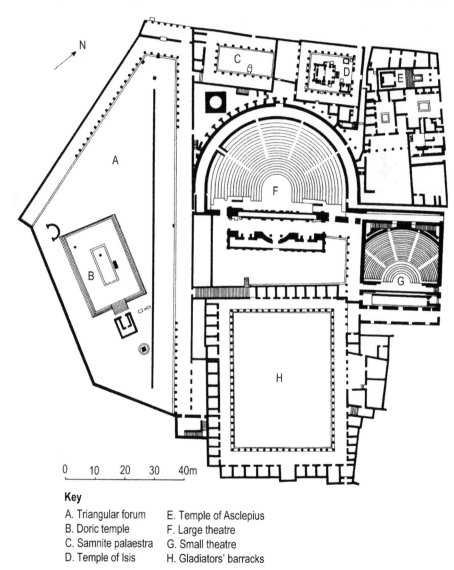

Key

A. Triangular forum
B. Doric temple
C. Samnite palaestra
D. Temple of Isis
E. Temple of Asclepius
F. Large theatre
G. Small theatre
H. Gladiators' barracks

A plan of the theatre district.

The large theatre, with the gladiators' barracks in the background.

extensively modified at the end of the 1st century BCE, when two brothers from a prominent Pompeian family, the Holconii, commissioned a new upper section of seating supported by vaulted passageways. To commemorate their gift to the city, the two had the following inscription set up prominently in two places near the stage:

'Marcus Holconius Rufus and Marcus Holconius Celer (built) at their own expense the crypt, boxes, and theatre seating.' *CIL* X.833, 834

The inscriptions indicate how the wealthy of Pompeii tried to win favour and prestige by paying for public services. These two made absolutely sure that everyone knew about their endowment – both the inscriptions were well over six metres long! Drama was popular in Pompeii, to judge by the many mosaics, paintings, and other works of art – as well as graffiti – found relating to the theatre. However, we have little direct evidence for the type of shows put on; it is likely that they reflected the pattern elsewhere in the Roman world, which you can read about on pp. 223-41.

To the side of the large theatre was the smaller covered theatre (so called since it was roofed over), sometimes also known as the odeon. It was constructed in the 70s BCE, funded by two wealthy colonists, and could seat around 1,000. It may have hosted performances more intimate than full-scale plays, such as poetry recitals or public speaking competitions. In addition, there is a theory that it was also used as a council chamber for the city's newly settled colonists.

Below the large theatre was a colonnaded portico, which may originally have been designed as a gymnasium or simply as meeting area for spectators; however, after 63 CE it was turned into a barracks for gladiators. To the south-west of the large theatre, a monumental staircase led up to what is known as the 'triangular forum', at the heart of which was the 'Doric' temple (so named after its architecture), which may have been dedicated to Minerva and Hercules. There was a close link between drama and religion in both the Greek and the Roman worlds, and two other temples were also located nearby – one to Isis (which is described in detail on p. 112), the other generally believed to be to Asclepius, the god of medicine. A *palaestra* (exercise ground), built in the Samnite era, was the other building in the district.

v. The amphitheatre

Pompeii's amphitheatre was built in about 70 BCE and is the earliest amphitheatre discovered in the Roman world (see p. 211 to read more about amphitheatres). It seems that the building was closely connected with Pompeii's new status of colony, since its construction was privately funded by the colonists Gaius Quinctius Valgus and Marcus Porcius, the same two who had commissioned the covered theatre.

It is difficult to come up with an exact figure for the capacity of the stadium, and estimates have ranged from 10,000 to in excess of 20,000.

The outside of the amphitheatre on its western side.

Even at the lower estimate, this was significantly more than the citizen population of the city, and so it is likely that many outsiders came to Pompeii to watch games. The seating itself was divided into three levels, with the Pompeian elite sitting closest to the action. There were also special boxes for the city's magistrates, and an awning to protect spectators from the elements. The amphitheatre therefore had many of the features later evident in the Colosseum (see p. 212), even though it was built 150 years earlier.

As in Rome, putting on shows was the duty and privilege of aspiring politicians, who hoped to win support and popularity by providing the common people with spectacular entertainment. Games seem to have taken place all year round, and the sponsor of the games, the *editor* (see p. 193), would advertise the forthcoming spectacle on walls around Pompeii. Many of these painted notices have survived for us to see today; they were typically done by professional sign-writers, and promoted the forthcoming spectacle. The following is typical:

> '20 pairs of gladiators of Decimus Lucretius Satrius Valens, perpetual priest of Nero, and 10 pairs of gladiators of Decimus Lucretius Valens, his son, will fight at Pompeii on 8, 9, 10, 11, 12 April. There will be a regular hunt and awnings.'   *CIL* IV.3884

It is interesting that the father has included his son in the process – presumably he was trying to ensure that the family's political influence continued into the next generation.

The gladiators of Pompeii

Two locations have been discovered where gladiators seem to have been housed. The first is a converted house simply called the House of the Gladiators, where more than 100 graffiti have been found relating to gladiatorial combat. Various types of fighter are mentioned, including the *murmillo*, *retiarius*, *secutor* and *Thracian* (see pp. 208-9). In some cases, fighters have scrawled graffiti to show off their successes in the arena – or with women. In the following example, the gladiator Celadus did both:

> 'The girls' heart-throb, Thracian gladiator Celadus, belonging to Octavus, fought 3, won 3.'   *CIL* IV.4342

After the earthquake in 63, the colonnaded portico behind the large theatre was also converted into gladiators' barracks. It had about 30-40 cells on two floors, as well as some communal living quarters. Archaeologists found here 15 richly decorated bronze helmets, as well as shinguards, shoulder-guards, daggers, and other weapons. The bodies of 18 people and two dogs were also uncovered in one of the rooms during excavations.

Next to the amphitheatre was a large *palaestra*, complete with a swimming pool at its centre. As well as being a public exercise ground, this may have been a place where gladiators warmed up before a bout; alternatively, on days when shows were being held, it was perhaps a place for spectators to congregate and wait before entering the amphitheatre.

The riot

In 59 CE, Pompeii caused a stir in the Roman world when a riot broke out between locals and visiting spectators from the nearby city of Nuceria. It was an incident serious enough for the Roman historian Tacitus to mention in his *Annals*. Further evidence comes from a famous fresco in the House of Actius Anicetus, which clearly shows fighting going on both in the stands and outside the stadium. Tacitus' account runs as follows:

'About this time there was a serious fight between the inhabitants of two Roman settlements, Nuceria and Pompeii. It arose out of a trifling incident at a gladiatorial show given by Livineius Regulus, whose expulsion from the senate I have mentioned elsewhere. During an exchange of taunts – characteristic of these disorderly country cities – abuse led to stone-throwing, and then swords were drawn. The people of Pompeii, where the show was held, came off best. Many wounded and

The famous fresco depicting the riot at Pompeii's amphitheatre.

287

mutilated Nucerians were taken to the capital. Many bereavements, too, were suffered by parents and children. The emperor himself instructed the senate to investigate the affair. The senate passed it to the consuls. When they reported back, the senate debarred Pompeii from holding any similar gathering for ten years. Illegal associations in the city were dissolved; and the sponsor of the show and his fellow-instigators of the disorders were exiled.'   Tacitus, *Annals* 14.17

As well as the sponsor being exiled, it is likely that both the city's leading magistrates, the *duoviri*, were removed from office. It seems that the ban was lifted by the emperor Nero in 64, while even before this time it was only gladiatorial contests which were banned, since advertisements do survive for wild beast hunts.

Review 4

1. Define the following terms: *cardo, castellum aquae, decumanus.*
2. What advantages did the layout of Pompeii have for its citizens? How does it compare with that of a modern city with which you are familiar?
3. How does the method of supplying water in Pompeii compare with that in different parts of the world today?
4. What do the entertainment facilities in Pompeii tell us about the interests of its inhabitants?
5. Have there been incidents in the modern world similar to the riot in Pompeii? Why do you think that sports fans sometimes behave like this?
E. Imagine you run an ancient tourism company and want to attract visitors to Pompeii. Design a brochure selling the city.

---

5. The forum

Pompeii's forum was located in the oldest part of the city, close to the Marine Gate in the south-west. It was the city's civic centre, about 150 metres long and 40 metres wide, with important religious, commercial, legal and political buildings (although in some cases the exact identification and purpose remains uncertain). While a modern visitor can still get an idea of what the forum would have looked like, it is hard to recapture the sheer splendour of the place. At its centre was a paved open square, around which ran a double colonnade in white marble. To the north end was the imposing Temple of Jupiter, flanked on either side by two grand ceremonial arches.

During the day, the square came to life; evidence for this comes from a series of frescos in the House of Julia Felix which portray forum scenes. In some are traders who have set up temporary stalls – an ironmonger, a cobbler, a man selling cloth and another selling pots and pans; elsewhere, people have come to the forum to read public notices.

A plan of the forum area.

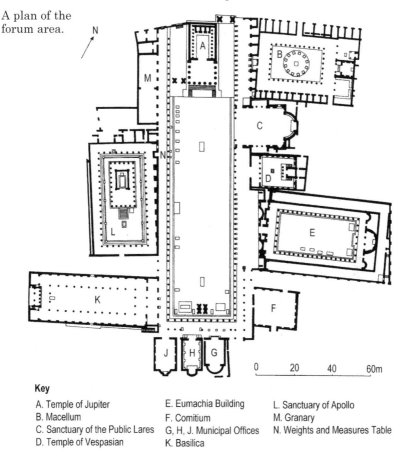

Key

A. Temple of Jupiter	E. Eumachia Building	L. Sanctuary of Apollo
B. Macellum	F. Comitium	M. Granary
C. Sanctuary of the Public Lares	G, H, J. Municipal Offices	N. Weights and Measures Table
D. Temple of Vespasian	K. Basilica	

The square was also presumably a place where friends came to meet, chat and shop, while politicians and public figures might have made speeches here; the whole area was pedestrianised, with blocking stones preventing vehicles from the adjoining streets from entering.

Statues

Another feature of the square was its statues of important public figures; visitors today can still see the bases of these – 57 in all, 16 of which could have supported a man riding a horse. Those honoured with these statues would either have been important members of Pompeian society, or else members of the imperial family. Although we know little of the public figures represented in the forum of Pompeii, the story of Marcus Nonius Balbus at Herculaneum (see p. 328) gives an idea of the prominent position such people were given in the life of a Roman city.

In this fresco scene from the House of Julia Felix a banner has been set across three statue bases and one man seems to be reading it to two others. The statues of public figures on horseback are visible in the background.

i. Religious buildings

The **Temple of Jupiter** at the north end of the forum was the most important in Pompeii. First constructed in the second half of the 2nd century BCE, it was given a significant makeover after the city became a Roman colony. At this point, the temple became a *capitolium*, modelled on the Temple of Jupiter in Rome (see p. 71), and dedicated to the Capitoline triad of Jupiter, Juno and Minerva, who each have their own

5. Pompeii

The Temple of Jupiter at the head of the forum, with Vesuvius in the background.

rooms in the temple. When it was excavated in the 18th century, a colossal marble head of Jupiter was discovered.

On the west side of the forum stood the walled **Sanctuary of Apollo**. The first building on this site can be dated to the 6th century BCE, although the complex visible today was first constructed some 400 years later. The temple is surrounded by a portico, on each side of which was found a bronze statue – one of Apollo, the other of his sister Diana (see p. 70 to read about the Roman gods), both of them posing as archers. Beside the temple was a sundial, which was donated by two magistrates.

On the other side of the forum was the sanctuary containing the **Temple of Vespasian**, which is believed to have been dedicated to the imperial cult (see p. 79). Although it takes its name from Vespasian, the emperor who died shortly before the eruption, it is now thought to have been built when Augustus was emperor, and dedicated then to the *Genius* (see p. 135) of the ruling emperor; the temple was therefore an important symbol of Pompeii's loyalty to the imperial family. A marble altar with an impressive frieze of a sacrifice taking place can still be seen in situ today (see image on p. 98).

Further north was the area known as the **Sanctuary of the Public Lares**, who were the guardian spirits of the city (see p. 134), and it was once thought that this was where they were worshipped. However, this identification is now disputed, and the purpose of the building remains unclear. One theory is that it was used to display statues of the imperial family (and so it is now often referred to as the 'Imperial Cult Building'), since there are many niches for statues in the walls of the sanctuary.

The Temple of Apollo.

The bronze statue of Apollo
poised to fire an arrow.

ii. Commercial buildings

The forum was also the business centre of Pompeii, containing buildings concerned with various trades and industries. To the north-east was the **Macellum**, a rectangular market selling food and drink. Its centre was open-air and contained a circular building holding a pool of water with fish for sale. To the west and the north side were porticoes, where stalls may have been set up, while there were shops along the south side (as well as a suite of three halls, which may have housed statues of prominent Pompeians or the imperial family). Some of the surviving frescos indicate the goods sold there, including fish, bread, poultry and wine.

A little further south was the grand **Eumachia Building**, which had an elaborate entrance and was surrounded by porticoes. Its purpose is unclear, although as it was the largest building in the forum it must have played an important role in civic life. It takes its name from Eumachia, a public priestess (possibly of Ceres), who came from a wealthy and influential Pompeian family. Over each entrance to the building was the following inscription:

'Eumachia, daughter of Lucius, public priestess, in her own name and that of her son Marcus Numistrius Fronto, built at her own expense the chalcidicum (*porch*), crypta (*covered passage*), and porticus, and dedicated them to Augustan Concord and Piety.'   *CIL* X.810 and 811

It is interesting to see a woman playing such an important role in the public life of the city, both as a priestess and as a benefactor wealthy enough in her own right to fund such a huge development. There have been various theories about what her hall was actually used for; the most common is that it was a guildhall for the fulling industry (see p. 298), based mainly on the fact that a statue of Eumachia was set up inside the building with the following inscription:

'To Eumachia, daughter of Lucius, public priestess, from the fullers.'
CIL X.813

However, the evidence for such a use is inconclusive; other theories have suggested that the building may have been used as an additional market-place (perhaps even as a slave market), as a multi-purpose hall, or even as a meeting centre for Pompeii's College of Augustales (see p. 80). Ultimately, there is not enough evidence to be sure of any of these.

To the north of the Temple of Apollo were two other commercial sites: the **Weights and Measures Table** and the **Granary**. The former was used to check the accuracy of the measures of the forum traders. The table has 9 holes, each one equal to a specific measure and with a mini

The statue of the priestess Eumachia set up by the fullers.

The Weights and Measures Table.

trapdoor at the base. A hole would be filled to the brim, the trapdoor released, and the exact amount fell into a pot below. The granary next door may have been used as a warehouse market to store cereals and pulses, but it seems not to have been in use at the time of the eruption, since it was lacking a roof and the walls had not been plastered.

iii. Political and legal buildings

The main political and legal buildings of Pompeii were found at the southern end of the forum. To the south-west was the **Basilica**, one of the city's most impressive buildings. Constructed in about 100 BCE, the main entrance had five grand doors fitted with wooden shutters. Inside, steps led up to a grand hall which was surrounded by huge columns, the bases of which can still be seen today.

It is likely that important legal cases were heard in the Basilica; at its far end was a raised podium, the *tribunal*, from where a magistrate might have presided over disputes (although the view to the platform would have been obscured by a large statue). Alternatively, it may have been used to hold auctions, since the Basilica probably also doubled up as a commercial centre where people met to talk business or sign contracts.

At the south end of the forum were three large offices, usually

The *tribunal* at the far end of the Basilica.

referred to as the **Municipal Offices**, where it is assumed that the magistrates worked, the Council met, and the public archives were kept. However, there is no conclusive evidence to support this – archaeologists base this view on what they would normally expect of a Roman city. To the east of these offices was an open-air meeting hall called the **Comitium**; it has often been thought that this was a polling station where people went to vote, although in fact the whole forum may have been used for this purpose.

Pompeian politics

From 80 BCE, Pompeii's political system was based on the system of government at Rome (see Appendix 2). Each year in March, all adult male citizens could vote for the city's magistrates; in addition, there was a city Council, modelled on the Senate in Rome. The main political bodies were therefore as follows:

- The two **duoviri** (singular: *duumvir*) were the most important magistrates. They presided over meetings of the city council, and ensured that its decrees were carried out. They also managed public funds and oversaw legal cases, both criminal and civil. Every five years, the *duoviri* were given special powers to update both the citizen roll of Pompeii and the list of Council members; these *duoviri* were known as *quinquennales* ('five-yearly magistrates'); being elected as one was held in great prestige.
- The two **aediles**, the two junior magistrates, were primarily responsible for maintaining the streets, public buildings, and markets. Becoming an *aedile* was an essential step for an ambitious Pompeian politician, since no man could become a *duumvir* unless he had previously served as an *aedile*.
- The **council** was made up of about 100 councillors, known as *decuriones*. Membership of the council was usually limited to ex-magistrates, who served for life. The council had a wide range of powers, and was the city's main legislative body. *Decuriones* were given certain privileges, including the best seats at the theatres and the amphitheatre.

To be a magistrate or a *decurion*, one had to be a free-born male citizen of good character, with a certain level of wealth, and to live in Pompeii or its immediate surroundings.

Election campaigns

We can get a unique insight into election campaigns in the Roman world through the election notices, or *programmata*, which are painted on walls all over the city. Over 2,800 such notices have been found, most of them carefully painted by professional sign-writers in red or black on a white background. They tend to relate to election campaigns in the last years of Pompeii's life, and in particular to the election of March 79.

The *programmata* normally indicate a candidate's personal qualities, rather than making any specific promises or offering a manifesto. This one was found behind the wall of the Basilica:

> 'I ask you to elect as *aedile* Gnaeus Helvius Sabinus, a young man worthy of every reward, worthy of public office.'   *CIL* IV.706

Sometimes, a guild of traders gathered together to put their support behind a certain candidate, as here:

> 'All the fruit-sellers with Helvius Vestalis call for Marcus Holconius Priscus as *duumvir* for lawsuits.'   *CIL* IV.202

Not all the notices were serious. The following is a parody of the type of message above, in which trade guilds supported a candidate:

> 'All the late drinkers ask you to elect Marcus Cerrinius Vatia *aedile*.'
> *CIL* IV.581

Needless to say, there was no such guild as the 'late drinkers' – it is really a joke, suggesting that the only people likely to vote for Vatia are drunks coming out of the pub late at night! Poor Vatia seems to have been the butt of such jokes, since other notices list as his supporters the 'little thieves' and 'all those asleep'. Perhaps not surprisingly, there is no record of his ever having been elected.

Review 5

1. Define the following terms: *aediles, decuriones, duoviri, programmata.*
2. How much do you think we can learn about the life of Pompeii from its forum?
3. Find out more about the three temples in the forum, and compare and contrast each of them.
4. How does the forum compare to a modern city centre which you are familiar with?
5. How do Pompeii's elections compare to those in the modern world?
E. Imagine you are a market trader in the forum of Pompeii. Describe what you see happen there on a typical day.

---

6. Industry

The economy of Pompeii was booming its final years. In addition to the commercial buildings of the forum, more than 600 privately owned shops have been excavated. In common with other cities around Vesuvius, the Pompeian economy was based on agricultural produce (particularly grapes, olives, and cereals) and the fishing industry. Many villas supporting farms have been found outside the city (see p. 318), while there were also market gardens within the walls.

However, there was a wide variety of trades, as is indicated by the following list of all the occupations recorded on graffiti, inscriptions and wax tablets discovered in the city:

Architect	Dyer	Lupin-seller	Sauce-maker
Baker	Engraver	Miller	Scorer
Banker	Farmer	Money-lender	Scribe
Barber	Felt-worker	Mule-driver	Soothsayer
Bath-attendant	Fisherman	Ointment-seller	Spinner
Builder	Fruit-seller	Onion-sellers	Surveyor
Carpenter	Fuller	Outfitter	Tanner
Carriage-driver	Furnace-stoker	Painter	Theatre official
Chicken-keeper	Gem-cutter	Pastry-cook	Waggoner
Clapper-beater	Goldsmith	Pig-breeder	Weaver
Cloak-seller	Grape-picker	Porter	Wine-seller
Cobbler	Guard	Priest's attendant	Wool-worker
Cushion-seller	Herdsman	Prostitute	
Doorman	Innkeeper	Rag-and-bone man	

i. The fulling industry

Fulling – the washing and dyeing of wool, and manufacture of cloth – seems to have been an important industry in Pompeii. Four large fulleries have been uncovered, while there were several smaller ones, as well as six dye-shops; in addition, wool-sellers and fullers figure prominently in *programmata* and inscriptions while, as we have seen, some have believed that the fulling industry was important enough to have its own guild-hall in the forum. However, the truth is that we just cannot know the extent and significance of the industry.

The most famous fullery is the **Fullery of Stephanus** on the *Via dell'Abbondanza*, which gives us a good idea of how the cloth treatment process worked. After checking the cloth for faults and removing any fluff, workers trod it in urine to stiffen it; it was then washed with fuller's earth or other cleansing agents to remove grease. The workers would most likely be slaves; a famous fresco seems to show young children being forced to do this work. After this it was stretched and beaten to even it out, next rewashed and rinsed in large vats, then removed again, and combed, brushed and trimmed, to bring up the nap. At this stage, white cloth was bleached by laying it out on a cage over burning sulphur and brimstone; dye was added if required. Finally, the cloth would be put in a press for finishing.

In this fresco of a fullery, slaves or children are trampling cloth in vats.

This fresco shows a girl combing cloth to bring up the nap, and a man carrying a cage for bleaching. He also carries a bucket of sulphur and brimstone.

A fresco depicting a clothes press from a fuller's shop in Pompeii.

The wool wasn't just produced for regular clothing. It could also be stiffened in vinegar to produce felt, which was used to make items such as hats, cloaks, slippers and blankets.

Taxed relief

Ordinary Pompeians were asked to help the fulling industry by urinating in pots left outside the fulleries – urine is rich in ammonia, which is a powerful cleaning agent. The emperor Vespasian soon devised a cunning plan to benefit from this: he taxed the collection of these pots, thinking it unfair that the fullers got this resource for free. As a result, the locals nicknamed the pots (and public urinals generally) *Vespasiani*, as a token of what they thought of the emperor and his tax – and the word still means 'public urinal' in Italian today!

The remains of a bakery. On the right hand side are four grinding mills, with a large oven behind them.

ii. Baking

The remains of more than 30 bakeries have been excavated, suggesting that most people went out to buy their bread rather than baking it at

A reconstruction of a grinding mill.

home. Some bakeries used their own mills to grind grain into flour. The mills followed a standard pattern in two halves. The top half of the mill rotated by means of an attached wooden frame. Corn was poured into the top of the mill, which was turned either by a blindfolded donkey or by a slave. The bottom half was a cone shape set into a stone base, with a lead trough, in which the ground grain, now flour, was collected.

The flour would then be kneaded into circular loaves, often marked into eight sections, and then baked in a large adjoining oven which was very similar to a modern Italian pizza oven. At its bottom was a hole used for storing spare fuel, above which was a large semi-circular opening, where the fire was kindled and the bread inserted, using a large wooden-handled long spade. These ovens had a huge capacity: in one large bakery, that of Modestus, 81 loaves were found preserved by the volcanic ash.

iii. Fast food

As a city which lived on trade, Pompeii had a thriving hospitality industry. There is good evidence for inns, stables, and snack bars dotted throughout the city, most especially near to the main gates and along the main streets. In particular, fast food was a way of life – it would have served its many visitors, as well as the many Pompeians who didn't have the time or facilities to cook at home.

A snack bar is conventionally known as a **thermopolium** (although there is no evidence that this is what the Romans called it); they are easily recognised by their masonry counters with jars inset – these are known as **dolia**, and would have contained dry products, such as nuts, fruits, grains and perhaps vegetables. A bar might also sell wine and hot food, and many of them had seats and tables for people to come and sit.

Fishy business

One delicacy for which Pompeii was famous was its fish sauce, known as *garum* or *liquamen*. Pliny the Elder gives a vivid (and rather revolting) description of how it was produced 'from the guts of fish, and anything else which would have been discarded, steeped in salt; in other words, it is the fermentation of decaying matter'. We can only guess at what these 'other parts' were – probably fish blood, intestines and gills; the stench must have been foul!

If Pompeii was a centre of the *garum* industry, then in the 60s CE Aulus Umbricius Scaurus was the city's 'Mr Fish-Sauce'. It is estimated from the number of pots which bear his trademark that he produced about 30% of the *garum* in the whole region, while one *garum* container bearing his trademark has even been found in southern France!

A mosaic of a *garum* container with the inscription *'liqua(men) flos'* – 'flower of liquamen'.

Two bars on the *Via dell'Abbondanza* are excellent examples of *thermopolia*. In the *thermopolium* of Lucius Vetutius Placidus is a beautiful and well preserved *lararium*, which is in this instance a shrine protecting the premises. In the centre is the Genius flanked by two Lares, which we would expect of a *lararium*; however, at each end of the painting is a god – Mercury to the left and Bacchus to the right. The support of these two gods was vital to the bar-owner – the former as the god of traders, and the latter as the god of wine.

A little further down the street is the *thermopolium* of Asellina. Asellina was one of four women named on electoral notices outside the bar, and it is believed that she may have been a waitress there. The bar's counter has four *dolia*; beyond it is a small oven, with a bronze container built in for heating water. Wine jars were stacked against the wall behind the counter, while two jugs were found, one in the shape of a rooster, the other of a fox. At the back of the bar, a wooden staircase led up to rooms above.

Graffiti and wall paintings in the bars and inns of Pompeii give us an idea of what went on there. One bar has a series of paintings with the ancient equivalent of cartoon captions; they show men fighting over

The *lararium* of Lucius Vetutius Placidus.

payment for drinks, arguing about a game of dice, and talking about women. The graffiti are revealing, and sometimes amusing. The following guests staying at inns were clearly unimpressed with the quality of service they had received:

> 'We pissed in the bed, I admit, and we're bad guests, but if you ask why, it was because there was no chamber-pot.'   *CIL* IV.4957

> 'I hope you get punished for your lies, innkeeper; you sell water and keep the pure wine for yourself.'   *CIL* IV.3948

iv. Finance

In 1875, a hugely important discovery was made in the upper storey of the House of Lucius Caecilius Iucundus, when 153 partially legible documents were found stored in a wooden box. These were wax tablets which contained information about the business dealings of a certain Lucius Caecilius Iucundus, who seems to have been a cross between a banker, an auctioneer and a money-lender. Although the wax had long

This painting in the bar of Salvius shows two men gambling.

since disappeared from the tablets by the time that they were discovered, traces of what was written remain where the stylus had gone through the wax and marked the wood below.

These tablets represent a goldmine for our understanding of the Pompeian economy, since they tell us what was being bought and sold, when and for how much. The majority (137) record transactions, usually auctions, which Iucundus carried out on behalf of other people; typically, he would profit from both parties by charging commission to the sellers and lending money at interest to the buyers. Most of these documents are 'receipts' from the seller, acknowledging that Iucundus has paid them the amount raised at the auction, less his commission. The following, for a sale of a slave in 54 CE (the exact date is unclear in the text), is a typical example:

'1,567 sesterces (*see Appendix 3 for currency values*) – the sum of money which is due for payment, as contracted with Lucius Caecilius Iucundus, by 13 August next, for the auction of Nimphius, slave of Lucius Iunius Aquila, less commission – Lucius Iunius Aquila declared that he has received this sum, in cash, from Lucius Caecilius Iucundus.

Transacted at Pompeii on 29 May (or 28 June), in the consulship of Manlius Acilius and Marcus Asinius.' *CIL* IV.3340.7

As well as slaves, diverse commodities are recorded on other tablets, including boxwood, linen, fixtures and fittings, and a mule (it is a sad reminder of how cheap a slave's life was that the mule was sold for 520

This wax tablet from the archive of Lucius Caecilius Iucundus is blackened but writing can still be seen.

sesterces, about a third of the price of Nimphius). The document gives us other useful information:

- **The amount** paid of 1,567 *sesterces* is not untypical – of the 44 exact and approximate sums known, the range is from 342 to 38,079 *sesterces* (although only three sales fetched more than 20,000) and the median is about 4,500. Iucundus' commission seems to have varied between 2% and 7%.
- **Witnesses**. On another page of the document is a list of witnesses – each document seems to have been witnessed by up to ten people. The lists tell us something of Pompeian society, since witnesses seem to be listed in order of their social status, while women are not present at all – not because they were illiterate, but because they were not legally allowed to sign.

In addition to these private transactions, a further 16 tablets record agreements between Iucundus and the Pompeian authorities, with whom he had a contract to collect taxes (taking a profit himself), and he also rented out (and perhaps sub-let) from them public properties, such as a farm and a fullery.

Who was Lucius Caecilius Iucundus?

We know very little of Lucius Caecilius Iucundus apart from what is revealed in the tablets. It is not clear where his auctions took place, or if he operated from an office away from his house. The house itself shows signs that he was wealthy, with elaborate paintings and artwork; in the *atrium* was found a bust of a middle-aged man, with thinning hair and a prominent wart on his cheek, and it is just possible that this is Iucundus himself.

The dates of the documents tell us a little more. The first to carry his name was signed in 27 CE, although most of them cluster around the years 54-58; it is not clear why these particular documents were preserved rather than those from other periods of his career. One final clue comes from the latest recorded document, dated to January 62 CE. This was just one month before Tacitus' dating of the earthquake, which was commemorated on the *lararium* in Iucundus' house (see p. 262). Why do the records stop then? Might Iucundus have been killed in the disaster? We will probably never know.

This bust may represent
Lucius Caecilius
Iucundus.

Review 6

1. Define the following terms: *dolia, garum, thermopolium.*
2. Create a list of occupations of all the people you know. How does it compare to the list of occupations at Pompeii?
3. What similarities are there between the ancient and modern approaches to the cloth industry and the baking industry?
4. How do ancient snack bars and inns compare with their modern equivalent?
5. Summarise why the wax tablets of Lucius Caecilius Iucundus are so important for our understanding of life in Pompeii.
E. How much can we learn about the lives of the people of Pompeii from the city's industries?

---

7. Houses

Andrew Wallace-Hadrill, a leading scholar on Pompeii, has described the city as having 'an interlocking jigsaw of large, medium and small houses'. These ranged from small one- or two-roomed residences on the upper floor above a workshop, to grand *atrium* houses, known as *domûs*. Sometimes, these were divided up and developed into smaller middle-class apartments. A further type of house was the country villa located outside the walls of the city.

A detailed overview of Roman housing is given on pp. 125-32. You are advised to read these pages before continuing with this section, not least because the house described as the 'standard' of a *domus* (large house) is Pompeii's House of the Tragic Poet. Once you have read about this house, you can then compare and contrast it with a range of other houses described below. The location of each house within the city is labelled on the map on p. 276.

i. The *domus*

The large houses of Pompeii offer a deep insight into the private lives of some of the city's leading individuals and families. As is the case today, no two houses were exactly the same; there were individual designs and layouts, while each family clearly chose to decorate their living space according to their tastes. The following three *domûs* – the House of the Faun, the House of the Vettii, and the House of Menander – are amongst the most spectacular to have been recovered in the city.

a. The House of the Faun

This house, which takes its name from the statue of a dancing faun found in its *impluvium*, is the largest in Pompeii, covering an area of almost 3,000m² and occupying an entire block. It was built at the beginning of the 2nd century BCE, and then reconstructed later in the same century when its famous mosaics were set in place. At the time of the eruption, the house had changed little and it is thus a classic example of the ways in which Hellenistic culture influenced Pompeii.

Layout

Since the layout is so huge and extraordinary – comprising two front doors, a back entrance, two *atria*, two *peristylia*, a large *exedra* (summer reception room) and four dining rooms – it is worth studying its plan carefully to understand where all these were located. There would also have been an upper floor at the front of the house.

Outside the main entrance to the house the word 'HAVE', or 'Greetings' was inscribed on the pavement. Entering from here into the main *atrium*, a visitor would initially have seen the classic layout of a house – at the back of this *atrium* was the *tablinum*, beyond which was a *peristylium*. However, beyond this was an *exedra*, a grand summer room, and then a second, huge *peristylium*, which may have been converted from an original use as a working garden. As if all this wasn't enough, the house seems to have had four *triclinia*, perhaps one for each season of the year.

The second entrance and *atrium* may have been used as private quarters for the family, while any house guests could also have used it to come and go without disturbance. Beyond this *atrium*, a passage led right through to the large *peristylium*; running alongside it was a stable, a small set of rooms for bathing, and the kitchen. At the rear of the large *peristylium* was a back entrance to the house, known as a *posticum*, where tradesmen and slaves could come and go without fuss. The two small rooms next to it may have been used by a gardener and a doorman.

Works of art

The house had an extraordinary art collection on display. Entering the main *atrium*, a visitor would immediately see the statue of the dancing faun in the *impluvium*; set into the floor in front of this was a mosaic displaying two tragic theatrical masks, surrounded by flowers and fruit. Other mosaics decorated key rooms such as the *triclinia*, including one of Dionysus riding a tiger, another depicting a variety of sea-creatures (a clue to the sort of food served there?). At the back of the small *peristylium*, in front of the *exedra*, was an elaborate mosaic of Nile animals, including ducks, snakes, crocodiles and a hippopotamus.

b. The House of the Vettii

Election notices on the outside walls and two signet rings found in the

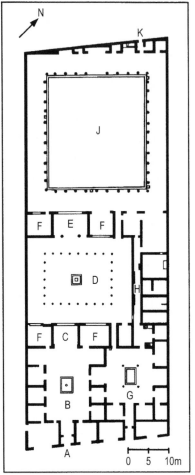

A plan of the House of the Faun.

Key

A. Main entrance
B. Main atrium
C. Tablinum
D. Peristylium
E. Exedra
F. Triclinia
G. Second entrance and atrium
H. Passage to large peristylium
J. Large peristylium
K. Posticum

The Alexander mosaic

The house's masterpiece was the mosaic covering the floor of its exedra. This depicts Alexander the Great defeating Darius III of Persia at one of the battles they fought against one another in the late 330s BCE; it is believed to be a copy of a famous Hellenistic painting of the 3rd century BCE, perhaps produced for King Cassander of Macedonia. The mosaic measures 5.82 x 3.13 metres, and it has been estimated that it is made up of at least one and a half million *tesserae*, the tiny stones used to make mosaics. After defeating the Persians, Alexander went on to conquer Egypt and found the port city of Alexandria, the epicentre of learning and culture in the Hellenistic world, and it is believed that the mosaics in the house were produced by skilled Alexandrian craftsmen.

This mosaic from one of the *alae* of the House of the Faun shows a cat attacking a quail and two ducks sitting among a still-life of birds, fish and seafood.

A replica of the dancing faun statue is still positioned in the *atrium* of the house.

The Alexander mosaic from the House of the Faun.

atrium tell us that the last owners of this house were two brothers, A. Vettius Conviva and A. Vettius Restitutus, both of them freedmen who worked as merchants. The house seems to have undergone major restoration and renovation after the earthquake of 63, much of it with very expensive materials.

The Vettii brothers were obviously very wealthy, and seem to have

Priapus weighs his phallus against a bag of coins.

312

enjoyed showing off their wealth, as seen by the painting on the wall inside the entrance (clearly visible from the street) of the god of fertility, Priapus, weighing his huge phallus against a sack of money. It was an image of both power and prosperity. Inside the house, two large bronze chests sat in the *atrium* – treasure troves for all to see, while they were able to maintain a sculptured garden in the *peristylium* – complete with plumbing for elaborate water features – on a scale rarely found elsewhere in the city.

Layout

This house is designed around its elaborate *peristylium* located straight through from the main *atrium*. The main reception rooms of the house gave onto the garden, which was beautifully decorated with plants and flowers, together with twelve fountain statuettes directing jets of water into eight marble basins standing around the edge of the open area.

The house also had two service quarters, both of them with stairways to an upper floor. The area to the right of the entry porch had its own small *atrium*, where a *lararium* was found complete with a now famous painting (see p. 133). This area also had a kitchen, with kitchen implements still in place from the day of the eruption, and a small room with erotic paintings. Harnesses and a horse skeleton were found in the other service area, indicating that this would probably have been the house's stables.

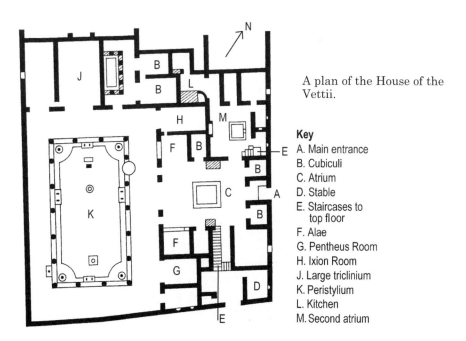

A plan of the House of the Vettii.

Key
A. Main entrance
B. Cubiculi
C. Atrium
D. Stable
E. Staircases to top floor
F. Alae
G. Pentheus Room
H. Ixion Room
J. Large triclinium
K. Peristylium
L. Kitchen
M. Second atrium

A section of the cupids frieze.

Works of art

The most important works of art were all wall paintings found in the reception rooms around the *peristylium*. In the large *triclinium*, there are nine friezes of cupids engaged in various activities: throwing stones, picking flowers and making garlands, making perfumes, racing chariots, working metal, baking bread, harvesting grapes, celebrating a festival, and buying and selling wine.

The room on the corner of the *peristylium* was probably also a

Pentheus being torn apart by his mother and aunts.

triclinium, and was painted predominantly in red and black. It is often known as the 'Ixion Room', after the painting on its back wall of Ixion being tied to a wheel for trying to rape Hera. There are two other mythological paintings in the room – one of Daedalus giving Pasiphae the wooden cow, and another of Dionysus discovering the sleeping Ariadne.

The third reception room on the *peristylium* may also have been used as a *triclinium*. The colour scheme here was primarily yellow panels with paintings inset. It is often known as the 'Pentheus Room' after the dramatic painting on the back wall of Pentheus being torn to pieces by his mother and aunts. On the side walls are paintings of Dirce being punished by being tied to a bull, and of the infant Hercules strangling the snakes sent by Hera to kill him.

c. The House of Menander

This house is one of the largest and most impressive in Pompeii, occupying about 55% of an *insula* and probably also owning many of the properties around it. It is named after a portrait on one of its walls depicting the Greek comic playwright Menander (*c.* 342-291 BCE), who greatly influenced Roman comedy. The house probably belonged to a certain Quintus Poppaeus, whose family may well have been related to Poppaea, the second wife of the emperor Nero; his bronze seal was found in the stable area.

Layout

The house was built according to the classic *atrium-tablinum-peristylium* design. There were some well decorated rooms around the *atrium*, which contained an elaborate *lararium*; nearby was a staircase to an upper floor. However, the main focus of the house is the *peristylium* and the grand rooms around it. In the north-west corner is a reception room coloured predominantly in green, with a floor mosaic depicting scenes from the river Nile. Further on is a suite of baths built around a small second *atrium*, while at the far end of the *peristylium* is a niche containing a second *lararium*. Along from this is a larger niche which was where the fresco of Menander was located. On the east side of the *peristylium* was a vast banqueting hall, at 11.5 x 7.5 metres one of the largest reception rooms yet discovered in Pompeii, indicating the high social status of the owner and his desire to entertain in lavish surroundings.

The house was so large that it even had two service areas. To the east side is a long corridor with a number of small rooms; at one end was a large stable, where a wagon, many amphorae and numerous agricultural implements were found, suggesting that the owner may have had a large farming estate as well. At the other end of the corridor was another small *atrium*, which may have been the headquarters for

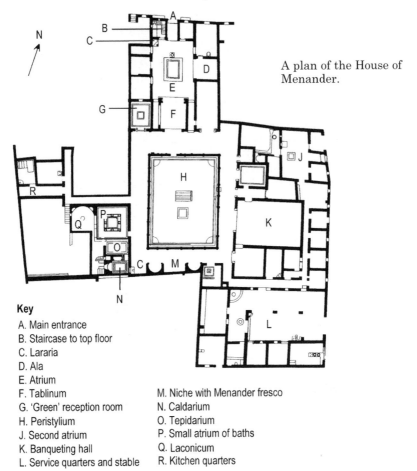

A plan of the House of Menander.

Key

A. Main entrance
B. Staircase to top floor
C. Lararia
D. Ala
E. Atrium
F. Tablinum
G. 'Green' reception room
H. Peristylium
J. Second atrium
K. Banqueting hall
L. Service quarters and stable

M. Niche with Menander fresco
N. Caldarium
O. Tepidarium
P. Small atrium of baths
Q. Laconicum
R. Kitchen quarters

the house's steward, or head slave. The other service area, on the west side of the house, consisted of a kitchen, latrine and service rooms, with access to cellars below.

Works of art

On the east side of the *atrium* was an *ala* with a set of three wall paintings depicting scenes from the Trojan war – the death of Laocoon to the south, the Trojan horse to the east, and the capture of Helen and Cassandra in the presence of Priam to the north.

The most famous work of art is the painting of Menander at the back of the *peristylium*, which would have been clearly visible to passers-by peering through the main entrance of the property. Alongside it are two other frescos – one depicting theatrical masks, the other presumed to be a portrait of the 5th-century Greek tragic playwright Euripides.

The portrait painting of Menander from which the house takes its name.

A silver cup from the collection found in the House of Menander. This one is decorated with the scene of an oarsman and a shepherd with a ram.

As well as these works of art, a significant stash of treasure was found by excavators in one of the cellars. This was predominantly a large collection of decorated silver vessels, wrapped in cloth and neatly stacked, including plates, trays, spoons, ladles, bowls and cups. They were mostly placed in a chest, together with other treasure, perhaps as an emergency measure during the eruption.

ii. The villa

There was much life outside the walls of Pompeii. In the surrounding region have been found numerous villas (large country houses), many of them operating as working farms. These produced goods such as wool, wine, olive oil, nuts, small animals and birds, hams, cheeses, beans vegetables and fine flours. However, not all villas were constructed primarily for farming – some were luxury properties for the wealthy elite, including the statesman Cicero, who tells us he owned a villa in the region of Pompeii.

Two villas are examined in this section – the Villa of Diomedes and the Villa of the Mysteries – both of which were situated outside the Herculaneum Gate, along or near the Street of the Tombs. Both were designed as luxury villas, although by Pompeii's final years the Villa of the Mysteries was being redesigned as a working farm. Both villas also

One side of the *cryptoporticus* of the Villa of the Mysteries.

share a common design structure: since they were both built on a slope, it was necessary to provide a level foundation; this was done by building an artificial base, known as a *cryptoporticus*, for the lower half of each villa.

a. The Villa of the Mysteries

This villa was first built in the 2nd century BCE, although it was completely modernised and extended soon after Pompeii became a Roman colony in 80 BCE. It was now a luxury suburban villa decorated with remarkable art work, in particular its famous set of frescos which are commonly believed to depict an initiation into the Mysteries of Dionysus (see box on p. 321), from which the villa takes its name. Little is known about the possible owners of the property before 63 CE, although after this it was probably owned by the Istacidii, one of Pompeii's wealthiest families. In these years, the villa was being turned into a large winery and seems to have lost some of its elegance.

The main entrance, from the east, led straight into a *peristylium*

Key

A. Main entrance
B. Peristylium
C. Atrium
D. Tablinum
E. Exedra
F. Terraced gardens

G. Portico
H. Kitchen
J. Baths suite
K. Second atrium
L. Hall of the Mysteries
M. Torcularium

A plan of the Villa of the Mysteries.

A scene from the mystery paintings. According to one theory, the initiate is on the left, listening attentively, while the ritual is read by a boy under the supervision of another woman.

(rather than the *atrium*, as in most city houses). Beyond this was the *atrium*, which in turn led into a *tablinum*. To the south of the *peristylium* was the kitchen, and next to it a small suite of baths built around a small second *atrium*. On the north side of the *peristylium*, a corridor led to the *torcularium*, a room used for pressing grape must and making wine. The grapes were brought in here for treading in a basin, after which the must was crushed repeatedly under a heavy press, with a ram's head, which has been reconstructed for tourists to see today. The villa had a large wine cellar for storing its produce.

The west side of the villa was built on a *cryptoporticus*. This included terraced gardens, as well as more reception rooms, among them the room sometimes known as the Hall of the Mysteries, which may also have been used as a *triclinium*.

320

A reconstruction of the *torcularium* in the villa.

The mystery paintings

The Hall of the Mysteries is famous for the paintings on the walls which wrap round three sides. No one has been able to prove conclusively the meaning of the scenes depicted, but the most common theory is that they represent the stages of initiation of a woman into the mystery cult of Dionysus, which is described in detail on p. 107; other theories hold that it is not the cult of Dionysus, but another female cult.

The scenes can be divided into three stages: first, scenes of preparation, where women are involved in ritual readings and making a meal; secondly, scenes of Dionysus and the rituals associated with him; and thirdly, the adorning of the bride, observed by another woman – was this the moment at which the initiate had completed the process?

It is noticeable that this room is found in a property located outside the walls of Pompeii, since Roman law banned people from taking part in the Mysteries of Dionysus inside towns or cities; equally interesting is the fact that women feature so prominently in the scenes, and some have thought that the owner of the villa may have been a priestess of the cult. Ultimately, however, we cannot be certain and it is likely that the purpose of the room will, appropriately enough, always remain a mystery to us.

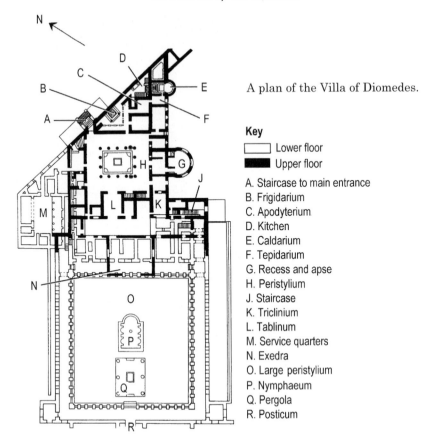

A plan of the Villa of Diomedes.

Key

☐ Lower floor
■ Upper floor

A. Staircase to main entrance
B. Frigidarium
C. Apodyterium
D. Kitchen
E. Caldarium
F. Tepidarium
G. Recess and apse
H. Peristylium
J. Staircase
K. Triclinium
L. Tablinum
M. Service quarters
N. Exedra
O. Large peristylium
P. Nymphaeum
Q. Pergola
R. Posticum

b. The Villa of Diomedes

The Villa of Diomedes is one of the largest and most luxurious in the hinterland of Pompeii. It was named after a certain Marcus Arrius Diomedes, whose tomb lies directly in front of the entrance, although there is no firm evidence that he was indeed the owner.

When it was excavated between 1771 and 1774, it caused a sensation, both because of its amazing splendour and for a tragic discovery: about 20 bodies, including those of women and children, were uncovered in the *cryptoporticus*, where they had been buried while sheltering from the eruption. Two other skeletons were found in the portico surrounding the garden, including that of a man holding a key, accompanied by one of the most impressive collections of coins found in Pompeii.

The villa was built on two levels, the lower of which was based on a *cryptoporticus*. The main entrance from the Street of the Tombs led into the upper level, at the heart of which was a *peristylium* with various living rooms around it. These included a suite of baths, a *tablinum*, and

5. Pompeii

The apse off the *peristylium* in the villa. Its roof was decorated with the signs of the zodiac.

A view from the far end of the garden in the Villa of Diomedes, looking back towards the house. The bases of the columns for the pergola can still be seen; beyond lies the hollowed area which was once the *nymphaeum*.

a magnificently frescoed recess with a large apse, from which three large windows gave superb views out to the coast. Behind the *tablinum* was a terrace leading to an *exedra*, which looked out onto the lower level.

A ramp on one side of the villa and a staircase on the other led down to the *peristylium* below; in the garden was a beautiful *nymphaeum* (fountain pool) and a pergola supported by six columns at one end; along the eastern side of the *peristylium* were living rooms decorated with beautiful frescos, while to the far end was a rear entrance to the villa. The inside of the *cryptoporticus*, which matched exactly the size and shape of the *peristylium*, seems to have been used mainly as a cellar.

Review 7

1. Choose two of the houses or villas above, and design an estate agent's pamphlet offering each one for sale.
2. Which of the houses above would you have preferred to live in, and why?
3. Choose one of the houses or villas above, and compare and contrast it to a large house today.
E. Why do you think that impressive art was so important to the owners of the houses covered in this section?
E. How much do you think we can tell about the owners of Pompeian houses from what has been discovered by archaeologists?

6

Herculaneum

'Near to Naples is the fortress town of Herculaneum, whose highest
point juts out into the sea, catching the breeze so wonderfully as to make
it a healthy place to live.'   Strabo, *Geography* 5.4.8

Although Strabo describes Herculaneum as a 'fortress town', by the 1st
century CE it was really a seaside settlement with a collection of
wealthy villas nearby; as he suggests, it must have been a charming
place to live. Although less well known than Pompeii, it is an important
archaeological site which differs in various ways from the larger city; in
addition, as we shall see, the way in which it was preserved gives us
unique information about life in a Roman town.

1. History

Herculaneum was located directly beneath Vesuvius, about 6 kilometres
(3.7 miles) from the volcano (see map on p. 256). The walled town was
bounded on either side by a small river and sat on the edge of a tuff spur
which met the sea. It was smaller than Pompeii, occupying an estimated area of 20 hectares (50 acres), in comparison with the 66 hectares
(157 acres) of its larger neighbour. At the time of the eruption, the
town's population is estimated to have been 4,000.

Sources suggest that it had a similar history to that of Pompeii (see
pp. 257-63); in particular, Strabo claimed that both cities had been influenced by Oscans, Greeks, Etruscans, Samnites and Romans. It has been
hard to track much of the early history of the town, as there has been
much less digging below the 79 CE ground-level than at Pompeii.
However, the name 'Herculaneum', meaning 'Town of Hercules', has led
some to believe that it was founded by Greeks; if so, it may have been a
satellite of one of the larger Greek settlements on the Bay of Naples,
such as Neapolis (Naples), since its streets are laid out on the grid pattern common to all Greek towns of that era.

Whoever founded Herculaneum, the town was almost certainly taken
over by the Oscan-speaking Samnites, along with Pompeii, in the late
5th century BCE; some Oscan graffiti and inscriptions still survive,
while houses dating to the 2nd century BCE were built in the typical
Samnite manner. In 89 BCE, Herculaneum joined Pompeii and many
other Italian towns in rebelling against Rome in what is known as the
Social War (see p. 35). Although defeated and pillaged, it was not, unlike

Images of Hercules were common in Herculaneum and this large fresco was found in the Basilica. The hero, tanned almost black by the sun, looks on as his son Telephus is suckled by a doe. The central female figure is a personi- fication of the beautiful Greek region of Arcadia, in whose forests the boy had been abandoned by his mother Auge.

Hercules

Hercules (or Heracles in Greek) was the ultimate strong man of Greek mythology, who had to complete twelve labours to atone for having murdered his wife and children in a fit of madness. His tenth labour involved him travelling to the region of Spain to steal fifty cattle from the three-headed giant Geryon.

After achieving this, Hercules is said to have led the cattle back through Italy to Greece in a triumphal procession and, according to one Greek historian, to have founded a small town where his fleet docked. Of course, this was just a myth, but temples to Heracles were often set up by Greeks colonising a new territory, and so it would make sense that they would want to name their town after the hero who became a god.

---

its larger neighbour, turned into a colony afterwards, probably because there was no space to settle army veterans within its walls. Nonetheless, the inhabitants of the town were given full Roman citizenship at this time, and the official language of its civic institutions was changed from Oscan to Roman.

By the imperial age, Herculaneum had established itself as one of the fashionable seaside resort towns on the bay of Naples, popular with the rich and famous; wealthy Romans built luxury summer villas nearby, among them Poppaea, the emperor Nero's wife. In the town itself, large houses with spectacular views were built over the sea wall above the shoreline. In fact, in one of these survives an amusing piece of evidence linking the town to another emperor, Titus: on the wall of a latrine in the House of the Gem, the following graffito can still be seen:

'Apollonaris, doctor of the emperor Titus, had a good crap here.'
CIL IV.10619

Since Titus became emperor only in June 79 CE, Apollonaris must have written this in the very last months of the town's life. As well as luxury homes, the town had elaborate public buildings, including at least three sets of baths, a *basilica*, a *palaestra*, and a theatre.

We hear little of Herculaneum in the history books until the earthquake of 63 CE; as we have seen on p. 261, in his description of the event, Seneca the Younger comments that:

'Part of the town of Herculaneum too fell down and even the structures that remain are unstable.' Seneca, *Natural Questions* 6.1.2

Although Herculaneum suffered significant damage, restoration may have proceeded much faster than at Pompeii and the buildings seem to have been in relatively good condition in 79. This may be because the smaller town required less repair work; alternatively, it may have had a larger number of wealthy residents who were prepared to help fund the necessary repairs.

Economically, there is little evidence of large scale industry in Herculaneum, perhaps because of its restricted hinterland. Compared to Pompeii, there is less evidence for industries such as fulling, wine-making, or the production of *garum*, while the excavated streets show few signs of heavy traffic. However, even in the relatively small part of the town which has been excavated, a number of *thermopolia* have been discovered, as well as a jewel maker's and a lead workshop.

Fishing also seems to have been important to the town, since a large number of nets, hooks and other fishing gear have been found during the excavations. Herculaneum's harbour has yet to be located, but it is believed to have been the first safe port of call after Naples, and was open all the year round, unlike smaller harbours in the bay which were open only in the summer.

Marcus Nonius Balbus

One prominent public figure in Herculaneum was Marcus Nonius Balbus, a leading benefactor of the town during the late 1st century BCE. Balbus had an impressive career in Roman politics, as praetor, consul and governor of the province of Crete and Cyrene, and then finally tribune in 32 BCE (he was a supporter of the future emperor Augustus). Many statues of Balbus have been found in the town, including two from the forum area of him riding on a horse, while statues of his entire family were also discovered in the Basilica. Nearby is an inscription (*CIL* X.1425) which states: 'Marcus Nonius Balbus rebuilt the Basilica, gates and walls at his own expense.' Another inscription carved on a funerary altar next to the Suburban Baths records the gratitude of the town council for Balbus' gifts to the town; in return, they awarded exceptional honours to his memory. His ashes (still in situ when the site was excavated) were enclosed in a base on which was placed yet another statue of him, erected next to the funerary altar. The story of Balbus is a good example of the important role that wealthy and influential men could play in their home towns.

One of the statues of Marcus Nonius Balbus riding on a horse.

A view down to the excavated ancient shoreline of Herculaneum. The volcanic rock which submerged the town can be seen to the right and beyond.

2. Destruction

Herculaneum's location meant that it was not destroyed in the same way as Pompeii (you should read about this first on pp. 263-70). For one thing, it was not downwind of the eruption, and so avoided the rain-shower of volcanic material during the initial Plinian phase; in fact, by the time that the pyroclastic surges and flows began in the early hours of the morning following the eruption, it had probably received only a light covering of pumice, rock fragments and ash, perhaps about 15 to 20 centimetres thick. In one way, however, this might have been even more frightening for the inhabitants, since they would have been able to see clearly the size and power of the eruption column.

Once the surges began, the town's proximity to the volcano meant that it was doomed. It was directly in the path of the pyroclastic surges and flows: the first surge probably killed anyone still in the town, while the second overwhelmed it; ultimately, Herculaneum was buried to a depth of up to 23 metres (about four times as deep as at Pompeii), while the flows pushed the coastline out by about 400 metres (where it remains today).

The manner of Herculaneum's destruction means that its state of preservation is different from that of Pompeii in two important ways:

- **Upper storeys.** A higher proportion of upper storeys have survived, probably for two reasons: first of all, the roofs were not subject to the heavy build-up of volcanic material during the Plinian phase which caused many upper floors in Pompeii to collapse; secondly, Herculaneum was on a steeper incline than Pompeii, so that the terraced layout of the town offered some protection and support from the surges and flows as they fell upon the site from a higher angle.
- **Carbonisation.** Organic materials such as wood, cloth, papyrus and foodstuffs have been preserved to a far greater degree by carbonisation, since the temperatures of the surges and flows at Herculaneum were significantly higher than at Pompeii and sealed the town in an oxygen-free environment.

Both of these features – an upper storey and carbonised material – are found in the House of the Wooden Partition, which is described on pp. 341-3.

However, as this modern writer on Herculaneum makes clear, not all the organic material found in the town has been preserved in carbonised form:

> 'It appears that wood ... was heated up to 400 degrees centigrade in some places. Yet the pyroclastic flow played strange tricks. For all its force and massive volume and high temperatures it was unpredictable. In some spots it was hot enough to carbonise wood and foodstuffs; in others, hot enough merely to scorch cloth and bread. And in still others wood, rope, eggs, and even fishnets appear essentially unharmed.'
> Joseph Jay Deiss, *Herculaneum: Italy's Buried Treasure*, p. 18

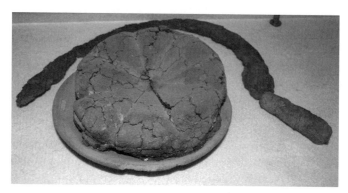

This carbonised loaf of bread was found in a villa near Herculaneum. Beside it lies a sickle.

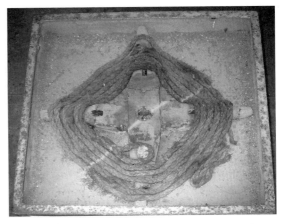

This windlass and rope
was used to draw water
from a well. It was left
almost completely undam-
aged by the volcanic debris
which buried it.

As Deiss suggests here, it seems that the various surges and flows had
different effects on different areas of the town. Some of them were so hot
that they instantly carbonised any organic material in their path, while
others seem to have been much cooler, and so simply formed an airtight
seal around any material, perfectly preserving it as it was.

Therefore, we should resist the temptation to see Herculaneum
merely as a smaller version of Pompeii. The town had a different character, was destroyed in a different way, and has lessons of its own to
teach us.

3. Rediscovery

Herculaneum was explored before Pompeii (the rediscovery of which
you can read about on pp. 271-7). In 1709, in the town of Resina
which lay on top of the site, a peasant woman was digging a well
when she came down onto ancient ruins. She brought to the surface
a large quantity of ancient marbles; these soon came to the attention
of the French Prince d'Elbeuf, who was constructing a villa nearby
and wanted marble to decorate it. He ordered the well to be widened
and tunnels to be dug: as much marble as possible was to find its way
to his villa. Without realising it, workmen started to ransack the
theatre of Herculaneum. As at Pompeii, the early incursions into the
town were entirely devoted to treasure hunting, causing the loss of
many valuable works of art.

The work in Herculaneum followed a different pattern from that
in Pompeii. Very little of the site was uncovered until the 20th century; instead, the early explorers dug a network of tunnels into the
buried town – thanks to their accurate mapping, we know a good
deal about the unexcavated areas. However, after attention turned
to Pompeii in the middle of the 18th century, progress in
Herculaneum was fitful. One major problem was that the site was

331

The Theatre of Herculaneum

In the sorry history of the early excavations at Pompeii and Herculaneum, the looting of Herculaneum's theatre is perhaps the saddest story. It was a relatively large building – estimates suggest a capacity of between 1,300 and 2,500 people – and the way in which it was buried meant that it had been preserved almost fully intact along with its decorative features, uniquely for a Roman theatre.

However, for almost forty years, first d'Elbeuf and then Alcubierre quarried it remorselessly, removing its multi-coloured marbles, stuccoes, and bronze and marble statues. By 1739, the entire stage had been cleared of decoration. If these early diggers had preserved the theatre, rather than plundered it, then without doubt it would have been considered one of the archaeological wonders of the modern world. As it is, what we have left is important structurally, but leaves us guessing a great deal about how the surviving decorations would originally have been displayed.

---

much harder to excavate, since it was buried so much deeper than Pompeii. In addition, it lies underneath a modern town, whose residents understandably have never been keen on being moved to allow the past to be uncovered.

Most of what can be seen today was excavated between 1927 and 1961 under the guidance of archaeologist Amedeo Maiuri, who took over when the Italian government, led by Mussolini's fascist party, wanted to reclaim the nation's Roman heritage. Maiuri is the person who had the greatest impact on the creating the site of Herculaneum as we now know it. Under his direction most of the site visible today was properly excavated, with a team of workers who dug, reconstructed and then presented the Roman buildings to visitors. In particular, his method was innovative in two important ways:

- **Display**. He was keen to present the remains in such a way that original artefacts were displayed within rooms to illustrate aspects of daily life in the Roman world, something which had rarely been done before.
- **Conservation**. He made sure that workers regularly checked the site and conducted maintenance and conservation work when necessary.

However, since 1961, with one or two notable exceptions, there has been little significant progress. Today, it is estimated that the excavated remains – four complete and four partially excavated blocks – represent only about 25% of the site. The rest lies buried under the modern town of Ercolano (which had previously been called Resina).

The second death of Herculaneum

By the year 2000, the excavated part of Herculaneum was in a sorry state. Owing to a series of complex reasons including a lack of regular maintenance and underfunding for conservation work, decay was evident in all areas, with structures collapsing, plaster surfaces crumbling, mosaics disintegrating, and weeds and plants growing in and around the buildings. The site seemed doomed to a second death – slower, but equally destructive.

In 2001, the Herculaneum Conservation Project was established in an attempt to reduce the decay to a minimum. Launched by the Packard Humanities Institute in partnership with the local heritage authority and the British School at Rome, the Project has set about repairing the damage in various ways, including conserving decorative wall paintings and mosaics, repairing roofs, improving the drainage at the site, and even clearing the ruins of pigeons, whose excrement causes corrosion. Good progress has been made, although like all archaeological sites, Herculaneum is fragile and will require continued high quality care in the years to come.

---

4. The skeletons along the ancient shoreline

One notable moment of progress after 1961 came in March 1982, when archaeologists became concerned by the level of flooding in the Suburban Baths (which had already been excavated). They decided to dig a trench beneath the complex to channel off water, and dug into what had been arched storehouses along the seafront – these are conventionally referred to as 'boathouses', even though the Roman boats

A modern view of six of the twelve boathouses.

This boat was excavated with its wood almost fully intact. It would have been about 9 metres long and over 2 metres wide, and was manoeuvred by three pairs of oars. It looks much like a *gozzo*, a traditional fishing boat still used in the seas of the Italian coast.

which have been found would have been too big to fit into them! Soon a skeleton was found, followed by another, and then more still. By 2002, more than 350 skeletons had been found in this area, most of them huddled together in the boathouses. It was an extraordinary and gruesome find – what had happened to these people?

Before 1982, it had been assumed that almost everyone in the town had managed to escape, since only 32 skeletons had been found. Among these were the bones of a baby still lying in its cradle, and a boy still lying in bed, with a chicken lunch on a nearby table. We can only guess why they had been abandoned in the town – perhaps they were considered too weak or vulnerable to be evacuated. Yet the people in the boathouses seem to have been awaiting rescue; it is interesting that only one boat has been found at the site – perhaps a fishing fleet had been caught out at sea when the eruption began, or other boats may have carried people to safety and found themselves unable to get back due to the pre-tsunami effect that accompanied the eruption, as Pliny the Younger describes:

> 'It seemed as though the sea was being sucked backwards, as if it were being pushed back by the shaking of the land. Certainly the shoreline moved outwards, and many sea creatures were left on dry sand.'
>
> Pliny, *Letters* 6.20.9

> **The force of the eruption**
> Not all the skeletons were found inside the boathouses. One woman had clearly been thrown down onto the beach from the terrace above – her skeleton shows a smashed skull, a crushed pelvis and a thighbone which had been jerked up to her collar bone, all of which is further evidence of the force with which the pyroclastic surge arrived.

Anyone left in the town would have been overwhelmed by one of the early surges and killed by thermal shock; death would have been instantaneous, but gruesome nonetheless: the people would have heard the pyroclastic surge come screaming down the hillside at an enormous speed; when it hit them at a temperature of between 400 and 500 degrees Celsius, their organs vapourised, while there is evidence of teeth shattering and brains boiling and bursting through skulls – in some cases, cracked skulls have been blackened on the inside. Moreover, the bones were exposed to such high temperatures that the DNA has degraded – which is unfortunate, since we cannot tell how many of these people were related to one another or what ethnic groups they belonged to.

Dr Sara Bisel's research

In June 1982, Dr Sara Bisel, an archaeologist and anthropologist, was called to the site to examine the emerging skeletons. In all, she worked with 139 Herculaneans – 51 males, 49 females and 39 children. She was able to gather a variety of evidence, both from the condition of the bones themselves and from the artefacts found alongside them. As a result, she tried to interpret what sort of lives these people may have led, although her approach has come in for criticism on the grounds that she has over-interpreted the evidence in a number of cases. In particular, it has been argued that she was too specific about the age, social class and character of some of the skeletal remains.

Nonetheless, what she discovered about these people was very interesting, and a few examples are given below:

- **'The lady of the rings'**. One woman was named after the two gold rings found on her left hand, both of which were set with gemstones; she was also wearing golden bracelets and earrings. Tests on her bones revealed that she was in her forties, relatively tall, and well nourished; she also had perfect teeth. She had probably given birth to two or three children. Bisel suggested that she may have been a wealthy member of Herculaneum society.
- **'The soldier'**. This skeleton was given its name because it was found lying with a sword attached to a belt – although there is no other evidence that he was indeed a soldier. Beside him were carpenter's tools, such as chisels and an adze. He was in his 30s

The skeleton of the 'soldier'.

The skeleton of a young
woman cradling the tiny
skull of a baby.

and had a particularly strong right forearm, possibly suggesting years of work as a carpenter. He had a huge nose and three of his front teeth were missing, although not from tooth decay – perhaps they had been knocked out.

- **A group**. Perhaps most poignant were a large group of twelve who may have belonged to the same household: three men, four women, four children and a baby. The baby was wearing jewellery, which led Bisel to speculate that she may have been from a wealthy family. However, she was being cradled by a young woman in her teens, whose bones showed signs of malnutrition and overwork. Bisel suggested that she may have been a family slave entrusted with looking after the baby in those final hours.

The skeletons of Herculaneum represent a rare treasure trove for archaeologists since Romans practised cremation in this period – this was therefore the first significant sample of a cross-section of a Roman population from the 1st century CE. They also represent a unique example of a 'healthy' population – whereas most skeletons in cemeteries are of people who died of disease or of old age, the Herculaneum skeletons were all killed by a single accident and offer a snapshot of the living population in 79 CE.

Analysis of 36 relatively complete skeletons reveals that the average height in men was 5 feet 7 inches (170 centimetres) and in women 5 feet 1.5 inches (156 centimetres) which is not dissimilar to the modern population. In general, they had good teeth, perhaps because the local water supply contained high levels of fluoride, while the Romans never discovered sugar; however, there was a strong build up of tartar on some of the teeth, suggesting that bad breath must have been an issue!

Other skeletons give hints as to injury and illness. Five showed some sort of bone trauma, but had recovered remarkably well – a testament to the high quality of Roman surgery. A further seven skeletons (five adults and two children) contained levels of lead high enough to cause

---

Review 1

1. Draw a timeline for what we know about the history of Herculaneum. Why do you think that it developed differently from Pompeii?
2. Summarise the ways in which Herculaneum gives us archaeological information which is not available at Pompeii.
3. Find out about the work of the Herculaneum Conservation Project at www.herculaneum.org. How much danger is the site in at the present time?
E. Why was the discovery of the bodies in the boathouses so important for our understanding both of how Herculaneum was destroyed, and of life in the Roman world more generally?

An aerial view of partially excavated ancient Herculaneum.

poisoning and even brain damage. This information would tie in with the use of lead pipes to channel the water supply (see p. 280), while lead was also used in crockery such as pots, plates, and cups, as well as in some medicines.

5. Layout

It is impossible for us to have a complete picture of Herculaneum because of the relatively small proportion of the site which has been uncovered. Even the theatre remains underground and hidden away from visitors. Also buried but located is the town's *Basilica*, which must have been used in a similar way to that of Pompeii. Perhaps most crucially, the forum, just beyond the excavated area, has yet to be fully uncovered; this would surely teach us much more about the town's public spaces.

The excavated area is the lower end of the town as it slopes down to the sea. As you can see from the plan opposite, it consists of three main streets (*cardines*) heading north-east up the hill, with two streets crossing at right angles (*decumani*); a third *decumanus* is known from 18th-century tunnel excavations. This part of the town contained two sets of baths – the Suburban Baths on the ancient shoreline, and another com-

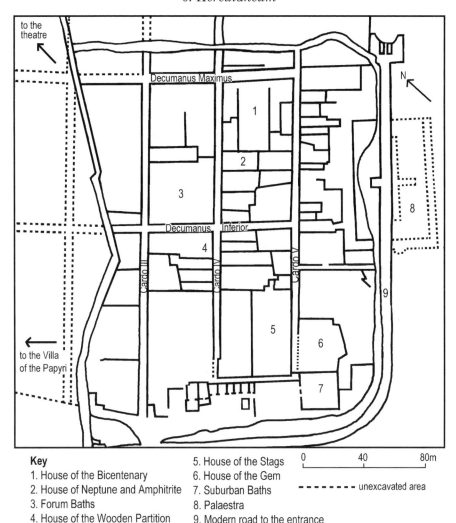

A plan of the excavated area of Herculaneum.

Key

1. House of the Bicentenary
2. House of Neptune and Amphitrite
3. Forum Baths
4. House of the Wooden Partition
5. House of the Stags
6. House of the Gem
7. Suburban Baths
8. Palaestra
9. Modern road to the entrance

plex further into town, known either as the Forum or the Central Baths. The latter had separate bathing areas for men and women, both of which were heated by a central furnace (like the Stabian Baths in Pompeii – see p. 250); unfortunately for the women, however, their baths did not have a *frigidarium*. To the south-east of the excavated area, a large *palaestra* has also been partially excavated, and this had a cross-shaped pool in the middle.

The rest of the excavated site consists of streets, houses and shops similar to those of ancient Pompeii and other Roman sites. One differ-

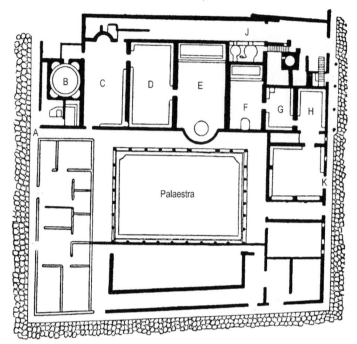

A plan of
the Forum
Baths.

A. Men's entrance
B. Men's frigidarium
C. Men's apodyterium
D. Men's tepidarium

E. Men's caldarium
F. Women's caldarium
G. Women's tepidarium
H. Women's apodyterium

J. Furnace
K. Women's entrance

Waste disposal

As part of the Herculaneum Conservation Project's work, the town's sewers
have recently been excavated, allowing them to be used again to help drain
the site. During their work, archaeologists came across a part of the town's
sewer network which is more like a huge septic tank, into which chutes from
the latrines and kitchens of the houses and shops above emptied waste.
Since this septic tank had no outlet, slaves would have been used to empty it
from time to time, no doubt a revolting task but useful for fertilising the
surrounding fields.

A huge amount of organic waste and refuse had collected inside. A large
proportion of this was human excrement, which can tell us a good deal about
the local diet: eggshell fragments, poppy and fig seeds (Cato the Elder, in an
essay on agriculture, is full of praise for the figs of Herculaneum), olive pips,
fish bones and scales, pig, sheep and bird bones, and a particularly high
number of chicken bones; those with more exotic tastes were also eating sea
urchins. This discovery is another example of how the eruption of Vesuvius
has allowed us to learn about the small details of daily life in the region, and
in particular the diet and health of the inhabitants.

ence, however, is found in the lower pavements and lack of stepping-stones for crossing the streets; Herculaneum had a far better drainage system – an expertly constructed, large sewer system which ran under the town's streets. Thanks to this, there was no need to prevent people from stepping into the streets.

6. Housing

Herculaneum had a range of houses, with grand mansions set alongside humble dwellings, as Pompeii did. However, while Pompeii includes some enormously wealthy residences indicating some very rich inhabitants, there was also a large number of poorer residences. By contrast, the average level of wealth at Herculaneum seems to have been higher – one piece of evidence for this is the much higher percentage of houses decorated with multicoloured marbles, a clear sign of wealth in the Roman world.

Some of the most impressive houses are found overlooking the sea, including the House of the Stags, whose beautifully decorated peristyle afforded fantastic views out over the bay towards the islands of Capreae and Pithekoussai. However, there are two houses in Herculaneum which give us particularly good information about certain aspects of Roman house design, while one villa outside the town offers a tantalising possibility.

a. The House of the Wooden Partition

This house was once very big, but it seems that in the middle of the 1st century CE some rooms on the street sides were converted into shops – a large clothes press was found in one of these. Moreover, an upper floor

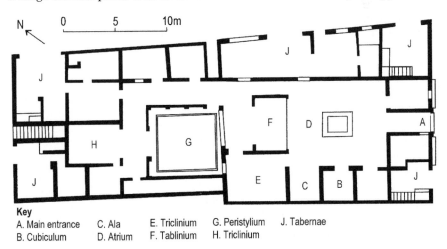

Key
A. Main entrance C. Ala E. Triclinium G. Peristylium J. Tabernae
B. Cubiculum D. Atrium F. Tablinium H. Triclinium

A plan of the House of the Wooden Partition.

The façade of the House of the Wooden Partition today.

The *atrium* of the House of the Wooden Partition, with the partition still in situ.

was added in the same period; this had a separate flight of stairs as its entrance, and suggests that the upper rooms were used as a separate apartment.

The house's east façade is one of the best preserved of any in Pompeii or Herculaneum; indeed, what we can see today on its ground and first floor level is probably almost the same as what people saw in 79 CE. Outside the front door are the benches where clients would wait to meet their patron in the morning (see p. 152); above these, small windows look onto the street, while the wooden cross beams are still in place, albeit carbonised. Entering into the house through the front door, one finds a typical wealthy *domus*, laid out in the classic *atrium-tablinum-peristylium* form. The *impluvium* was decorated with marble, while a marble table placed in front of it remains in place today. To the back of the house, a *triclinium* was found beyond the *peristylium*.

However, the item of most interest is the 'wooden partition' from which the house takes its name. It is assumed that this was used as a screen to separate the tablinum from the *atrium*, giving the *paterfamilias* some privacy when required. The partition was originally made of three beautifully panelled double doors, although the middle panel was sadly hacked through by early tunnellers. Thankfully, the other two panels have survived in carbonised form, together with their hinges and bronze lamp supports, each in the form of a ship's figurehead. Another carbonised relic can be seen in a small room off the *atrium* – a bed or couch which stood on legs shaped by a lathe.

b. The House of Neptune and Amphitrite

This house seems to have been a typically middle-class residence. It was reconstructed in the second quarter of the 1st century CE. Since its front wall was destroyed by the eruption and only partially reconstructed,

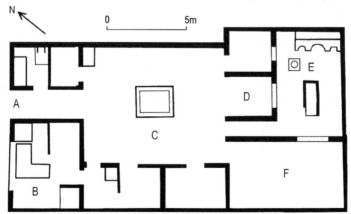

Key A. Main entrance   B. Taberna   C. Atrium   D. Tablinium   E. Courtyard   F. Triclinium

A plan of the House of Neptune and Amphitrite.

The mosaic of Neptune and Amphitrite from which the house takes its name.

visitors today can see directly into the shop at the front. This was probably owned by the family and run by a house slave. It has a counter, a hearth, a sink, and some amphorae of wine, as well as a low mezzanine level which was probably used either for sleeping space or for storage. The back part of the shop was closed off by a wooden partition.

Walking through the front door of the house, a visitor entered the *atrium*, which contained an ornate *lararium*. The house also had two upper floor areas; one was at the back, perhaps reached by a ladder in the courtyard, and consisted of two simply decorated rooms. The upper floor at the front and side of the house, which was reached by a staircase inside, is much better preserved. It consisted of eight rooms, one of which was probably a *triclinium*, while there was also a kitchen and a bedroom. Since both upper areas were accessed from inside the house, it seems that they were used by the family.

The house's focal point was its courtyard at the back, which may have been used as a *triclinium*. Here, the owners have made up for the fact that there was no room for a *peristylium* or garden by creating outdoor scenes in a set of wall paintings along with stunning water features. On the back wall was a large mosaic of Neptune, the god of the sea, and his

The *nymphaeum* in the House of Neptune and Amphitrite.

wife Amphitrite, both depicted on a gold background. Surrounding them were intricate floral designs in red, blue and gold. On the adjoining wall was a *nymphaeum*, a monumental fountain, with scenes of the country-side: deer being chased by hounds, garlands of fruit and flowers, and peacocks. In the centre of the room was a small marble column forming a fountain feature.

The idea here is simple – if the owner of this house could not afford space for a real garden, then he was going to reproduce one artistically with a riot of brilliant colours and water features.

c. The Villa of the Papyri
In 1750, a magnificent villa was discovered just outside Herculaneum and partially excavated. It is believed to have been owned at one time by Julius Caesar's father-in-law, Lucius Calpurnius Piso. Terraced in four different layers down to the sea, it had a baths complex and library, with floors of marble or mosaic, as well as several large garden areas with pools surrounded by fountains and statues.

However, for all its stunning beauty, the villa is most famous for the papyri from which it takes its name. More than 1,000 carbonised papyri scrolls have been found in all, the majority them found in a room along with busts of three Greek philosophers – Epicurus, Hermarchus and

In 1750, from an underground tunnel near Herculaneum, Karl Weber drew plans of the majestic Villa of the Papyri. Millionaire John Paul Getty built a museum in California based on these plans.

This bronze statue was one of two identical statues from the large *peristylium*. Both have glass paste eyes; traces of red paint were also found on the athlete's lips. Eighty statues have been found during the excavations of the villa.

Rolled and unrolled papyri. The papyri are extremely fragile, and many were destroyed in the initial attempts to unroll them. Of those which have been unrolled, not all are legible.

Zeno – as well as one of the orator Demosthenes. Scientists have been able to unravel and interpret some of the scrolls, and three-quarters of them are works of Philodemus of Gadara (a city in what is now Jordan), an Epicurean philosopher (see p. 104) of the 1st century BCE.

Although Philodemus tells us a good deal about Epicurean philosophy, archaeologists and classicists had hoped that the library would

347

contain some of the famous lost books of ancient writers – for example, only 35 of the 142 books written by Livy in his *History of Rome* (see pp. 1-2) are known to us, and the lost books could tell us a great deal about other periods of Roman history. All is not lost, however – many ancient libraries had both a Greek and a Latin section, and it is hoped that a room with Latin texts lies unexcavated.

To dig or not to dig?

The Villa of the Papyri therefore perhaps offers enormous potential for teaching us much more about wealthy and literate Romans and their world. There are many archaeologists, historians and papyrologists who would like to see excavations extended specifically to investigate whether there is a second library with Latin texts waiting to be found.

However, other archaeologists have been equally strong in their opposition to excavation at the villa. This may seem a strange position for the profession to take, but they argue that what has already been excavated has suffered greatly owing to a lack of adequate maintenance and conservation. Until the excavated site can be properly cared for in the long term, they believe, no more should be exposed, so that it remains safe and stable for future generations to uncover. They also point out that further excavation of the villa and other buried areas of Herculaneum could only be done by destroying the medieval town centre of Ercolano and many important historic buildings that lie along the so-called 'Golden Mile' of 122 18th-century villas.

At this stage, archaeologists have decided not to risk exposing any more of the building until they can guarantee the conservation of what has already been excavated. This may change in the future – but only if appropriate techniques for excavating without negative impact on the town are found. If the villa is eventually excavated, it may illuminate aspects of the Roman world so far unknown.

Review 2

1. How does the layout of the uncovered areas of Herculaneum compare to that of Pompeii?

2. How does the House of the Wooden Partition give us information about Roman housing which we do not find at Pompeii? What similarities does it have to the houses of Pompeii?

3. What can we learn about Roman housing from the House of Neptune and Amphitrite?

E. Should the Villa of the Papyri be excavated? What are the advantages and disadvantages of such a course of action?

Appendix 1

The City of Rome

The city of Rome developed around seven hills alongside the river Tiber, which flowed into the sea about 25 kilometres (16 miles) away. The first settlements on the site of Rome date from the 10th century, and there were various reasons why this was an obvious point for settlement. For one thing, the area was abundant in natural resources which allowed the early settlers to flourish. Writing in 54 BCE, the statesman Cicero clearly appreciated this point:

> 'In choosing a site for the city, how could Romulus' inspired judgement have been improved on? For, by placing his city on the bank of a broad river which flows steadily into the sea all the year round, he secured the advantages of a coastal town, and avoided its drawbacks. For the city can use its waterway for importing what it needs and for exporting its surpluses ... So it seems to me that at this early stage Romulus predicted that the city would one day be the centre and heart of a mighty empire. For no other site in Italy would have enabled us to maintain our widespread dominion so easily.'

Elsewhere, he also comments that the site is well supplied by natural springs. He then continues by evaluating the natural defences provided by the site:

> 'Furthermore, anyone with any powers of observation will have a clear impression of the natural strength of the city's defences. The line of its walls was cleverly planned by Romulus and his successors to run along steep and rugged hillsides for all its length, so that the single approach, between the Esquiline and Quirinal hills, was protected by a huge rampart and ditch, blocking an enemy advance. The city's citadel is so well fortified by its surrounding precipices ... that it remained safe and impregnable even during the terrifying onslaught of the Gauls.'
>
> Cicero, *On the Republic* 2.5-6

As Cicero suggests here, a key element in the development of the city were the seven hills on the west side of the Tiber (see map on p. 350). The hills all had names, some of whose origins are clearer than others. For example, the citadel of Rome which Cicero refers to was the Capitoline, the seat of government; it therefore took its name from the Latin *caput*, meaning 'head'. The Quirinal hill was named after Quirinus, a god of early Rome (Roman citizens were sometimes also known as Quirites), while the Viminal was named after the small willow trees (*vimina*) which grew there.

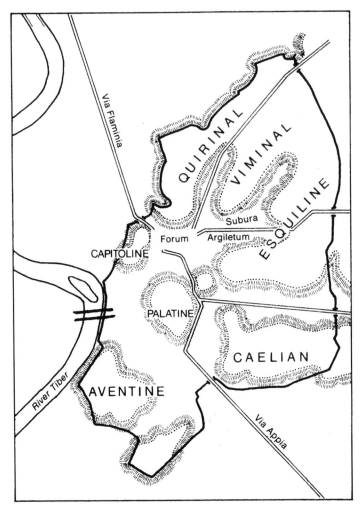

Rome in the early days, showing the seven hills and the 4th-century stone wall, known as the Servian Wall.

The growth of the city

The small settlements on the hills merged into a unified community, probably in the middle of the 8th century. This united settlement was recognised by a sacred boundary, called the *pomoerium*, which had been marked by a plough to indicate the area under special protection of the city's gods. However, it wasn't until Rome came under Etruscan influence in the 6th century that the city really took on a recognisable urban form.

At this stage, temples and public buildings were constructed, and the whole area was surrounded by a defensive rampart. In particular, Tarquinius Superbus is credited with making some key developments: building the Temple of Jupiter Optimus Maximus on the Capitoline hill (see p. 71), and draining the swamp which lay between the Capitoline and the Palatine. On this reclaimed land was built a forum (see below), the city centre where social and civic business was conducted.

The Cloaca Maxima

The Etruscans were fine engineers, and they managed to drain the forum area by means of a huge underground channel, which collected all the standing water and carried away to the Tiber. This was known as the Cloaca Maxima ('Greatest Sewer') and was one of the world's earliest sewage systems. It was so good that it was still used by Romans centuries later!

Roman engineering skills were equally brilliant in bringing water into the city. The Romans were masters of designing aqueducts and, by the end of the 1st century CE, the city was served by no fewer than nine, with a total length of 425 kilometres (264 miles) – it is estimated that they delivered one billion litres of water to the city over a 24 hour period.

The city was further developed after its sack by the Gauls in 390 BCE. About ten years later, a proper wall was built around the city for the first time. This was known as the Servian Wall (as it was mistakenly thought to date from the reign of the king Servius Tullius – see p. 8), and it allowed the city to be enlarged – the original *pomoerium* had included 180 hectares, while the new wall surrounded an area of 280 hectares. As Livy explains, the Romans also took the opportunity to renew their city:

> 'The rebuilding of the city began, without any planning at all. Tiles were supplied at government expense ... in their haste they took no care in laying out the streets ... this explains why the old sewers, which former-ly ran under publicly owned land, now frequently pass beneath private houses, and why Rome looks more like some haphazard settlement than a properly planned city.'   Livy 5.55

When writing this, Livy would have been aware of the Greek cities of the Mediterranean, many of which had been laid out on an organised grid-plan. Yet although the Romans later copied this model with the new set-tlements they built, it had not been the case with their own capital. Nonetheless, the Greeks did have a profound influence on the city dur-ing the period of hellenisation in the 2nd century BCE (see p. 31); in par-ticular, Greek style basilicas were constructed – public halls which served as markets, offices and law courts.

Augustus and the emperors
When Augustus took control of the Roman world in 31 BCE, he was determined to turn Rome into a city worthy of a great imperial capital. He therefore initiated a huge building programme for the city, during

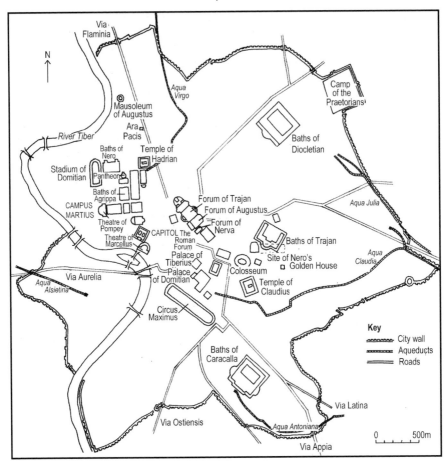

Imperial Rome in the first three centuries CE.

which he renovated the main forum (he also built a second, smaller one which was named after him), as well as having many public buildings renovated or constructed from scratch. In particular, his closest ally Marcus Agrippa oversaw the redevelopment of the city's water supply, restoring and building aqueducts, enlarging and cleansing the Cloaca Maxima, and constructing new baths. This programme transformed the city; the achievement was aptly summed up by Suetonius, who wrote a biography of Augustus:

> 'Since the city was not as splendid as the dignity of the empire demanded, and was subject to flood and fire, he made it so beautiful that he could justly claim to have found it made of brick, and left it made of marble.'   Suetonius, *Augustus* 28

Suetonius mentions here that the city was prone to fire, and Augustus also established a fire brigade consisting of 7,000 men, known as *vigiles*. They were permanently on patrol in the city, although at times they could not prevent disasters from happening, as in 64 CE.

Following on from Augustus, subsequent emperors also tried to leave their mark on the city, with a number of new forums being constructed. In addition, Claudius built an aqueduct, Vespasian commissioned the Colosseum (see p. 212), and Domitian set up a new race track. Trajan was particularly innovative, building public baths, a shopping centre, and a vast and an elaborate new forum – more than two centuries later, when the emperor Constantius II visited it for the first time, he was awestruck, as Ammianus Marcellinus relates:

> 'When he entered the Forum of Trajan, a structure unequalled, I believe, anywhere on earth ... then he stood still in amazement: he gazed around at the mighty complex surrounding him, impossible to describe, impossible ever again for men to equal. Giving up all hopes of attempting anything like it, he simply said that all he could and would imitate was the equestrian statue of Trajan standing in the centre of the court.'
>
> Ammianus Marcellinus, 16.15

However, there were remarkable structures built after Trajan's time; his successor Hadrian rebuilt the Pantheon (see p. 87), which remains one of the most remarkable buildings in the world today due to the size and design of its dome. A century later Caracalla built the baths which bear his name (see p. 243), and these were almost matched by the Baths of Diocletian, built in the early 4th century.

Palaces

The most exclusive place to live in Rome was the Palatine hill, with its easy access to the forum and views over the Circus Maximus. Augustus built himself a modest house there, but later emperors had a series of elaborate palaces constructed. In fact, the English words 'palace' and 'palatial' are directly derived from the name of the hill where Rome's grandest residences were situated.

Entertainment

As well as grand civic buildings, the centre of Rome was furnished with lavish entertainment facilities. The Circus Maximus had developed from ancient times in the valley between the Aventine and Palatine hills (see p. 194), while the emperor Domitian constructed another racetrack (the shape of which now forms the Piazza Navona in central Rome). As for theatres, in the 61 BCE Pompey commissioned the first permanent theatre in the city (see p. 226), and this was soon followed during Augustus' building programme by the theatre of

Marcellus. The ancient city's most iconic building, the Colosseum, was completed in 80 CE.

There were also plenty of places where Romans could relax and refresh themselves. To the west of the city, a bend in the Tiber enclosed the Campus Martius ('Field of Mars'), a vast open park used as an exercise ground for soldiers and a training ground for athletes. Moreover, the city was home to a vast number of baths, grand and small, including, as we have seen, the huge complexes built by emperors such as Trajan, Caracalla and Diocletian.

The Forum Romanum

The main forum of Rome, the Forum Romanum, was the heart of the city's social, political and commercial life. The site was first developed in the 6th century BCE, when the valley between the Capitoline and Palatine hills was drained; originally, the forum was simply an outdoor meeting place – in fact, the word 'forum' is linked to the Latin *foris*, which meant 'outdoors'.

The remains in the forum today are relatively sparse and date from various periods in Rome's history. The plan opposite gives an outline of the area during the 1st century CE, the high point of the Roman empire. The forum is split by a main road, the **Via Sacra** ('Sacred Way'), which

The Forum Romanum today, as seen from the Capitoline hill. The Arch of Septimius Severus is in the foreground to the left, and to its right are the remains of the rostra. In the far distance at the other end of the forum is the Arch of Titus.

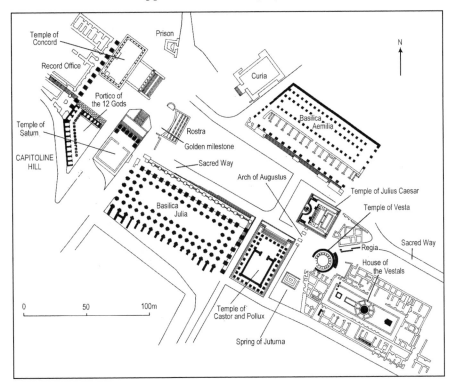

A plan of the Forum Romanum in the early 1st century CE.

was the grandest street in the city. At one end of the forum was the **Temple of Vesta** and the **House of the Vestals** (see p. 92), which were close to the **Temple of Julius Caesar**, built by Augustus in his memory. This was one of a number of temples in the vicinity. The two **Basilicas** were used both as law courts and as commercial centres; large crowds could come and watch the day's big trials, while merchants and bankers also came there to do their business.

The forum was a centre of political life as well. Senators met and discussed matters in the **Curia**, while politicians made speeches on the speaker's platform, known as the **Rostra**. This name comes from the six *rostra*, or ship's rams, which were captured in the battle of Antium in 338 BCE and attached to the front of the platform. Emperors also liked to use the area to commemorate their achievements; modern visitors to the forum can still see three **triumphal arches** in or near the forum – those of Titus, Septimius Severus and Constantine.

During the day, the forum would have been alive with people of all kinds. As well as politicians and businessmen, other citizens might come to visit the temples, listen to the speeches, watch trials, shop, or just meet friends. At other times, more formal ceremonies might take place, such as young men assuming the toga of manhood (see p. 147), funeral processions of important men (see p. 185), or triumphal processions of victorious generals.

All roads lead to Rome

The forum was in fact the heart of the whole empire. To symbolise this, the emperor Augustus set up by the Rostra a golden milestone which marked the origin of the roads which made their way out of the city to all parts of the empire. Romans liked to say that 'all roads lead to Rome'.

Appendix 2

The Roman Political System

1. The monarchy

The seven kings were believed to have been advised by a council of elders known as the **senate** (the word 'senate' comes from the Latin *senex*, meaning 'old man'). It was said to have been set up by Romulus, who appointed 100 rich aristocrats to advise him. It apparently grew in size, so that by the end of the reign of Tarquinius Superbus in 509 BCE, there were 300 senators.

2. The republic

When the kings were expelled in 509 BCE, the Romans set up a new political system. Each year, they voted for new political leaders, known collectively as **magistrates**.

a. The magistrates
By the late republic, there was a four-step career path for aspiring politicians hoping to become consul. This was known as the *cursus honorum*. The roles of the magistrates were as follows:

- **Quaestors (20)**: were officers responsible for financial affairs, supervising the state treasury, the collection of taxes, and managing public expenditure.
- **Aediles (4):** The aedileship did not become a full magistracy until 367 BCE; the aediles were responsible for public services, such as the corn dole (see p. 151), streets, public order, water supply and public games.
- **Praetors (8):** were in charge of the judicial system. They served as judges but could also convene meetings of the senate. They could also take on the administrative duties of consuls absent from the city.
- **Consuls (2):** were the chief civil and military magistrates who were the heads of state. A consul had to be at least 42 years old to stand for election, and then had to wait another ten years before he could stand again. The consuls initiated and passed legislation, after consultation with the senate. They were also military commanders and took control of foreign policy.

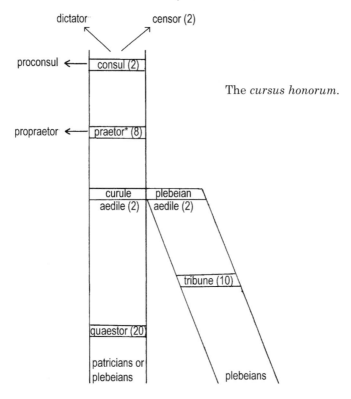

The *cursus honorum.*

Ex-consuls and ex-praetors were eligible to serve as governors in the provinces. In this capacity, they were known as **proconsuls** and **propraetors**. In addition, two other key positions at the heart of the constitution were:

- **Dictator (1):** if the city was facing a grave military crisis so that it needed one man to take control, then the consuls could appoint a dictator (see p. 16 to read the story of Cincinnatus). He could serve for up to six months, during which time the constitution was suspended.
- **Censors (2):** were elected every five years to serve for a period of 18 months to update the electoral roll and to make property assessments for tax purposes. They were also responsible for revising the lists of senators and equites (see p. 360).

The final key position was that of **tribune** (see below), a magistracy which came about as a result of a power struggle between rich and poor Romans known as the Conflict of the Orders.

Lictors, carrying *fasces*.

The lictors and fascism

Senior magistrates were given an escort of bodyguards known as lictors (the number of lictors depended on the office – consuls were each accompanied by 12, praetors by 6, etc). Lictors were usually freedmen, and had to follow their magistrate wherever he went, including the forum, the baths, temples, or at home. To symbolise the power of their magistrate to flog or execute, each lictor carried the *fasces*, a bundle of white birch rods, tied together into a cylinder, with the blade of a bronze axe coming out of the top.

The modern political word 'fascism' is derived from the *fasces*. For when the Italian Benito Mussolini and his group of ultra-right wing authoritarians formed a new political party in 1921, they wanted to connect themselves to Italy's ancient past. They saw the *fasces* as a symbol of how the Roman republic had maintained good order, and so called themselves *'fascisti'* – fascists – to indicate the authoritarian nature of their movement.

The Conflict of the Orders

Early Roman society was highly polarised between the small group of wealthy, land-owning aristocrats, known as the **patricians**, and the poor majority of citizens, known as the **plebeians**. In the early days of the republic, it was the patricians who held all the positions of power in the city, and who filled the senate. The plebeians soon came to resent this, and insisted on having their own representatives in the political system. Therefore, from 494 BCE, each year there were elected the tribunes of the people:

- **Tribunes of the people (10):** The tribunes had the power to veto the legislation of any magistrate, while they could also convene meetings of the senate. They therefore had great power to block anything not in the interest of the plebeians. From 471 BCE, they also supervised a new plebeian assembly, which passed its own laws known as *plebiscita*.

However, the new office of tribune did not solve all the plebeians' problems at once. For many years a power struggle ensued, known as the Conflict of the Orders, during which the plebeians won concessions from the patricians over a large span of time. For example, in 455 BCE the ban on inter-marriage between the two orders was lifted. Five years later came another key moment, when a law code was written down for the first time, thus preventing patricians from making up and changing the laws as it suited them. This legal code was known as the **Code of the Twelve Tables**, and it was still being learnt by Roman schoolboys some four centuries later.

In 367 BCE, a law was enacted that one of the consuls should be plebeian; the final victory came in 287 BCE, when all *plebiscita* passed by the plebeian assembly were made legally binding on the whole population. It is no coincidence that this happened just as Rome was taking control of the whole of Italy, and needed all citizens to work together in managing the growing sphere of her power.

However, the conclusion of this conflict did not put an end to class differences in Roman society. During the 3rd century BCE, the wealthiest citizens, drawn by now from both patrician and plebeian families, formed a new aristocracy, known as the **nobiles** ('nobles'). They were not allowed to take part in commerce and trade, but relied on their land to provide income. Crucially, the **nobiles** were the only Romans wealthy enough to be able to run for the magistracies, which were unpaid.

b. The senate

Although the senate was in theory an advisory body, in reality it was the most powerful section of the government of Rome. Any citizen who had been elected to one of the magistracies became a senator for life. (the number of senators fluctuated at different times in Rome's history, but was generally around the 600 mark). It was therefore in the interest of magistrates to work closely with the senate, since they would soon be senators themselves; in addition, they would probably hope that they

A painting imagining the Roman senate in session.

The equites

As the Roman sphere of control grew, it gave many opportunities for men outside the traditional aristocracy to make money out of trade and commerce throughout the Mediterranean world. Such men were known as equites ('knights' – since in early Rome they were wealthy enough to own a horse and fight in the Roman cavalry).

The equites often lived in tension with the senators; the former were not allowed to run for public office, while the latter were forbidden to engage in trade. Yet, there were other instances of the two groups working together; since senators could not engage in business, they were often silent partners on commercial transactions, and would make alliances with certain equites for the benefit of both parties.

(and perhaps other members of their family) would hold further magistracies in the future, so they would not want to alienate their senatorial colleagues. For this reason, magistrates would rarely go against the senate's wishes.

Roman coin showing
a citizen voting.

The senate was heavily involved in law making. The two consuls
would introduce to the senators proposals for legislation; if the senate
approved them, then the consuls would put them to the vote in one of the
popular assemblies. Therefore, the senate really controlled what laws
could be voted on. The senate also controlled public finances and foreign
affairs, administering the provinces and sending out its own members
to be provincial governors. As Rome's territory increased, the senate
grew more and more powerful, since only the senators, it was believed,
had the education and experience to deal with the complex issues of
imperial administration.

c. The popular assemblies
Roman citizens did not vote for candidates and on legislation on a 'one
man, one vote' system, whereby every man's vote counted equally.
Instead, they had a complex collegiate system, with each citizen belong-
ing to an electoral college (rather like the voting system for the US president); this was weighted in favour of the wealthy, since the colleges
were divided up by wealth, with the colleges of the poor having many
more members than those of the rich. In essence, the rich had more voting power than the poor.

There were also different voting assemblies depending on the nature
of the legislation. As we have seen, the *concilium plebis* (plebeian assembly) could vote laws into effect from 287 BCE. However, for the most
part, it was the old senatorial families which controlled the elections and
the magistrates – through their enormous wealth and patchwork of
clients, they could often ensure that the people voted for their preferred
candidates. During the final two centuries of the republic, it became
common for politicians to try to buy votes by staging ever more impressive shows and games (see p. 193).

d. Polybius' analysis of the constitution
Polybius, a Greek living in the 2nd century BCE who admired Rome, was
certain that the Romans owed their success to their mixed constitution,

whereby the magistrates, senate, and people all had a say. In what follows, he sums up the roles of each, starting with the magistrates:

'The consuls have authority over all public business. All other magistrates, except the tribunes, are under them and take their orders. They consult the senate on matters of urgency, and carry out the senate's decrees ... They summon assemblies of the people, bring proposals before them, and carry out what the majority decrees. In the preparations for war they can appoint military tribunes, levy soldiers, and select those who are fittest for service ... They can spend as much public money as they choose, and have a financial officer (*quaestor*) to act on their instructions.'

He then goes on to assess the role which the senate plays as follows:

'The senate controls the treasury, and regulates all revenue and expenditure. Except for payments made to the consuls, financial officers are not allowed to draw on public money unless the senate gives permission by decree ... The senate hears cases of treason, conspiracy, poisoning and assassination ... and acts as an arbitrator in private disputes. It is responsible for sending ambassadors abroad to settle differences, to give advice, to make demands, to receive submission or to declare war. The senate too receives all foreign delegations, and decides what answer to give them.'

He next comes to the role played by the people through the popular assemblies:

'But there is a role, and a very important one, left for the people. The people have the sole right to confer honours and inflict punishment. They are the only court to decide matters of life and death ... It is the people, too, who by their votes bestow honours on those who deserve them. They have the right to accept and reject laws, and, most important of all, they debate questions of war and peace. And in the case of alliances, armistices or treaties the people can ratify or cancel them.'

He then reaches the following conclusion:

'Each of these three groups can have its power counteracted by another group, and none had absolute control. Even the senate is unable to put any of its resolutions into effect if one of the tribunes of the people uses his veto, and in fact a tribune's veto can prevent the senate from meeting altogether. And those tribunes are always obliged to act as the people decree, and to fall in with their wishes.'   Polybius, 1.66ff.

In reality, Polybius was too idealistic in his analysis of the constitution. As we have seen, the magistrates made sure that they did not upset the senate, and even tribunes were generally careful in this regard, since often they too had their eye on a political career ending in the consulship. Moreover, the senate was made up of a narrow aristocracy who held on to power closely and admitted few members from non-senatorial families.

SPQR

The phrase signifying the Roman state was SPQR, standing for *Senatus Populusque Romanus* – 'The Senate and People of Rome'. It appeared on coins, public documents, and the standards of Roman legions. Today, Rome's city council uses the formula as the motto for the city, and it can still be seen on the city's coat of arms, as well as many other civic buildings and monuments – even on the manhole covers of the Roman drains!

---

3. The empire

After Augustus defeated Antony and Cleopatra in 31 BCE, it was clear that the old system of republican government was dead. Yet Augustus was careful not to dismantle the old system, but simply to ensure that he used it to give himself the key powers. Therefore, each year he would hold one of the key positions of government – consul or tribune – as well as taking control of the empire's most important provinces. He commanded the armies, who swore an oath of loyalty to him, and controlled almost all foreign policy. Moreover, he also took the right to name his successor.

This new constitution was a monarchy in all but name:

- The power of the **senate** was diminished considerably, since they had little power to act against the wishes of the emperor. As time went on, the senate generally became less and less significant, although some of the most successful emperors were those who tried to work with it.
- If Augustus diminished the power of the senate, his successor Tiberius did the same to the **people** when he transferred the voting for magistrates from the popular assemblies to the senate. From now on, the people were limited to expressing their views at public events such as games and triumphs.

One group who did relatively well out of the new arrangement, however, was the equites. Augustus recognised that he needed an effective civil service to administer the empire. The equites were also keen to support the new emperor, since he brought peace and prosperity to the empire, allowing them to pursue their business interests in a flourishing and stable world.

Appendix 3

Roman Currency Values

The Romans started using coinage as the city expanded and they came into contact with the Greeks of southern Italy in the 4th century BCE. The system of coinage started from the smallest coin, the *quadrans*, and progressed as follows:

4 *quadrantes*	=	1 *as*
2 *asses*	=	1 *dupondius*
2 *dupondii*	=	1 *sestertius*
4 *sestertii*	=	1 *denarius*
25 *denarii*	=	1 *aureus*

The relative values of these coins was reflected in the metal used to mint them: an *aureus* (which was rarely minted but normally used as a large unit of accounting) was made of gold, a *denarius* of silver, a *sestertius* and a *dupondius* of bronze, while the *as* and the *quadrans* were minted in copper.

Three Roman coins: a *sestertius* of Nero, a *denarius* of Trajan and an *aureus* of Marcus Aurelius.

The name of each unit also had a logic: a *quadrans* was a quarter of an *as*, which in turn meant a 'unit'; *dupondius* meant 'double weight' (*duo* + *pondus* – which gives us the English word 'pound'), since it was twice the value of an *as*; *sestertius* originally meant 'two and a half', since in early Roman times it was two and a half times the value of the *as*; in the same way, the *denarius* ('containing ten') was originally ten times the value of the *as*; *aureus* simply meant 'golden'.

Values

It is almost impossible to give an exact value of Roman coinage in modern money, partly because values changed so much from place to place over the centuries. However, sources do give a reasonable amount of evidence for currency values in the late republic and early empire:

Entry to the public baths: 1 *quadrans*
A loaf of bread: 1 *as*
Day's wage for a labourer: 1 *denarius*
Annual pay of a Roman soldier: 300 *denarii*
Cost of a slave boy: 600 *denarii*
Cost of staging 3-4 days public games: 25,000-50,000 *denarii*
Membership of the equestrian class: 100,000 *denarii*
Membership of the senatorial class: 250,000 *denarii*

Perhaps the most helpful point to remember is that the *denarius* was the daily wage of a labourer. It is likely that the *quadrans* and the *as* were today's equivalent of loose change, while a *dupondius* and *sestertius* might be considered similar in status to a two pound coin and five pound note respectively (or, in US dollars, to a five and ten dollar bill).

The legacy of the denarius

The Romans introduced a single European currency long before the Euro appeared in 2002. Moreover, the name *denarius* has lived on in many countries once ruled by the Romans. The 'dinar' is the unit of currency in Algeria, Tunisia, Libya, Iraq, Jordan, Kuwait and Serbia. Moreover, the Italian word *denaro*, the Spanish *dinero*, the Portuguese *dinheiro*, the Slovenian *denar* and the Catalan *diner* are all derived from *denarius* and all mean 'money' in their respective languages.

Appendix 4

Roman Clothing

Men's clothing

The **tunic** was the basic garment for all men. It was a type of long shirt, made of linen or wool, formed of two widths sewn together. It was slipped over the head and fastened round the body with a belt. At the front, it came down to the knees, but usually fell a little lower at the back.

The **toga** was the most famous form of Roman dress. All freeborn Roman citizens were entitled to wear the toga, although in practice it was a very cumbersome item and so was only used ceremonially or by members of the upper classes, particularly senators and magistrates performing public duties. It was made of fine wool, semi-circular in shape, and draped over one shoulder and wrapped around the body, falling down to the ankles. The toga a symbol of the Roman people – in Virgil's *Aeneid* (1.282), Jupiter talks of the future Roman race as *Romanos, rerum dominos, gentemque togatam* ('Romans, masters of the world, the toga-wearing race'). Of the various types of toga, the most important were as follows:

- The *toga virilis* ('toga of manhood') was worn by the average Roman citizen. It was plain white and first worn by a youth at his coming-of-age ceremony (see p. 147).
- The *toga praetexta* ('bordered toga') was worn by magistrates and boys who had not yet reached adulthood.
- The *toga candida* ('whitened toga') was a toga bleached white with chalk and worn by candidates for public office – the idea being that a dazzling white toga would suggest their virtue and honesty. The Latin for bright white, *candida*, meant that politicians seeking election were known as *candidati*, from where we get the English 'candidate'.

There were other forms of clothing too – including underwear and shoes, while for formal dinner parties a long and light linen garment, the *synthesis*, allowed guests to recline comfortably (see p. 155).

Women's clothing

The main item of clothing for a woman was a dress, the *stola*, which was tied at the waist and fell down to the ankles; a woman usually also slipped an undergarment tunic on underneath. If she went out, then she would wrap a rectangular woollen shawl, the *palla*, around her shoulders and often over her head. At dinner parties, women would wear the *synthesis* as men would.

No respectable woman would ever wear a toga, which was a sign of disgrace for a woman: women working as prostitutes or caught in adultery were forced to wear it as a mark of shame.

Appendix 5

Time

Hours of the day

The Romans mainly used sundials and water clocks to tell the time. However, these were far less precise than modern clocks, and so time in the Roman world was much more fluid – there would be no way, for example, that people would be able to agree to meet at exactly 10.15.

As we do today, the Romans divided their day into 24 hours, although they did not have 24 equal units of 60 minutes. The Roman day had twelve hours of daylight, counted from sunrise to sunset, and twelve hours of night, from sunset to sunrise. This meant that the length of the hours changed slightly every day – hours of day were short in winter and long in summer, with the opposite being true for the hours of night. At the winter solstice, when the day had only 8 hours 54 minutes of light, the length of each daylight hour was about 45 minutes, while by the summer solstice this had lengthened to about 75 minutes. The only days when the hours of day and night were of an equal length were the spring and autumnal equinoxes.

Romans adjusted their timekeeping according to the time of year – we know from sources that it was common to go to the baths at the eighth hour in winter but the ninth hour in summer. The day started at the beginning of the first hour – which in midwinter would be at about 7.30 am, while in midsummer it would be nearer to 4.30 am!

Months of the year

From early Roman times, the annual calendar had consisted of, at first ten, then twelve months fitted into a 355 day year. However, this was an inefficient system since an extra 'intercalary' month had to be fitted in, usually every other year, so that some years were longer than others. In 46 BCE, Julius Caesar oversaw the reorganisation of the calendar, creating a year of 365 days, with a 'leap year' inserted every fourth year which included an extra day in February. This was known as the 'Julian calendar' and, with a few small adjustments, is the one used in the modern world today.

The Romans did not count the days of their months from 1 to 28, 30 or 31, as we do. Instead, they had three points in the first half of the month from which they numbered their days:

- The 1st day of the month was known as the **Kalends** (from the verb 'to call', since originally a new month was 'called' at the arrival of a new moon), from which the English word 'calendar' is derived.
- The 5th day of the month (or the 7th in March, May, July and October) was called the **Nones** ('ninth', since the *Nones* was always nine days before the *Ides*, counting inclusively).
- The 13th day of the month (or the 15th in March, May, July and October) was known as the **Ides** (from the Latin *idus*, meaning 'half division', i.e. of a month).

The days of the month would be named according to which of these three dates was next to fall in the calendar. For example, the 1st of January would be known as the 'Kalends of January', but the 2nd of January would be called 'the fourth day before the Nones of January' – since the Romans counted inclusively.

The months of the year

Until 713 BCE, the Romans had a ten month annual calendar. The first four months were *Martius, Aprilis, Maius* and *Iunius* – *Martius* and *Iunius* were named after the gods Mars and Juno, while *Aprilis* is probably derived from the Latin verb *aperire*, 'to open', since this is the time of year when the flowers and plants 'open up'; *Maius* was named after the Greek goddess Maia, a fertility goddess associated with the Roman *Bona Dea* (see p. 94). The names of the other six months – *Quintilis, Sextilis, September, October, November, December* – simply meant 'fifth', 'sixth', etc.

In 713, the King Numa introduced a further two months at the beginning of the year – *Ianuarius* (from the god of entrances, Janus), and *Februarius* (named after a verb meaning to purify, since February was a month of purification). With the reorganisation of the calendar in the late 1st century BCE, *Quintilis* and *Sextilis* were renamed *Iulius* and *Augustus* after Julius Caesar and his successor Augustus. No attempt was made to rename the final four months of the year, which were now out of line with their place in the year – as they still are today!

Until the late republic, years were always named after the annual consuls so that, for example, 205 BCE was 'the year of the consulship of Publius Cornelius Scipio Africanus and Publius Licinius Crassus'. However, in later times, some annalists preferred to record years from 753 BCE – the traditional date of the foundation of the city (see p. 6). Under this system, 205 BCE would have been dated as 548 AUC (*Ab Urbe Condita* – 'from the foundation of the city').

The festival year

For most of Roman history, there was no seven day week with two days of rest as we have today. Instead, the Romans had a day off every eight days for a 'market-day'. This was known as the *nundinae*, meaning 'ninth day' since, counting inclusively, each market day was held on the ninth day after the previous one (1+7+1). In addition, the *Kalends*, *Nones*, and *Ides* were always rest days, as were various other 'festival days' which were set aside each month – some of these were given over to worshipping gods, while others were for games such as chariot racing, drama and gladiatorial shows.

The seven day week

The concept of a seven day week emerged among eastern Mediterranean peoples such as the Egyptians, Persians and Jews – the earliest evidence for the continuous use of this system appears with the Jews in 586 BCE during their captivity in Babylon. From the adoption of the Julian calendar, the seven day week was used in some parts of the empire alongside the nundinal cycle; in 321 CE, the emperor Constantine, who had made Christianity the official religion of the empire, adopted it for official usage.

The seven day system was devised by Middle Eastern astrologers, who named each day after the seven visible 'planets' which were believed to rule the universe: the Sun, the Moon, Mars, Mercury, Jupiter, Venus and Saturn. Starting with Sunday, the Roman days of the week were thus named: *dies Solis* ('Sun's day'), *dies Lunae* ('Moon's day'), *dies Martis* ('Mars' day'), *dies Mercurii* ('Mercury's day'), *dies Iovis* ('Jupiter's day'), *dies Veneris* ('Venus' day') and *dies Saturni* ('Saturn's day'). The names of the weekdays in the romance languages follow these Roman names, although in English they are based on Norse mythology.

Chronology

Year	Events	Writers
900 BCE	First settlements on Palatine and Esquiline Hills	
753	**The Kingdom** Traditional date of the foundation of Rome; Seven Kings: Romulus, Numa Pompilius, Tullus Hostilius, Ancus Martius, Tarquinius Priscus, Servius Tullius, Tarquinius Superbus	*c.* 8th century: Homer composes the *Iliad* and *Odyssey* in Greek
509	**The Republic** The Republic formed	
493	First tribunes appointed	5th century: high point of Greek
458	War with Aequi: Cincinnatus	drama in Athens (Aeschylus,
450	Twelve Tables of Law published	Sophocles, Euripides,
449	Tribunes increased to 10; sacrosanctity guaranteed by law	Aristophanes)
410	Rome overcomes Latin League	
406-396	Siege and capture of Veii	
390	The Gauls sack Rome	
390-338	War with Latin neighbours	
358-351	Successful wars in Etruria	
343-341	1st Samnite War	
338	Victory over Latins; Latin League dissolved	
327-304	2nd Samnite War	
321	Defeat at Caudine Forks	
312	Appian Way to Capua built	
298-290	3rd Samnite War	
287	Lex Hortensia; *plebiscita* become law Pyrrhus fights in Italy	
280-275	Tarentum surrenders	
272	1st Punic War	
264-241	Sicily becomes first Roman province;	Livius Andronicus: translation of
241	Sardinia follows in 238 2nd Punic War	Homer's *Odyssey*; plays
218-202	1st Macedonian War	
214-204		
200-194	2nd Macedonian War	Plautus: comedies
197	Spain organised as two provinces	Ennius: plays and epic poetry
171-168	3rd Macedonian War	
167	Sack of cities in Epirus: 150,000 enslaved	Terence: comedies
146	Rome destroys Corinth and Carthage in the same year	Pacuvius: tragedies
133	Pergamum becomes province of Asia Minor Tiberius Gracchus tribune	Polybius: *Histories*
123-122	Gaius Gracchus tribune	Accius: tragedies
107-100	Consulships and conquests of Marius	

91-89	Social War against Latin allies	
89	Mithridates invades Asia Minor	
88	Sulla marches on Rome	
87	Marius captures Rome; dies in 86	
82-80	Sulla dictator and then consul	
63	Cicero consul; conspiracy of Catiline	Cicero: numerous works
	1st Triumvirate (between Caesar,	Lucretius: *De Rerum Natura*
60	Pompey and Crassus)	Catullus: love poetry
	Caesar's conquests of Gaul	
58-49	Caesar crosses the Rubicon; civil war	Caesar: *Gallic War, Civil War*
49	with Pompey and the Senate	
	Death of Pompey after Pharsalus	
48	Assassination of Caesar	
44	Octavian defeats Anthony and	
31	Cleopatra at the battle of Actium	
		Horace: *Odes, Epistles*, etc.
	The Principate	Virgil: *Eclogues, Aeneid*, etc.
	Augustus (Octavian)	Livy: *History of Rome*
27-14 CE		Ovid: *Metamorphoses*, etc.
14-37	Tiberius	
37-41	Caligula	
41-54	Claudius	
54-68	Nero	Seneca the Younger: *Letters, Essays*
69	4 emperors	Petronius: *Satyricon*
69-79	Vespasian	Pliny the Elder: *Natural History*
79-81	Titus	Pliny the Younger: *Letters*
81-96	Domitian	Tacitus: *Histories, Annals*, etc
96-98	Nerva	Quintilian: *Education of an Orator*
98-117	Trajan	Martial: *Epigrams*
		Juvenal: *Satires*
117-138	Hadrian	Plutarch: *Lives*
		Suetonius: *Twelve Caesars*
138-161	Antoninus Pius	
161-180	Marcus Aurelius	
180-192	Commodus	
193	Pertinax; Didius Julianus	
193-211	Septimus Severus	
211-284	27 other emperors	
284-305	Diocletian; 6 other emperors	
306-337	Constantine	
313	Edict of Milan legalises Christianity	
337-378	12 other emperors	
379-395	Theodosius I; Christianity becomes the official state religion	Ammianus Marcellinus: *History*
395-475	24 other emperors	
475-476	Romulus Augustulus is the last Roman emperor in the West	

Index

Illustration Sources and Credits

References are to the page numbers of this book.

After M. Beard, J. North & S. Price (eds), *Religions of Rome* 1998), 227; After S. Bidel, *The Secrets of Vesuvius* (1990), 336 (below); After P. Bradley, *Ancient Rome: Using Evidence* (1990), 355; After J. Deiss, *Herculaneum* (1985), 336 (above), 338, 340; After W. Jashemski, The *Gardens of Pompeii, Herculaneum and the Villas Destroyed by Vesuvius* (1993), 310; After R. Ling, *Pompeii: History, Life and Afterlife* (2005), 256, 283, 289; After S. Nappo, *Pompeii* (2008), 131 (above), 250, 313, 316, 319, 322; After N. Rodgers, *Life in Ancient Rome* (2005), 212; After D. Taylor, *Roman Society* (1990), 155; After G. Tingay & J. Badcock, *These Were the Romans* (1972), 12, 21, 22, 30, 37, 38, 39 (above), 43, 50 (above), 58, 165, 350, 352, 359; akg-images, London/Eric Lessing, 166; akg-images, London/Peter Connolly, 71, 85, 92 (above), 111, 185, 195 (above), 196, 197, 219 (above), 229, 249, 301 (below); Antikensammlungen, Staatliche Museen zu Berlin, 238; Arch of Titus, Rome, 117; Archaeological Museum, Florence, 90; Archaeological Museum, Naples, 110; Archaeological Museum, Sousse, 231 (below); Archaeological Museum, Tripoli, 209, 217, 219 (below), 220 (above); Bardo Museum, Tunis, 3, 77; Bibliotheca Alexandrina, Antiquities Museum, 137; Bildarchiv Preussischer Kulturbesitz, 201; Deborah Blake, 27, 339, 341, 343, 358; British Museum, London, 5, 143, 152, 181 (above), 152, 181 (above), 362; Capitoline Museums, Rome, 6, 9, 46, 47, 51, 52, 73, 105, 188; Castel Sant'Angelo, Rome, 72; Corbis/Roger Wood, 179; R.L. Dalladay, 144, 149, 151, 176, 210 (below), 112; Rick Dikeman, 18; El Djem Archaeological Museum, Tunisia, 218; Epigraphical Museum Rieti, 114; Galleria Borghese, Rome, 4; J. Paul Getty Museum, Malibu, California, 346 (above); Giovanni Lattanzi, 291; Glyptothek, Munich, 53, 248; Hinton St Mary, Dorset, 119; Michael Holford, 162; Institute of Etruscan and Italian Antiquities, University of Rome, 66 (above); Michael Ivy, 66 (below); Kunsthistorisches Museum, Vienna, 202; Louvre, Paris, 7, 11, 75 (left), 97, 99, 142; Metropolitan Museum of Art, New York, 107; James Morwood, 147; Musée D'Orsay, Paris, 168; Musée Royal du Mariemont, Belgium, 181 (below); Museo Archaeologico Nazionale, Naples, frontispiece, 132, 154, 156, 184, 210 (above), 220 (below), 228, 232, 233, 239, 245, 326, 328, 347; Museo Archeologico Ostiense, 138; Museo della Civiltà Romana, Rome, 190; Museo delle Terme, Rome, 199; Museo Etrusco Guarnacci, Volterra, 14; National Museum of Rome, 88; National Museum, Naples, 28, 29; Ny Carlsberg Glyptotek, Copenhagen, 36 (left); Palazzo dei Conservatori, Rome, 56; Palazzo Farnese, Piacenza, 100; Palazzo Madama, Rome, 361; Palazzo San Marco, Venice, 55; Piazza Armerina Archaeological Museum, Sicily, 203, 216, 224, 228 (above); Provincial Museum of Campania, Capua, 183; James Renshaw, 65, 79, 109, 127, 131 (below), 171, 195 (below), 246, 247,260, 273, 274, 275, 278, 279, 281, 282, 284, 285, 292, 294 (below), 295, 301 (above), 304, 318, 321, 323 (below), 329, 330, 331, 333, 334, 342, 344, 345, 354; Römische Villa Nennig, Germany, 207; Scala Archive, 34 (left), 36 (right), 145, 163; Soprintendenza Archeologica Napoli e Pompeii, 70, 98, 128, 129, 133, 139, 158, 258, 262, 269, 270, 287, 290, 294 (above), 299, 300, 303, 305, 306, 307, 311, 312, 314, 317, 320, 323 (above), 326, 346 (below); Temple of Fortuna, Praeneste, 25; Tomb of the Triclinium, Tarquinia, 13; Vatican Museums, 34 (right), 41, 63; Visual Publications, 231 (above).